Modern News Editing

Fifth Edition

Modern News Editing

Fifth Edition

Mark D. Ludwig

Gene Gilmore

Blackwell
Publishing

Mark D. Ludwig is an assistant professor in the Communications Studies Department at California State University, Sacramento, where he teaches classes in reporting and editing. He has worked as an editor in various capacities at nine newspapers—including the *Los Angeles Times* and the *San Jose Mercury News*—and a magazine, *Business 2.0*.

Gene Gilmore, author of the first four editions of *Modern Newspaper Editing*, started his journalism teaching career at Syracuse University and spent more than 20 years at the University of Illinois, Urbana-Champaign. He has worked on 13 newspapers, including a weekly, the *Los Angeles Times*, the *Washington Post* and the now defunct *Philadelphia Bulletin*.

©2005 Blackwell Publishing

Blackwell Publishing Professional
2121 State Avenue, Ames, Iowa 50014, USA

Orders: 1-800-862-6657
Office: 1-515-292-0140
Fax: 1-515-292-3348
Web site: www.blackwellprofessional.com

Blackwell Publishing Ltd
9600 Garsington Road, Oxford OX4 2DQ, UK
Tel.: +44 (0)1865 776868

Blackwell Publishing Asia
550 Swanston Street, Carlton, Victoria 3053, Australia
Tel.: +61 (0)3 8359 1011

Authorization to photocopy items for internal or personal use, or the internal or personal use of specific clients, is granted by Blackwell Publishing, provided that the base fee of $.10 per copy is paid directly to the Copyright Clearance Center, 222 Rosewood Drive, Danvers, MA 01923. For those organizations that have been granted a photocopy license by CCC, a separate system of payments has been arranged. The fee code for users of the Transactional Reporting Service is ISBN-13: 978-0-8138-0772-0; ISBN-10: 0-8138-0772-7/2005 $.10.

First edition 1971, The Glendessary Press, Inc., Berkeley, California.
Second edition 1976, Boyd and Fraser Publishing Co., San Francisco, California.
Third edition 1983, Boyd and Fraser Publishing Co., San Francisco, California.
Fourth edition 1990, Iowa State University Press, Ames, Iowa.
Fifth edition 2005, Blackwell Publishing, Ames, Iowa.

Library of Congress Cataloging-in-Publication Data

Ludwig, Mark D.
  Modern news editing / Mark D. Ludwig, Gene Gilmore.— 5th ed.
    p. cm.
  Rev. ed. of: Modern newspaper editing. 1990.
  Includes bibliographical references and index.
  ISBN-13: 978-0-8138-0772-0 (alk. paper)
  ISBN-10: 0-8138-0772-7 (alk. paper)
    1. Journalism—Editing. I. Gilmore, Gene, 1920- Modern newspaper editing. II. Title.

PN4778.G5 2005
070.4'1—dc22

                                                            2005004585

The last digit is the print number: 9 8 7 6 5 4 3 2 1

Contents

Preface

I am not the editor of a newspaper and shall always try to do right and be good so that God will not make me one.
—Mark Twain, 1870

When I worked as a copy editor in the newspaper business, it was my fantasy to see the paper published just once without the benefit of copy editing. All those reporters who were so fond of disdainfully calling us hacks and whining about their "butchered stories" could see how—although we did occasionally make mistakes—we kept near-mortifying mistakes from getting into the paper. Mistakes such as misidentifying the name of a street, or misstating somebody's title or, worse yet, misspelling somebody's name. That way, they would all see the value of our work.

Of course, that could only remain a fantasy. Professional standards would never permit it. Mistakes tear at the fabric of news publications. A newspaper, news Web site or news broadcast organization that makes mistakes loses its credibility with its audience and eventually the audience itself. With no audiences come no advertisers.

Editors play a vital role in minimizing errors in news publications. By working with reporters, photographers, artists and other editors, they decide what's newsworthy; how what's newsworthy will be reported, written and presented; whether the stories are free of spelling, grammar and style mistakes; whether all the information that the public needs is available.

My own career as a journalist and editor began at a young age, when I produced a monthly newsletter for a fan club of a Chicago children's television program, pounded out on my mother's typewriter and photocopied by my father at work. For the next 30 years, I worked as an editor in various capacities: at my high school newspaper, my college newspaper and professionally at an assortment of suburban and metro dailies in Illinois and California. A number of mentors along the way deserve some credit in helping my development as a journalist and editor:

Carolyn Stanek, my high school journalism teacher, who prodded me into journalism over science as a career choice; Robert Reid, a former journalism professor at the University of Illinois, who helped me to see the real importance of journalism in American society; John Lampinen, an editor at the *Daily Herald* in the Chicago area, who gave me my first professional job and who helped me decide what I really wanted to do as a journalist; Jack Breibart, a retired editor at the *San Francisco Chronicle*, probably the finest boss I ever had; and Clay Haswell, now of the Associated Press, who as executive editor of the *Contra Costa Times* in Northern California built the best news staff I ever worked with.

I would be remiss not to mention Gene Gilmore, the original author of this textbook, who taught me and hundreds of others editing at the University of Illinois at Urbana-Champaign. The things that Professor Gilmore taught me a quarter-century ago still resonate with me today.

Despite the effects of rapidly advancing technology on newsgathering and publishing, Professor Gilmore's wisdom about editing has not gone out of style. The rules of grammar, the importance of style, the completeness of information and ethical practice all remain the same, no matter the news medium. But in other ways, the book tries as best it can to catch up with current technology. It recognizes the return to a 24-hour news cycle that the Internet has brought, the importance of immediacy in reporting and the nonlinear presentation of news that the World Wide Web makes possible.

This book is intended to help new editors get their start by setting forth what it is that editors do and what they watch out for. But editing cannot be learned simply by reading textbooks. The best way to learn to edit—and to improve as an editor—is practice, practice, practice. The exercises that accompany this book give you a chance to do that. Another good way to practice is to read news reports critically. What mistakes do you see that the reporters and editors made? Is the information complete or does it leave you wanting more? What is it about particularly good stories that resonates with you, and how can you bring that to your own work as a journalist? How as an editor can you help others learn from that experience? Through such a critical approach, you develop yourself as an editor.

Acknowledgments

No author can expect to complete a textbook like this one without some outside help. I'd like to extend my thanks to Rich Hanner, Chet Diestel, Jennifer Bonnett, Simon Birch and Brian Craig at the *Lodi* (Calif.) *News-Sentinel;* Vlae Kershner at SFGate.com; Linda Gonzales, Joyce Terhaar and Linda Ash at the *Sacramento Bee* and Sacbee.com; Steven Wright, Rob Klindt, Randy Keith, Dennis Akizuki, Guy Lasnier and Josh Susong at the *San Jose Mercury News*; David Martin Olson, a student photographer for the *State Hornet* at California State University,

Sacramento; and Clay Haswell, chief of the AP's California and Nevada Bureau. Robert Humphrey, on the journalism faculty at California State University, Sacramento, assisted with the media law chapter. Most important, I would like to thank my wife, Catherine Snapp, an editor at the *Sacramento Bee*, who helped me keep the project on track.

Mark D. Ludwig

Modern News Editing

Fifth Edition

CHAPTER 1

Editing in the Age of Convergence

What does an editor do? That's a complex question. In the simplest sense, an editor is someone who makes changes in someone else's work before publication or broadcast. But an editor is also a coach. An editor is a manager. An editor is an artist. An editor is quality control—and more.

Let's take a look at the work of editors at three different news operations: a small newspaper in California's Central Valley, a metro newspaper in the heart of Silicon Valley and a news Web site based in San Francisco.

A Day at a Small Newspaper

It's going to be another busy day for Jennifer Bonnett, the assistant city editor at the Lodi *News-Sentinel*, a small news operation in Northern California that publishes a daily newspaper and local news Web site. Bonnett doubles as the City Hall reporter. She starts her day with an informal meeting of the City Council at 7 a.m., where officials talk about the city's budget reserve. From there it's back to the newsroom to catch up with what the police reporter is doing and review what other reporters are working on before heading into the editor's office for the meeting to discuss the day's news at 8:45.

The morning meeting

At the morning editors meeting—known as a budget meeting because editors review lists of news stories known as budgets—are Richard Hanner, the *News-Sentinel's* editor; Chet Diestel, the city editor; Bonnett;

and Debbie Freeman, a photographer who is filling in for the vacationing chief photographer. The early meeting is less formal than a second they'll hold that afternoon, at which the editors will decide what stories to put on the front page.

Hanner starts the meeting with a review of the morning's newspaper. Diestel comments about the reporters' hustle the day before. Hanner compliments a story about Lodi residents reacting to the death of Ronald Reagan over the weekend, particularly praising the details about how residents recalled that Reagan had served as a parade marshal in town decades earlier. Hanner noted how the lead had been changed from the original to focus more on the local angle—the story ran below a more general Associated Press report about people streaming to see Reagan's coffin in Southern California. Hanner says he thinks the local Reagan story is the best in that day's paper in the way that it connects with readers in Lodi.

Other stories on the front page that day include a story about a continuing controversy in town over a proposed Wal-Mart Supercenter, a follow-up story about a breach in a river levee that flooded thousands of acres of farmland and a story about the graduation at an area high school. Hanner notes that the headline on the levee story needed to say something about levees. (It read: "Problems persist: Dozens evacuated due to unstable road.") He also points out that he got lost reading a story about utility fees that ran on Page 3 and says it could have been written more clearly. But overall, the editors like the way the morning's paper came out.

After the critique, the editors move on to the day's stories. At the *News-Sentinel,* reporters fill out a weekly budget that informs the editors about what they're working on. For the early meeting, the editors review this budget to see what the potential stories are. Business reporter Greg Kane is working on a story about the job market for recent graduates. He also will cover the visit of an Asian wine expert to the area, which is in a wine-producing region of California. Ross Farrow will be starting his day after noon to cover a meeting of the City Council in Galt, one of the communities that the *News-Sentinel* covers. The editors also discuss a story Farrow has been working on about fire safety at the weekly flea market in Galt. Reporter Tom Hall is working on a story about Alzheimer's disease pegged to the Reagan death and will also be working on a longer-term story about charter schools.

Reporter Les Mahler, who is shared with another newspaper in the county, will be covering the County Board of Supervisors meeting that day. Of interest to the editors is an item about the county's sending a washing machine repairman for the county jail out of state for training. This item leads to a broader discussion of the costs of laundering at the county hospital and of uniforms for public employees. The ideas from the discussion will be passed along to the reporters.

The police reporter, Layla Bohm, received a tip overnight that public safety officials were worried about more breaks in the levee system, and a local fire district had been put on high alert for potential evacuations. The editors also talk about how the flooding from the levee break is coming closer to the area. Although the levee story has been previously covered by the county reporter, the editors decide to assign Bohm to keep track of the effects closer to home. Bohm also will be covering a sentencing in a drunken driving case, for which she will write a story, and is keeping tabs on another court case.

Reporter Sara Cardine is covering a ground-breaking for a new school to be built in town. Bonnett talks about what happened at the early City Council meeting and also notes that some governments would be closed that Friday to observe the state-declared day of mourning for Reagan.

Bonnett, who is working on a story out of the morning council meeting, agrees to do a roundup on government closures on the day of Reagan's funeral. Hanner, who notes that Bonnett will also be editing a few stories, asks her whether she will have enough time to get everything done by 4 p.m., when she is supposed to go home. She says she thinks she can but also volunteers to stay later if need be.

The editors then discuss what stories they think look good for the front page: one or two Reagan death follow-ups, a story that has been on hold about a local brew pub, the levee breach, the wine visitor from Asia and the laundry machine repair story. They then briefly talk about other events coming up later in the week and then break up to get the staff moving.

The morning's stories go online

At about the same time that the meeting is wrapping up, Simon Birch, the *News-Sentinel's* Internet services manager, is finishing up work on Lodinews.com, the newspaper's Web site. As the publication's Web master, Birch does it all—advertising, editorial, classifieds. The previous night, the newsroom's computer system, BaseView's NewsEditPro, prepared stories from the next morning's paper for World Wide Web production. Between 7 a.m. and 9 a.m., Birch checks the stories, tweaks and edits them, adjusts headlines as necessary and uploads them to Townnews.com, a Web hosting service. He also sizes and formats the local photographs for Web publication. The Web host provides a separate feed of national and international news from the Associated Press. By 9 a.m., the morning paper's content is also available online. (See Figure 1.1)

The city editor's morning

After the budget meeting, City Editor Diestel has each of his reporters come by individually to talk about what they're working on that day.

Figure 1.1.

Late in the afternoon on its Web site, the *Lodi News-Sentinel* gives readers a preview of the next morning's stories. Used with permission.

Tom Hall, the schools reporter, has discovered that seniors at Galt High School are holding a graduation rehearsal. The high school has not turned in a questionnaire regarding graduation, so Diestel sends Hall to the high school to check things out.

Business reporter Greg Kane drops in to talk about the wine visitor from Hong Kong. Several wineries operate in the Lodi region, and the Hong Kong visitor is there to learn about them. Kane will be headed out soon to cover the visit. He also tells Diestel about the job market story that he's working on, what approach he is taking, what background he has read and what sources he plans to consult.

Diestel then calls an editor at the *Tracy Press*, with which the *News-Sentinel* shares the reporter who covers San Joaquin County; the two newspapers also share stories of interest to the readership of both. Diestel finds out a little bit more about the washing machine repair worker's trip and what the plans are for follow-up stories about the broken river levee. Officials are worried about more breaches. The county reporter will do a main story, and the *News-Sentinel's* police reporter, Layla Bohm, will do a story about area fire districts being placed on alert.

Diestel also takes a call from a health care workers group, which is planning a demonstration the next day at a local lawmaker's office, and assigns a brief story to let readers know this is going to happen.

While all this is going on in the morning, Diestel also squeezes in time to eat a breakfast burrito and write a 25-column-inch story about Ronald Reagan that will run on the opinion page—for which he is also the editor.

The assistant city editor's morning

Police and courts reporter Layla Bohm calls Jennifer Bonnett from the courthouse to report that a drunken driver who was convicted of manslaughter was sentenced to 15 years in prison. She tells Bonnett that she has talked with the victim's family and that the defendant got into an argument with the judge. Bohm also tells Bonnett what she knows about the fire department's state of alert prompted by the broken levee. Bohm then heads in to the office to put her stories on the daily budget.

Bonnett talks with reporter Sara Cardine about the school ground-breaking that she covered earlier in the morning. They agree on a 15-column-inch story, and Bonnett suggests that Cardine look up the background on the new school. Cardine tells Bonnett that she has collected details to give her piece color from the scene. Bonnett tells Cardine to be sure to keep in mind why this new school is important to readers. Cardine returns to her desk to start writing. Schools reporter Tom Hall checks in with Bonnett about area closings for the Reagan story.

Between consultations, Bonnett begins work on her two original stories and a third one she has picked up about the local lawmaker who is joining a Republican Party committee that could help out the city-owned electric utility.

The city editor's afternoon

At about 2 p.m., reporter Ross Farrow arrives in the newsroom. He started his day later than usual because he will be covering a city council meeting that night. He checks in with City Editor Diestel and discusses what's on the council agenda. Among the items is the city budget. Diestel also tells Farrow that Bonnett is working on a story about closures for the Reagan mourning day and that he should check with the agencies he covers and feed her the information. They also discuss a transportation financing story that Farrow is working on.

Diestel wraps up working on the opinion pages and starts to compile budgets for the afternoon news meeting. These budgets contain a list of all the local stories available for the next morning's paper, feature stories, sports stories and the best offerings from the wire services that the *News-Sentinel* receives.

Reporters start to finish up their stories, and it's time to start editing. Diestel prefers an approach that lets the reporters retain control of their stories. Comments about an approach are always couched in the terms of questions, such as, "Did you consider taking another approach in your lead?" Reporters are more receptive to inquiries like these than they are of direct criticism of their work.

He finishes up the budgets and heads to the afternoon budget meeting at 3:30 p.m.

The assistant city editor's afternoon

Early in the afternoon, the police reporter has gone to an area marina to talk with some people evacuated because of the levee breach. She calls at 2:45 to say that she has talked with them but that they're not too worried that the floodwaters will reach their homes. Bonnett tells her to come back in to finish her stories. In the meantime, Bonnett has finished her stories on the city council meeting and the legislative appointment. She passes along the story about the agency closings, essentially finished, to Ross Farrow, who will add more to the story that evening.

The front page meeting

At the afternoon meeting are Hanner, Diestel, News Editor Brian Craig, Assistant News Editor Deanne Lowenstein, business reporter Greg Kane and sports reporter Jeff Sutton. Diestel discusses what he thinks are the best local stories for the front page: a local story about Ronald Reagan, which Hanner is writing; the levee stories; the wine visitor from Hong Kong; and the sentencing in the drunken driving case. The story about the washing machine repair worker is being held for more work. Craig talks about the best of the stories available from the Associated Press, the Scripps-McClatchy Western wire service and the Copley News Service. Kane talks about what business stories are available, both from local and the wires, and Sutton reviews the best of the sports news. (See Figure 1.2.)

The editors discuss the merits of the stories and pick the best for the front page: a package on Reagan, a package on the levee breach, the wine visitor story and a wire story about the report of the commission inves-

Figure 1.2.
Editors at the *Lodi News-Sentinel* meet to discuss what stories will appear on the front page for the edition of June 9, 2004. From left are News Editor Brian Craig, Assistant News Editor Deanne Lowenstein, City Editor Chet Diestel, and sports reporter Jeff Sutton.

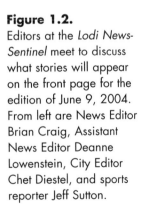

tigating the Sept. 11, 2001, attacks on the World Trade Center and Pentagon. Because the editors have not yet seen photographs, they defer a decision on what the lead picture will be. Stories inside the paper about the NBA playoffs, the school ground-breaking and the sentencing of the drunken driver will be teased on the front page as well.

Into production mode

After the meeting, Diestel runs off final budgets, and Craig breaks down the paper. The front of the paper will be devoted to local news; next comes state news and then national and international news. Craig will be in charge of the front page and jump pages; Lowenstein will handle the local pages; and another copy editor will produce the pages with wire news.

Diestel and Hanner determine which stories each will edit. Ordinarily, Bonnett also would be assigned stories to edit, but she has left for the day. Diestel also assigns two stories that will be coming in later to be read by the copy desk. Bohm returns from the Delta (the area of the levee breach) and updates Diestel on what her story will say.

Diestel and Hanner read the stories as they come in; most arrive by the 4:30 p.m. deadline. They also edit picture captions as they become available. By 6 p.m., Diestel has read six stories, including a roundup of briefs from the region, and has handled about 20 pictures.

Some of the stories need some rewriting and some need a few minor questions answered, but overall the stories are clean and need only minor tweaks.

On the copy desk, Craig is making a sketch of what the front page will look like. The levee art is better than the Reagan art, so he decides to make the levee package the centerpiece of the page. After making his sketch, he shows it to Hanner, who gives him the go-ahead. He checks the wires again, to make sure no other front-page contenders have emerged. He then begins to build the front and jump pages, using the QuarkXpress software program.

At the same time, Lowenstein is designing the local pages. At the *News-Sentinel,* inside pages are designed on paper, known as page dummies, and sent to composing, where a production worker builds the pages by computer. Lowenstein will edit the stories on her pages, write the headlines and check the captions to make sure they are correct. When the pages come back from composing, she and Craig check them over, mark final corrections and send them back to composing for adjustment. Another proof comes back for a final OK.

Copy editor Paul Bruton follows the same process for the national and world pages. He decides what stories to use, although Craig sometimes makes suggestions about stories he likes.

At about 8 p.m., Craig calls the *Tracy Press* looking for the photos to go with the levee story. These are the last elements he needs for the front page.

Shortly after 10 p.m., reporter Farrow comes back to the newsroom with his Galt City Council story. Craig reads the story; it looks clean. He turns the story over to Lowenstein, who has left a place for it on an inside page. After she reads the story, it is placed on the page for proofing.

The last of the copy goes to composing at about 11:30 p.m., and the desk finishes up with the page proofs about 12:30 a.m.—10 minutes ahead of deadline. (See Figure 1.3.)

After the paper is put to bed, Craig sends the stories about the sentencing and a story about the Wal-Mart Supercenter to the Associated Press for possible use on the wire. He then takes a final look at the wires to make sure nothing important has happened and fills out a report about what the night was like. Another edition of the *News-Sentinel* is complete. In the morning, Birch will put the stories online. (See Figure 1.4.)

The *Mercury News* and MercuryNews.com

Reporter Chuck Carroll, a reporter for the *San Jose Mercury News,* starts his day at about the same time that many of his newspaper's readers are picking up the morning edition at 7 a.m.—a full 16 hours ahead of the next press run. Carroll's main job isn't to report for the next morning's edition, however. He reports breaking news for immediate posting to the newspaper's Web site, MercuryNews.com. Carroll checks in with local police departments for incidents that have happened since the last reporter went home at about midnight, and follows up on stories that broke late in the night.

His editor, Dennis Akizuki, the law and justice editor for the *Mercury News,* is headed to work at about 8 a.m. On the way, he listens to the local news on the radio to be alert to any news that may be breaking in the San Francisco area, and particularly in the Silicon Valley, the publication's strongest market. He arrives about 8:30 a.m. and checks the wire services and Bay City News Service, a local news service, to see if anything's going on that they don't know about. He knows of one sure story that will be updated on MercuryNews.com through the day: the trial of Scott Peterson in the highly publicized death of his wife, Laci. But other than that, as of 10 a.m., not much is going on.

Rob Klindt, the *Mercury News'* online editor, starts his day at home at about the same time Akizuki is arriving in the newsroom. He checks the wires, picks some breaking stories he wants to add to the Web site, and contacts Knight Ridder Digital, which handles production of the site. At about 10 a.m., he heads to the newsroom.

The morning meeting

The *Mercury News* conducts its morning news meeting at 10:30 a.m. At the meeting are Susan Goldberg, the executive editor; David Satterfield,

Figure 1.3.

The front page of the *News Sentinel* on June 9, 2004. Used with permission.

Figure 1.4.
Lodinews.com was updated with the stories from the June 9, 2004, newspaper. Used with permission.

the managing editor; and representatives of each of the sections that the *Mercury News* produces. Klindt, the online editor, also attends the meeting. Metro reports that it still has two enterprise stories available that have been holding. One is about the murder rate in San Francisco; the other is about how some gasoline-burning cars are actually cleaner than hybrid vehicles. The metro staff is also chasing a story on the San Jose mayor's fund-raising practices.

The deputy national editor—whose staff includes the Sacramento bureau, covering state government—reports that negotiations over the state budget are continuing and there's new violence in Iraq. He also has a story about the ascendancy of Iran in Mideast politics. Last, presidential candidate John Kerry is speaking that morning at a fund-raiser in San Jose. Editors believe he will be talking about innovation—a hot topic in Silicon Valley.

Business has a package about stock options—also a big deal in Silicon Valley. The first piece will be about a federal hearing into how companies report stock options as an expense. The other, and potentially more interesting story, is a rally planned at the hearing by area workers who want the status quo on stock options—an only-in-Silicon-Valley story.

Sports has a special section on prep sports and is watching the

National Basketball Association draft and some major league baseball games. It also is chasing a story that appeared in the competing *San Francisco Chronicle* that morning regarding a steroids scandal. Features has its home and garden section and Friday entertainment section coming out. Photo reports that it is staffing the stock options rally and the Kerry visit, and graphics reports that it is working on art for the Iraq and clean cars stories.

Satterfield, the managing editor, then picks stories to look at for the next morning's front page: Kerry, the stock options story, the San Francisco murder story, the mayor's fund raising, Iraq and the state budget. This is just a tentative list and likely to change through the course of the day.

The editors then turn to a critique of that morning's newspaper. They discuss work in the paper that they like and point out some that could have used a little more work. Steve Wright, the deputy managing editor for convergence, reports an incorrect Web reference. Goldberg questions whether a story that ran inside the metro section should have run on the front of that section. Bert Robinson, the assistant managing editor for metro, explains that the story went inside because the section front had a number of other crime and justice stories on it.

The metro editors meet

After the morning news meeting breaks up, the editors on the *Mercury News*' metro desk gather to discuss what they have happening that day. At the meeting are Randy Keith, the metro editor for news, and five assigning editors responsible for various areas of the *Mercury News*' coverage. An editor in a local bureau participates by speaker phone. Also at the meeting are representatives of the graphics and art departments. Keith starts the meeting by talking about which stories are being considered for the front page. The other editors then each talk about what their reporters will have that day, including stories about a pharmacy expansion and a city's prohibition of the use of plastic chairs at restaurants with outdoor dining, a follow-up about a local woman hurt in an accident who is in a coma in Salt Lake City and a story that San Jose had been unable to pass Detroit on the list of the nation's most populous cities.

The Web site is updated

As the editors are meeting, Klindt, the online editor, is making adjustments to MercuryNews.com. He posts the overnight lottery numbers and pulls a brief out of a roundup about a rabid bat to give it better play; stories about animals are popular with visitors to the site. He updates a police report item with information from the Associated Press

Figure 1.5.
Rob Klindt, the online editor at the *San Jose Mercury News*, talks with a producer at Knight Ridder Digital. The newspaper's newsroom and Knight Ridder Digital work together to produce MercuryNews.com.

and adds an Associated Press story about the national do-not-call list. (See Figure 1.5.)

He also sends a list of the potential Page 1 stories to Knight Ridder Digital so that news producers there can start to prepare material for changes to the Web site that will take place the first thing the next morning. He also alerts the producers that an afternoon update from the Scott Peterson trial is anticipated and that an antitrust trial involving a Bay Area technology company is continuing and may generate stories. He checks with Deputy National and Foreign Editor Guy Lasnier to assure that the reporter covering the Kerry speech plans to write immediately for the Web site. In the meantime, he'll keep an eye out for an AP story. If the wire service files first, he will use that until the local version is ready. During all this, he also works on regular features of the Web site that update through the course of the day.

Meanwhile, on the national and foreign desk

It's late morning, and the reporter covering the Kerry event calls Lasnier to tell him she's on the way into the newsroom to write. Lasnier confirms that she's planning to file an early version to put on MercuryNews.com and then will spin it around for the morning print edition. They agree to talk about the print story before she sits down to write; it may require a little more reporting. Lasnier is also monitoring the wires—the *Mercury News* gets a lot of them: the AP, the New York Times service, the Knight Ridder Tribune service, the Washington Post-Los Angeles Times

Service and the Scripps McClatchy Western Service. He starts to prepare the department's budget, listing stories it is likely to use on its pages and stories he thinks worthy of the front page. In the early afternoon, two wire editors and an assistant national and foreign editor will arrive to help prepare the newspaper's state, national and foreign report.

The stock market closes

Visitor tracking at MercuryNews.com has found a spike in visitors after the close of the stock market—which is at 1 p.m. on the West Coast. At about that time, Jon Ann Steinmetz, the wire editor for the business section, creates the 60-Second Business Break, a compilation of short items that will appear at the top of the MercuryNews.com home page. The Business Break contains four to five items about the top business news of the day. The Business Break mostly comes from the wires, but occasionally staff members contribute. The items are short and written in a relaxed, conversational style. Steinmetz tries for a local focus, particularly on technology companies. Steinmetz completes the column and sends it to Klindt to be added to the Web site at about 1:30 p.m.

The Web updates come fast

At about 12:30 p.m., Klindt receives a story from the metro desk about a decomposed body found along a road. He gives it a quick read and alerts Knight Ridder Digital that it's ready to be posted under Updates From the Newsroom on the Web site. He also finds a story from the Peterson trial written by a reporter at the *Contra Costa Times*, a sister paper to the *Mercury News*. Because the local reporter has not filed yet, he processes that story instead for immediate posting. Klindt is still waiting for the Kerry story, so he starts work on a slide show of photographs that will accompany the story about San Francisco's murder rate—although it remains uncertain whether that story will run or hold again. At about 12:50, the reporter covering the Kerry story sends the Web version to Lasnier for editing, and she lets Klindt know that it's almost ready. Klindt calls up photos from the Associated Press and finds one of Kerry speaking at the event. He downloads the photo, opens it in Adobe Photoshop, crops it and sizes it for Internet use. About 10 minutes later, Lasnier alerts him that the story is ready. Klindt gives it a final read and lets Knight Ridder Digital know that the story and photo should be placed in a lead position on the home page as soon as possible. It's up by 1:20 p.m. At 1:30, he receives the 60-Second Business Break from Steinmetz, gives it a final read and alerts Knight Ridder Digital that it's ready. The column is at the top of the home page shortly. (See Figure 1.6.)

San Jose/Valley

 email this   print this

Posted on Thu, Jun. 24, 2004

Kerry calls for capital gains cut to spur tech investment

GETS IACOCCA ENDORSEMENT AT SAN JOSE STATE APPEARANCE

By Laura Kurtzman
Mercury News

John Kerry said in San Jose today that he would invest in technology by cutting the capital gains tax for investors who put money into small businesses. Kerry also said he would promote universal broadband access through tax incentives and increase government spending on scientific research.

The Massachusetts senator spoke at San Jose State University, where he was endorsed by former Chrysler Chairman Lee Iacocca, who backed George W. Bush in 2000. Iacocca said he was making the switch because, ``We need a new CEO and president.''

Kerry, the presumed Democratic nominee to face President Bush in November, also talked about out-sourcing, the transfer of jobs overseas. It's a common practice among Silicon Valley companies, a practice Kerry attacked during the primaries when he was facing stiff competition from rivals who took a more populist line. Since then, he has balanced his criticism of outsourcing with a fuller embrace of free trade.

IMAGES AND RELATED CONTENT

Associated Press

Democratic presidential candidate Sen. John Kerry D-Mass., gestures while speaking at San Jose State University Thursday during his California campaign swing.

RELATED LINKS

• **Full Election 2004 coverage**

Kerry used a comparison with India, which has become Silicon Valley's biggest competitor for engineering talent, to say why the United States should do better on investing in technology.

``We need a leadership that says if Bangalore in India can be completely wired, then so should all of America,'' Kerry said.

The Bush campaign said Kerry was a poor spokesman for cutting the capital gains tax, since he had voted against it in the Senate. Bush campaign officials distributed a statement quoting venture capitalist Floyd Kwamme, one of Bush's biggest supporters in the valley as saying: ``The technology industry has always needed a strong economy for it to flourish. The President's programs have helped Silicon Valley recover.''

Figure 1.6.
The *Mercury News* posted a story about presidential candidate John Kerry's visit early in the afternoon, long before the print edition would be ready for the presses. Copyright 2004, *San Jose Mercury News.* Used with permission.

The Page 1 meeting

At 2:30 p.m., editors from across the newsroom gather to discuss the front page. Running the meeting is Herschel Kenner, assistant managing editor for news, who will see the print edition through production. Although he starts his day in the newsroom in the early afternoon, in fact Kenner has been working since much earlier. He has listened to radio and watched television to keep abreast of the news and logged onto the *Mercury News'* computers from home to check his e-mail and read the various departments' budgets. He consults by telephone with the executive editor and managing editor about the best stories of the day. So, by the time the editors meet at 2:30, he knows what the best stories of the day are. He starts the meeting with a proposed list of Page 1 stories—some of which weren't even stories at the earlier news meeting. Kenner proposes a lineup that includes a story from the Sacramento bureau about problems in the state prison system, a story about the scaling back of spending at San Jose's new City Hall, a story about violence in Iraq, a story about the steroids scandal and the stock options rally story. Also under consideration: the Kerry story and Supreme Court story. Kenner then turns to the other editors to hear about those stories and others that may warrant the front page.

Randy Keith, the metro news editor, talks about the San Jose-Detroit story and the plastic chairs story. The San Francisco murder rate story will run on the local section front because he is concerned about the competition's getting the story. Lasnier talks about the Iran ascendancy story, the state prisons story and the Iraq story. The executive business editor talks up the stock options rally story. The lead is a clincher: "They came by foot, by bus and by BMWs—BMWs paid for with stock options." The executive sports editor describes the steroids scandal story; the features editor talks about the available promos to stories inside. Representatives of graphics and photo talk about what they have available.

Kenner sticks with his original lineup and then has the section editors give story length estimates and times when the stories will be ready for the copy desk. Most will be ready by 6 p.m. Tonight, the deadline for everything to be finished for the first edition is 10:15, 15 minutes earlier than usual.

Lasnier leaves the meeting to talk with his wire editors about what stories they will work on through the night; then she goes to talk with the reporter who covered the Kerry speech about her story. She tells him that Kerry did not really say that much new and she's not sure what approach to take with the story. President Bush was spending part of the day reacting to Kerry's lead on technology issues. After further discussion, Lasnier and the reporter agree to an approach. It's once again become OK to paint yourself as a candidate interested in technology. She agrees to a length of 20 column inches and gets on the phone for additional reporting before she begins to write.

Back in the conference room, the wire editors are meeting with two page designers to decide where to place the day's stories. The Kerry story is headed for Page 3. Behind Page 3 will be state and national news; foreign news will appear in a second A section. Using a white board, the designers and wire editors place stories throughout the paper and agree to lengths for each story. (See Figure 1.7.) The group breaks up and heads back to the newsroom. Over in metro, Marc Brown, the metro planning editor, and Josh Susong, the night city editor, meet to decide what stories will appear on the local section fronts.

At about the same time, the business desk sends the stock options rally story to Klindt to be posted online.

Figure 1.7.
Editors at the *Mercury News* use a whiteboard to plot out where to put state, national and foreign stories. News designer Shan Carter has that duty this day.

Production of the daily newspaper

The *Mercury News* primarily produces its pages using the pagination system developed by CCI. One page designer is assigned to the front page and its accompanying jump pages; two designers will split the work on the state, national and foreign pages; and two other designers will handle the pages in the local section. Final budgets are produced by the national and metro desks for the designers to work off.

In the late afternoon, local reporters begin to turn in their stories for editing. Sometimes, the editors call for revisions. Stories for the front page go through several layers of editing. At the same time, the wire editors prepare stories for the state, national and foreign pages, sometimes combining elements of stories from different news services.

When finished, the assigning editors and wire editors send their stories to the designers, who look them over and then place them in an electronic basket for copy editors to begin work on. Work is split between two copy desks, one of which handles stories from the national and foreign desk and the other from the metro desk. After the pages are designed, headline and caption specifications are automatically placed on the stories. Copy editors write the headlines and captions and send them to a copy desk chief for a final check.

The afternoon update on MercuryNews.com

At about 4 p.m., online editor Klindt finishes up the slide show for the San Francisco murder rate story. At about the same time every day, the Web site is rearranged to emphasize entertainment opportunities around town. The main traffic to the site in the late afternoon is from people looking for ways to spend their free time that evening or in the next few days. The "Today in the Mercury News" section is changed to "Tomorrow in the Mercury News," with previews of stories that will appear in the next morning's print edition. Klindt also starts to prepare a lineup for Knight Ridder Digital for production of the Web site the next morning.

The *Mercury News* on television

The *Mercury News* has affiliations with the local NBC and Telemundo television stations. These partnerships allow the newspaper and the broadcast outlets to share content—although most of it flows from the newspaper to the TV stations. Verónica Villafañe, the TV face of the *Mercury News*, starts her day in the newspaper's newsroom in the early afternoon. Her main focus is to promote the newspaper on television. On this day she attends the 2:30 p.m. news meeting and then sends the news budgets to the producer of the late newscast of the NBC station. Every night, she does a 30-second to 60-second report from the *Mercury News* newsroom about one of the stories in the paper. She tries to get the TV station to use the newspaper's top story, but it's up to the station's producer to pick the story.

The producer e-mails Villafañe that he is interested in the story about the ban on plastic chairs at Palo Alto restaurants and in the piece about San Jose's ranking in population remaining behind Detroit. He also asks what new details the newspaper had about the steroid scandal story. Villafañe calls him to argue for the City Hall spending story because of its importance to taxpayers in the city. While he deliberates, she tapes some Spanish-language pieces for Telemundo about stories that are appearing in *Nuevo Mundo*, a sister publication to the *Mercury News*.

The news producer bites on the City Hall story. When the metro desk is finished with it, she takes it and writes a short television version of the story and reports it on the 11 p.m. news. The television station uses archived videotape of construction of the new City Hall to illustrate the story.

Script for Verónica Villafañe's report

OUT GOES THE 12-THOUSAND DOLLAR PLASMA SCREEN TV AND THE 44-HUNDRED DOLLAR REMOTE CONTROL IN THE MAYOR'S TOP-FLOOR CONFERENCE ROOM.

THE COSTLY TV'S, VCR'S AND HIGH TECH VIDEO SCREEN ORIGINALLY PROPOSED FOR THE NEW CITY HALL WERE REVEALED SUNDAY IN A MERCURY NEWS INVESTIGATION ...

AND TODAY ... CITY OFFICIALS CANCELED TOP-OF-THE-LINE ELECTRONIC COMPONENTS ... BUT EVEN SO, AUDIO-VISUAL EQUIPMENT, WILL COST A LOT MORE THAN BUDGETED ... BECAUSE BIDS HAVE COME IN MUCH HIGHER THAN ANTICIPATED.

ALSO ... THE CITY PLANS TO PAY FOR WIRING THE ENTIRE 18-STORY BUILDING TO RECEIVE PLASMA SCREENS AND OTHER TECHNOLOGY IN THE FUTURE ...

FIND OUT MORE ABOUT THESE EXPENSES ... IN TOMORROW'S MERCURY NEWS.

LIVE FROM THE SAN JOSE MERCURY NEWSROOM, I'M VERÓNICA VILLAFAÑE.

Back on the copy desks

As the evening proceeds, stories continue to flow to the designers, who send them along to the copy editors. The copy editors' responsibilities include not only looking for spelling, grammar and style errors but also for missing information and fact errors. They also write the headlines and picture captions.

The initial version of the Kerry visit story arrives in Assistant National Editor Michael Winter's electronic basket at 6:30 p.m. Winter reads the story over and has a few questions. He goes to the reporter's desk to discuss his concerns and to help her bring more of a focus to it. He asks the reporter to conduct a little more research about which candidate was the first to bring up providing more broadband access as a campaign issue. She finishes it about an hour later, Winter reads it one more time and then sends it along to the design and copy desks.

The designer takes the story and runs a computer script that places headline and caption coding on the file; the designer then sends it to the copy desk. A copy editor picks it up, reads it, writes the headline and caption and sends it to the copy desk chief, Charley Lindsey. Lindsey's job is to check the copy editor's work to make sure that the headline is accurate and compelling and that the captions tell the story. He also gives the story a final read—the last stop before publication. Immediately, he notes a problem: the names of two people are misspelled. Both people are prominent in Silicon Valley and to misspell their names would be an embarrassment to the paper. He fixes the spelling, makes a final check and approves the story for placement on the page.

Back at the design desk, designer Shan Carter waits for the copy desk to finish with all the pieces on the page before making final adjustments and printing out a proof page. The proof goes back to the copy desk, and if there's time before the first edition deadline, copy editors will read the proofs. Pages that cannot be proofed by the first deadline will be read subsequently for potential corrections for the second edition.

A hectic night in metro

Over on the metro desk, things are getting busy late. Night City Editor Josh Susong describes what happened:

> We had a breaking news story, a particular kind that we've faced frequently in recent weeks: The dead-soldier story. The bombings and attacks in Iraq that lead to late updates in our foreign stories at night often lead to breaking local stories the next, as word gets back home about a local soldier who has died.
>
> So far we've made an attempt to do a full story as soon as we find out about any soldier from within our circulation area who has been killed. The problem with such stories is that they almost always seem to happen at night.
>
> This one was a little more drawn out than most of our late-night mad scrambles to find phone numbers, get interviews and write a story. AP reported two California National Guard soldiers killed in Iraq, based on a guard press release we couldn't find. One, Patrick McCaffrey, was from Tracy, which is well outside our area, and I was going to pass on it. But about 9, we got a tip that he had Bay Area ties and actually worked in Palo Alto.
>
> The night reporter ran an online search for McCaffrey and easily found a home number. Turned out the man's mother lived at his home, too, to help his wife care for the children while he was gone; the mother was very cooperative with us. While the reporter did an interview with her, I did online searches for the body shop we'd been told was his employer. It took awhile, because I had been using the wrong spelling, but eventually I found a business listing on a subscription service called Reference USA; it came with an owner's name.
>
> Then I turned to our voter registration database (this is priceless on deadline) to find the woman. With an unusual name, she was easy to find, but had her phone number withheld. Often, though, another search using the address will turn up somebody else in the family who has listed the phone number, and sure enough, a husband or other relative living there turned up. While the reporter was on the phone with McCaffrey's mother, I did a quick interview with the body shop owner. Turns out our soldier was set to become general manager when he returned and that he had legions of loyal customers in Palo Alto. In fact, people had been coming by the shop all day to offer their condolences. So we had our strong local link to round out the story from the mother. The reporter, who is fabulous on a phone interview and is lightning-fast with a nice story, wrote it up with an insert about the Palo Alto ties.
>
> While Sandra wrote, we figured out how to get the story in. Most critical, Herschel Kenner (the assistant managing editor) and I thought, was getting it onto the cover of the Peninsula edition's local section. Because of color positions, we were locked in without any good spot. We were able to turn one color mug shot into a "color mug shot with refer to story inside" and take that story's start for our new story. It was an awkward solution, but it got the newest story onto the cover, which was a much better story, so we went with it. On stuff like this, there's no replacement for:

Figure 1.8.
The final edition of the *Mercury News* on June 25, 2004. Copyright 2004, *San Jose Mercury News*. Used with permission.

Figure 1.9.
Early in the morning of June 25, 2004, producers at Knight Ridder Digital have assembled the MercuryNews.com home page. Copyright 2004, *San Jose Mercury News.* Used with permission.

- A good arsenal of online resources (Nexis, multicounty voter-registration database, good searchable phone book database better than the Web ones.)
- A seasoned reporter who can write quickly

The paper wraps up and the cycle begins anew

Despite the late-breaking stories and other problems that crop up during the night, the *Mercury News* editors make their first-edition deadline and each subsequent deadline, and the presses start to run at about 11 p.m. for the morning delivery. (See Figure 1.8.) Meanwhile, overnight, the *Mercury News'* computers will automatically copy the day's stories into the MercuryNews.com servers. Using tags that editors have assigned to the stories, they will post automatically to various pages on MercuryNews.com. For instance, stories marked for the Peninsula edition will automatically post to the Peninsula news page of MercuryNews.com. At 6 a.m., a producer at Knight Ridder Digital assigned to the *Mercury News* will begin to build the home page, using content from the newspaper that he or she thinks will be the best fit for the newspaper's Internet audience. An hour later, the early reporter will be starting his day. (See Figure 1.9.)

SFGate.com: The All-Day News Cycle

It's a much earlier start to the day for the first editor on the job at SFGate.com, an online news publication in San Francisco owned by Hearst Communications, which publishes the *San Francisco Chronicle* out of the same building. Although SFGate uses content from the *Chronicle*, it operates independently, with editors who select their own stories and give a different presentation to online users from that of the print publication.

On this day, it's Aileen Yoo's turn to put SFGate into operation. She gets up at about 4 a.m. and turns on the local news radio station to hear what's going on. She turns on her computer and checks what other news sites have, including MSNBC, the *Washington Post* and the *New York Times*. She then checks the story statistics from the previous day, which tell her what pieces SFGate's audience viewed the most. She notes the most popular so that she can be on the lookout for follow-up stories.

Her next task is to choose a centerpiece package. She's looking for a combination of a good photo and an interesting read. She checks the pictures that appeared in that morning's *Chronicle*, as well as what's available on the wires, and chooses a photo that goes with a *Chronicle* story about rental prices in Berkeley. From there, she chooses other breaking stories and mixes in stories from the *Chronicle* to complete the Web site's "first edition" at about 7 a.m.—about the same time that commuters are getting up in the morning and signing on to see what's news in San Francisco that day.

The SFGate crew also produces the *Chronicle*'s home page, with that day's stories from the *Chronicle* presented in a more newspaperlike fashion. Stories and photos have been sent overnight to SFGate by the *Chronicle*'s librarians. Yoo will sometimes recast the *Chronicle* headlines, spinning them ahead to make them more fresh.

After the home pages of SFGate and the *Chronicle* are built, Yoo goes back to rewrite, revise and fix typos as needed. She keeps on top of what stories are coming from the Associated Press and places them on the home page if warranted. She updates the site as much as the news dictates—and keeps at it until about 11 a.m., when SFGate editor David Curran takes control of the home page.

Curran picks up where Yoo leaves off—by keeping tabs on the wire services and revising the page as needed. At about noon, it's time to flip the centerpiece. Curran then continues to update the site as news become available. Later in the afternoon, the *Chronicle* newsroom sends over an early story from the Scott Peterson murder trial and posts it to the site. During the afternoon, another editor is working on the Day in Pictures features of the site, a slide show taken from wire photos that SFGate has received. (See Figure 1.10.)

At about 12:30 p.m., the editors convene for their weekly meeting. News director Vlae Kershner reports the latest statistics about traffic to the site and starts a discussion about how SFGate accidentally broke an

SFGate.com
Room Rates from $129
CLICK HERE for details
▸TRAFFIC ▸WEATHER ▸LIVE VIEWS ▸CLASSIFIEDS
San Francisco Chronicle ▸ Get Home Delivery
Quick Search
GO
Search in:
▸SFGate Home
▸Today's Chronicle
▸Sports
▸Entertainment
News & Features
▸Business
▸Opinion
▸Politics|Election '04
▸Technology
▸Crime
▸Science
▸Weird News
▸Polls
▸Photo Gallery
▸Columnists
▸Travel
▸Lottery
▸Obituaries
▸Personal Shopper
▸Classifieds
▸Jobs
▸Personals
▸Real Estate
▸Rentals
▸Vehicles
▸WebAds
Regional
▸Traffic
▸Weather
▸Live Views
▸Maps
▸Bay Area Traveler
▸Wine Country
▸Reno & Tahoe
▸Ski & Snow
▸Outdoors
▸Earthquakes
▸Schools
▸Entertainment
▸Food & Dining
▸Wine
▸Movies
▸Music & Nightlife
▸Events
▸Performance
▸Art
▸Books
▸Comics
▸TV & Radio
▸Search Listings
Living
▸Health
▸Home & Garden
Thursday, August 26, 2004
Updated: 06:30 PM PDT
California Dreamin'
TagTeamMedia
SF-based the Court & Spark plays the Great American Music Hall tonight, and the band is bringing a new album to the hometown fans. "Witch Season" blends dreamy elements of rock, folk and country. Derk Richardson. (With audio)
CACHE CREEK CASINO RESORT
MORE NEWS & FEATURES
Tyra Near The Altar?
Banks may be marrying Chris Webber; Romijn-Stamos starts dating; was Paris' Tinkerbell lost? Daily Dish!
Julian Peterson shows up at camp.
Ryan: Error of too much tolerance.
Soft drinks linked to diabetes.
Take a trip over Labor Day weekend.
Wrong 'terrorists' nabbed: Jon Carroll.
Mullin says Warriors' vets are key.
Inside SFGate
Chic In The City
Designer boutiques, funky galleries, a growing nightlife -- get to know Hayes Valley.
Find Entertainment Listings:
Movies, Food & Dining, Music, Theater...
Contract On Suspect's Life?
The teen suspected of killing Terrance Kelly is in protective custody as rumors spread other inmates want him dead. Chronicle
Red Flag Warning Issued
National Weather Service warns of high fire danger as hot weather settles over the Bay Area. AP
•Check the forecast: Weather
Breaking News
•Krispy Kreme earnings disappoint
•Inmates executed in Texas, Oklahoma
•Bush to ask for $2 bil. in hurricane aid
•Families sue to save WTC footprints
Najaf Deal Reached
Al-Sadr agrees to a peace accord presented by Grand Ayatollah Ali al-Sistani to end three weeks of fighting. AP
•Multiple pipelines sabotaged in Iraq
•Clock showing war cost unveiled
American Gold Rush
Hamm, Chastain and other U.S. soccer vets clinch the gold medal in OT over Brazil. AP
•Knapp: Who are you to judge?
•Ostler: In search of a medal goddess
•Olympics Page | TV | Results | Medals
'Russia Now Has A Sept. 11'
A Russian official acknowledges the cause of the two airliners crashing and killing 89 was probably terrorism. AP
Geragos Attacks Phone Records
Attorney spends Thursday attempting to cast doubt on records used to paint Peterson as a serial liar. Chronicle
•Is Scott a pathological liar?
Athens 2004
XXVIII Olympic Games
Full Coverage
News, photos, results, interactive guides, history, links, and more.
Medal Count
Schedule: Events | TV
Day In Pictures
Party lions, creamed tomato soup. Ladle up some DIP!
shop
Chronicle print ads
By category
autos
find a vehicle
jobs
find a job
homes
find a home
The Question
Who has the worst performance in the Olympics so far?
Incompetent judges 11%
Whining gymnasts like Khorkhina 9%
Boxer Estrada, barely tried or cared 3%
The "Dream Team" 19%
NBC, the U.S. chauvinists 59%
Total Votes: 997
Click to Vote
disclaimer
KAISER PERMANENTE

embargo on a story, allowing its publication before the source wanted. The solution is that the Associated Press has agreed not to send embargoed stories as part of SFGate's Web feed. The editors discuss the upcoming Republican convention and college football previews that are being produced. The production designer says that the food page has been redesigned. To wrap up, Kershner goes around the room to ask editors to discuss what had been done well during the past week on the site.

Figure 1.10. SFGate.com in San Francisco is run independently of its sister publication, the *San Francisco Chronicle*. Used with permission.

On this day, Dave de la Fuente takes over maintenance of the site from Curran late in the afternoon. The centerpiece is flipped again between 4 and 5 p.m. to a piece on a band, including an audio stream, that is playing locally. Late in the day, SFGate takes a more entertainment-oriented focus. At about 3 p.m., a gossip column known as the Daily Dish—one of the site's most popular features—is added to the home page. Later in the day, de la Fuente will work on the Top of the Bay, a newsletter that will be e-mailed to subscribers that has links to the next morning's best stories from the *Chronicle*, and content exclusive to SFGate. Later in the evening, he will work on material to prepare it for publication on the site the next morning.

Converging News Media

The *News-Sentinel*, the *Mercury News* and SFGate have each recognized the value of producing news for multiple platforms, although each has chosen its own way to use those platforms. At the *News-Sentinel*, convergence is the repackaging of the print edition for online dissemination. The *Mercury News* and SFGate both view the Internet's potential for providing a 24-hour news cycle—as with television and radio, the Internet provides the ability to report the news as it's happening. The *Mercury News* has chosen to do this as an extension of its newspaper brand—with a little bit of television partnership thrown in—whereas the SFGate has taken a separate identity from its sister publication, the *San Francisco Chronicle*. Still other news operations have taken convergence further. In Chicago, in addition to the *Tribune*'s print and Internet publications, the operation shares content with broadcast television station WGN and cable television news channel ChicagoLand TV—all of which are owned by the *Tribune*'s parent company.[1] The television stations have a studio in the *Tribune* newsroom, and reporters and columnists from the print publication appear on the television stations to discuss their stories. A similar situation is found in Tampa, Fla., where the *Tampa Tribune* shares material with television station WFLA and Web site Tampa Bay Online.[2]

None of these models can be categorized as the correct one. For one thing, different markets have different needs when it comes to news coverage. For another, this continues to be an evolving area in which news organizations are trying to ascertain the correct mixtures of news, features and multimedia content. One thing that hasn't changed, however, is the need for editors at all levels, whether for print, online or broadcast. It's editors who determine what stories get covered and which are shunted aside; it's editors who work with reporters to assure that stories are fairly and accurately and thoroughly covered; it's editors who assure the quality of the work; it's editors who are ultimately responsible for the way the news is presented.

This book is for editors and those who want to be editors. Its primary focus is editors who work for print and online publication, although its lessons can be carried into broadcasting as well. It begins with a discussion of what editors do and moves on to talk in detail about how they do it, from the detail-oriented world of copy editing to the care and handling of reporters, and from the selection of photographs to the design of pages. The book later discusses some of the issues that editors face, from how to keep up with the pace of breaking news to dealing with legal and ethical issues. Finally, it wraps up with a look at why American journalism continues to be as relevant today as it was when the nation was founded more than two centuries ago.

Notes

1. Ken Auletta, "Synergy City," *American Journalism Review* (May 1998).
2. Dinah Eng, "The Tampa Tribune," *Presstime* (July/August 2004).

CHAPTER 2

Deciding What's News

Sometimes it's easy to decide what's news. When terrorists fly airplanes into the towers of the World Trade Center, or the United States invades Iraq in pursuit of Saddam Hussein and biological, chemical and nuclear weapons, that's news. When a well-known celebrity becomes governor of California during a recall election, that's news. Other times, it's not so easy. When does a car crash in the community deserve to be covered? What actions of the city council are newsworthy and what should be ignored? When a local manufacturer holds a ground-breaking for an expansion of its facility, is it news or would covering it serve as free advertising for the company? What is the threshold for newsworthiness on items that appear on a police blotter?

Generally speaking, news is current information of interest to readers (or listeners or viewers). That definition is not meant to be a legalistic pronouncement but rather a stimulus to thinking about events. The concept "news," like the concepts "mental health" or "spirituality," is more easily recognized than precisely described. The editor's attention must be centered on the citizens served.

Some may object that the definition, by emphasizing audience interest, minimizes the significance factor in news. However, if an item is truly important to readers or listeners, it will interest them, too. How could it be otherwise? There is no dull significant news; there is only dull significant newswriting. If an epidemic threatens a reader's town or if a change in the federal budget affects taxes or services that concern the public, the medical or fiscal details should be presented in an appealing way. If an epidemic is far away or if the budget change really will not affect the reader, it deserves little attention. Why should an editor sweat over it? This does not refer, of course, to people concerned only with themselves or perhaps their immediate families. Typical readers, with some concern about the whole nation and the world, must still focus on what is most significant for them, and the editor should try to help them see and understand that significance.

Newsworthiness

Newsworthiness comes as second nature to practiced journalists, who, when deciding what stories to cover or what wire stories to choose, rarely think about the values that drive their decisions. But most news coverage falls within—and often overlaps—certain categories, sometimes called news values: timeliness, proximity, conflict, impact, prominence and novelty.

Timeliness

One of the authors worked for an editor who was known to quip that "news is that which has just happened that hasn't happened before." What he was speaking of, somewhat sardonically, was timeliness. The fact that a river runs through town isn't news, but when the river overflows its banks, it's news. This emphasis on timeliness can be seen in leads of news stories every day. "President Bush defended his budget proposals on *Tuesday* after coming under increasing attack from Democratic lawmakers." "Three Conrail cars carrying sulfuric acid derailed *this morning* in Decatur, forcing the evacuation of 350 nearby residents." So important is timeliness as a news value that rarely are stories published without including some sort of time element.

Timeliness as a news value is particularly important for online and broadcast news media. Their strength is their ability to put the news out there *right now*, as it's happening. Online editors understand that visitors to their Web sites want a unique experience each time they visit, so they make efforts to make sure that content is regularly updated, whether that be news taken from wire services or produced by reporters in their own newsrooms throughout the day. In this view, "news is only news while it is new."[1]

Proximity

Events that happen close to home are much more likely to be newsworthy than events that happen far from home. A murder in Topeka, Kan., is news to the people in Topeka but of very little interest to people in Albany, N.Y.—unless the victim happens to be a tourist from Albany. A car wreck that kills five people in Fargo, N.D., means more to Fargo residents than San Diego residents. Disasters must be of increasing magnitude the farther they get from the audience's home base to be considered newsworthy.

Local content often differentiates print and online news media from each other. Rob Neill, the online editor for ContraCostaTimes.com, the news site affiliated with the *Contra Costa Times*, notes that visitors to that site most often come looking for news about the San Francisco area, where they are located, or news about the Oakland Raiders football team. Although ContraCostaTimes.com carries wire news—provided by its host, Knight Ridder Digital—that content receives far fewer page views. Readers can go to the CNN or BBC Web sites for that kind of news, but they cannot get news about Contra Costa County there. "What subjects does your publication own?" Neill asks. That's what editors should concentrate on for their Web sites.

Conflict

As any fan of literature knows, the best stories hang on conflict. The same is true of news stories. Conflict can range from the seemingly mundane—a fight to get a stop sign installed at a dangerous intersection—to the critical—when the nation goes to war. When residents of a community go head-to-head with the city council over the pace of growth in the town, that's conflict. Every presidential election involves candidates pitted against one another. Stories about people overcoming seeming unbeatable odds are stories with conflict.

Impact

How does the news affect readers or viewers? That's impact. When a story about a tax increase explains what it is going to cost taxpayers and what the benefit of that increase will be, that's impact at work as a news value. A story about how sharp state budget cuts affect the beneficiaries of state programs recognizes impact as a news value. More than the other news values, impact is very reader- or viewer-focused.

Prominence

For some people, simply being who they are makes what they do newsworthy. At the top of this category is the president. The president's health checkup found nothing wrong? That's newsworthy. The president is taking a few weeks "off" at his ranch—news. The president makes an off-the-cuff remark caught by news microphones—embarrassing, and news. Today, because of the interest in celebrities, what they do is often newsworthy. Rumors about Jennifer Lopez's next pending marriage? Britney Spears' brief marriage to a childhood friend? For better or worse, audiences want to know about these things.

When are local people considered prominent? Certainly the highest elected or appointed officials, such as mayors and school superintendents, are prominent, but their acts as public officials—and not their personal lives—are what is likely to be covered.

Novelty

There's an adage in journalism: When a dog bites a man, that's not news. But when a man bites a dog, that's news. That's novelty at work as a news value. Readers have an insatiable appetite for the unusual, and reporters and editors are glad to feed it. *The Sacramento Bee* runs a weekly feature in its news section under the heading "Strange stuff." One week's compilation included a story on a hot-dog eating contest, one about a blind man who drove a golf cart across town under the direction of a drunken friend, and a piece about a lobster that stood guard over a watch at the bottom of an English harbor.

Visuals

Visual presentation is important on all news media platforms, but it dominates in television. Good videotape of a news event trumps other news values on TV. Film of a dramatic house fire beats more mundane news from the school board, for example. But visuals are also important in print and online. In newspapers, eye-tracking studies have shown that readers' eyes are first drawn to the largest photograph on the page.[2] Online, photographs, slide shows and short videos are an important part of the presentation of the news.

What about Younger Readers?

Newspaper executives have been wringing their hands for decades about some unattractive demographics: Their audiences are getting older, and younger people are not replacing them. Such data naturally make news organizations uncomfortable, and they continue to try new products to attract younger readers. In Chicago, the long-established *Tribune* and *Sun-Times* are trying to draw younger readers with *RedEye* and *Red Streak*—publications that take hip, irreverent tones and are more visually charged.

In 2003, the *Columbia Journalism Review* asked young journalists in newsrooms across the country what their "dream newspaper" would be like. Among the things the young journalists reported:

- Their newspaper would be a tabloid format. A Web site would exist to supplement, but not replace, the newspaper.
- They wanted stories that helped them connect with the world. This involves both increased international coverage and stories about people around the world, to help them relate to a global community.
- Their reporting and writing would have more attitude and style, with a conversational tone. Some even suggested abandoning objectivity when merited.

- Each story should be told in the most effective way possible, combining writing with photographs, graphics and interesting design.
- The publication would successfully walk the fine line between being informative and condescending.
- Their dream newspaper would be entertainment-heavy but not frothy. Stories would go behind the scenes of the entertainment industry.
- The publication would use its Web site to supplement the print publication, with links to original documents, full text of interviews, and other information that space in the newspaper would not allow. The online presence would also foster interaction with readers, to allow them to experience the news.
- Their newspaper would have more young journalists who better understand young people.
- Publications would set up task forces to stay connected with the needs of younger readers.[3]

Interactivity

Online news publications have an advantage that print and broadcast have long lacked: a direct connection with audiences. It's relatively easy to communicate almost immediately with reporters and editors using e-mail. Online chats and forums allow readers to react to and comment on the news, as well as suggest news stories of their own. Some publications even have tried allowing the public to create their own publications and report their own stories. Pablo J. Boczkowski notes that this has led to a change in journalism from being journalist-centered to being user-centered, and from being unidirectional to multidirectional in the way media communicate with their audiences. He also notes how online media allow a much more local focus.[4]

A Vast Collaboration

Deciding what stories to use online and in the newspaper is a collaborative effort. Beyond routine local news, a network of writers and editors normally selects stories, photographs and artwork.

Suppose, for example, that an avalanche in the Swiss mountains kills and injures several tourists. Depending on such factors as the number of deaths and the prominence of the people, a local reporter for the Associated Press would get the news and file a story to his or her bureau. The editors there would send a full story to the general desk in New York for distribution to its clients around the country.

Let's assume a prominent business executive from San Francisco is among the dead. The general desk may decide to send a more complete story out on the West Coast regional wire and a much abbreviated item to the rest of the nation. Editors locally then decide how much, if any, of it serves their audiences, be it in print, broadcast or online. In San Francisco, it is obviously a major story, but editors in most other cities will toss it. Broadcast and online news media that decide to use it will probably do so immediately, while a newspaper will have to wait until the next edition, usually the next morning.

The fate of this story, moreover, depends on the flow of other news. At each point—the local AP bureau and in New York—editors have to compare the news value of the story with other stories that reach their desks at about the same time. This variation in the flood of news means that one day a relatively small story gets big play, while another day a significant item is buried.

While the wire editor locally selects from AP or a supplemental wire service, a city editor dispatches reporters to newsworthy events. Writers on beats decide which events they find deserve coverage, and how much. The city editor evaluates the overall flow of city news from these local sources while a state editor weighs copy from the state or region and a sports editor evaluates sports news. Other editors and writers—the business editor, church editor and lifestyle editor—survey their fields for news significant to their readers. In a converged newsroom, reporters are sent into the field equipped to record audio and video for use on the Web site.

A Day on the *Tribune*'s Metro Desk

By Don Wycliff, Public Editor, Chicago Tribune
Jan. 15, 2004

The front page of last Friday's *Tribune* carried two stories generated from the paper's metropolitan news desk.

One, by science writer Peter Gorner, was headlined "U. of C. sex study sees love, loneliness." It described the results of a study by University of Chicago researchers that showed the typical Chicagoan now spends half of his or her life single, a development said to have enormous implications for social, cultural and other institutions and for people's way of interacting.

The other story, by the *Tribune*'s new environmental reporter Michael Hawthorne, was headlined "Study cites toxins in farmed salmon." It reported the alarming news that, according to a study in the journal *Science*, farm-raised salmon contains vastly higher levels of cancer-causing pollutants, including PCBs, or polychlorinated biphenyls, than does wild salmon.

Two stories. It was an average haul for Metro in the daily competition to get stories on the most valuable piece of newsprint in the paper: Page 1. There have been days when Metro has virtually owned Page 1—at the death of a mayor, for example, or when a disaster occurs, like the E2 nightclub stampede tragedy.

But last Thursday wasn't one of those. Locally, it was a fairly quiet early January day, the kind when most people are still partly in holiday mode and want only to stay inside and warm. Farther afield things were not so quiescent.

In Iraq, guerrillas shot down an American Black Hawk helicopter, killing nine soldiers. That story, from the foreign news desk, was a virtual lock for Page 1.

There also was big news out of Washington, where aides let it be known that President Bush would shortly reprise an old JFK gambit by announcing an ambitious effort to send humans to Mars. That national desk story ultimately would end up at the top of Page 1, with the biggest headline of all.

National got another on the front page as well—about the Food and Drug Administration's surprise rejection of an advisory panel's recommendation to allow silicone gel breast implants back on the market.

And the business desk also cracked Page 1 with a story on what looked like the striking of a deal in plea bargaining between federal prosecutors and Enron scandal figure Andrew Fastow.

But Page 1 decision-making is one of the last acts of the daily drama of putting out the newspaper. A lot of journalism has to be done in the hours before that.

On Metro, the day "starts" when Chicago bureau chief Claudia Banks arrives at 7 a.m. On most days and barring an exceptional news event, she will be the only editor on duty on Metro until 10 a.m., when Hanke Gratteau, associate managing editor for metro news, and her deputies arrive.

Last Thursday was routine. Shortly after arrival Banks conferred with the overnight editor and began updating a schedule of potential stories that she had started putting together the day before. At 8 a.m. she got together to share notes with Frank Hanes, the early man on the photo assignment desk. And she dispatched her one early reporter, Tara Deering, to check out a report that a 6-year-old student had been dropped off and left at the Loop Lab School by a parent who was unaware that the city had shut the school down the day before for a fire code violation.

As the hours wore on, more reporters drifted in, and always the first stop was the Metro desk. Metro has the biggest staff in the *Tribune* editorial department—about 150 reporters, editors, copy editors and others, Gratteau said. They are spread among seven suburban bureaus, as well as Springfield and the main newsroom at Tribune Tower. But not all of them work on metropolitan news all the time.

When war breaks out in Iraq, Metro gets tapped for extra people to cover it. In presidential election season, Metro gets tapped to help augment the coverage. When it's decided to pursue a special project that can be nationwide or worldwide in scope, Metro gets tapped for bodies.

"We're very much the job jar of the paper," Gratteau explained. Not even the most talented staff, however, can make news where none exists. For several hours on Thursday, it appeared that Gratteau would have a nifty piece of enterprise reporting to offer for Page 1. A young suburban reporter had found Census data indicating some surprising changes in the makeup of suburban populations. But at the last minute, Marie Dillon, one of Gratteau's deputies, discerned a flaw in the story. It would need more work.

Gratteau went into the 4 p.m. Page 1 meeting with three stories to offer: the salmon story, the sex story and a piece on the visitation for Staff Sgt. Michael Sutter of Tinley Park, a casualty of the conflict in Iraq. She came out with two of them selected. The Sutter story would go on the front of the Metro section, along with other stories produced by her staff on Thursday.

Two stories for Page 1. About average. But there'll be another paper tomorrow, and the day after, and the day after that . . . .

The Day's Top Stories

Who decides whether the accident in Switzerland deserves more or less space than a local court trial? In part, this question is solved or evaded by departmentalization. The city editor, for example, typically will have a page or two for display of local news, and the sports editor and lifestyle editor have special sections for their copy.

On the front page or home page, however, the biggest stories from all the channels meet in competition. Here the mountain accident faces the local murder, the bill in the state legislature, the statement from the president and perhaps a World Series baseball game. The publication has to have clear staff organization to decide how the stories should be played.

At a newspaper, to keep track of all the stories during the day, each assigning editor and the wire editor compile lists of stories being produced for the next edition. These lists, known as budgets, contain a story slug (or name), a brief description of the story, the estimated length of the story, and whether art is available to illustrate the story. The editors also recommend stories they think worthy of the front page. These budgets are copied and distributed to editors across the newsroom.

The managing editor is usually responsible for making front-page story decisions, but on larger papers "the ME" rarely makes hour-by-hour decisions on all the major stories from varied sources. These routine decisions are left to a news editor, who makes tentative choices based on what he or she sees on the budgets.

During the afternoon, most newspaper newsrooms conduct one or two budget meetings, at which editors meet to discuss the potential front-page stories. These meetings will often start with the news editor's recommendations, and then each assignment editor, or his or her representative, will make arguments as to why their stories are important. In the end, the news editor or the managing editor will choose a tentative lineup—but even that can change, depending on new developments or whether stories met initial expectations.

This system provides greater objectivity in evaluating news, for the enthusiasms and foibles of a single editor can be contained. As the news flow continues, changing stories moderately or dramatically in the next few hours, two or three editors again may confer for a minute or two on how to handle the latest developments.

In some ways, this is judgment by committee, and no committee can edit a paper or Web site continuously. Individual editors must have the responsibility to make rapid decisions required by the varied flow of news. They operate something like people going through a cafeteria line, deciding swiftly which foods to select and which to reject.

Wire editors, for example, have to run their eyes quickly over a stream of story summaries on the computer screen. They must pass over a half-dozen and take a slightly longer look at the seventh story. The eighth may require the revival of a story already cast aside. Experience is essential, for little time exists to ponder for more than a few seconds what to do with most of the hundred or more stories popping onto the tube.

Editors as Skeptics

Skepticism about government claims is almost the first rule of reporting, although too few reporters follow through on their skepticism to dig deeply for the truth.

Editors should keep asking, "Who are the sources and what is their motive in giving information? Is the story planted as a diversion, to take the public's eye off an embarrassment? Is it the result of some public relations "spin"? Are some facts deliberately omitted or exaggerated? Is the story based on a "media event," a contrived happening to attract press attention?

If newsroom separation from advertising is easy to preach about, the issues involved in keeping circulation up are more complex and more subtle. Every journalist knows that the publication must sell. If it barely sells, neither the business nor the editorial staff is happy. This pressures editors to give the public "what it wants."

Editors often argue that the public wants serious, solid news coverage. On the other hand, many journalists say that the public interest is shallow, as shown by the great interest in comics and entertainment reports. That view may be too cynical. The *Los Angeles Times*, the *Wall Street Journal*, the *Philadelphia Inquirer* and the *New York Times* are all serious yet successful.

Papers in small cities might break even imitating the *New York Times*, but the pressure on almost all news organizations is to build profit. Most news organizations today are owned by large corporations that have been criticized for putting profit motives above public service. Bill Kovach and Tom Rosenstiel argue that journalism organizations should keep in mind that they work for the public and not for the corporations' shareholders or the foibles of Wall Street traders.[5] News organizations that focus on public service and quality journalism can be successful financially as well.[6]

Guidelines of Judgment

The editor makes news evaluations most of the time with little concern over pressures. Several guidelines help in deciding what gets published. One guide advises against printing the obvious story; events as predictable as the sunrise aren't news. Other obvious stories might be in the "What did you expect him to say?" category. If the Chamber of Commerce president predicts a booming Christmas business, no one should be surprised. Should one expect any other prediction from this person? If the president, back from a trip, announces that he had a "valuable discussion" with a prime minister, the editor probably has to print something, because the president spoke officially. But his statement is barely newsworthy because no one would expect him to say anything else. The only newsworthy prediction by a political candidate about a coming election would be, "I'm gonna lose."

When editors decide a subject is good enough for detailed coverage, they apply another guideline: story stamina. Will the issue have long-range interest or will it be forgotten in a few days? Subjects with staying power have been abortion rights, gay civil rights and the "war" on drugs. Some subjects of continuing interest have their vitality limited to short bursts of coverage. The ups and downs of the stock market may be everyone's concern for a few days, but major daily coverage for weeks on end is too much for the ordinary citizen. A subject with long-term potential may even be killed by too much coverage. Readers can stay interested in events, such as local airport development, if major decisions are not lost in a stream of unimportant daily stories.

Good editors also strive to stay alert to change. Our society changes rapidly, yet anyone concentrating on the daily events might miss the economic and social alterations occurring over several years. Most editors were a bit slow to realize that a substantial portion of the population was keenly interested in retirement income, pensions and estate planning.

Some editors ignore competition and others jump nervously in anticipation of what another paper or television station will do with certain stories. The best editors will note the competition and adjust the news play accordingly. A big story that has been on radio, television and online all day should be treated differently in the next morning's paper. Often, a newspaper will take a look at what the event means or what comes next. This is sometimes called putting a forward spin on the story.

Editor Biases

To make proper decisions on news play of major stories, editors must take a little time to reflect. Unfortunately, some veteran editors tend to think that decisive editing means fast editing. The best editors, however, know when decisions require delay. They read or watch sensitive stories two or three times and even discuss them with a colleague. The interests of both the news media and the public are best served by editors who have confidence in their judgment and who take time to let it operate effectively.

Some editors recognize that their own biases form one of the greatest pressures toward slanted coverage. How else can they view the news except through glasses colored by their own opinions and prejudices? Maybe they can see how the staff plays to their views on snakes or economic development or pollution controls. Complete objectivity is impossible, but editors can strive for it by regularly analyzing their feelings and checking influences on their judgments. They can watch the news play in other news media and assess how their judgments stack up. Finally, and perhaps most important, they can check their perceptions by conferring with other staffers.

But even the way colleagues view the news is not sufficient for really self-critical editors. Colleagues also have their local or national biases. Editors can try sometimes to imagine how a person in Asia or at the United Nations would view the news. Other cultures do not operate as the American culture does, and American journalists should not assume that a foreign nation's ways are clumsy, wasteful or evil. Regular exercise in trying to rise above their own biases, and even those of their profession and nation, would be salutary for news editors.

Such detachment is possible, and research has shown that editors with strong positions on an issue still can fairly handle a story on that subject. In fact, they might even do a better job simply because they are concerned enough to know whether the story adequately gives the facts.

Professional Integrity

Sound evaluation of news is bound up in professionalism. Professional editors come to look at their tasks not as plumbers contemplating a neat fit, important as that is, but as physicians or educators contemplating their role in the improvement of society. Such editors use as a frame of reference for decisions not the personal tastes of advertisers, the publisher or themselves but rather the professional ideals held by the best practitioners of the news profession.

Professional integrity is the ultimate safeguard of the news stream.

For many Americans, the Golden Rule is the ethical touchstone. Wouldn't a news organization be ethical if editors handled the news as they would want news of themselves handled? Not necessarily. The principle is not easily applied to the evaluation of news for a large public. Whether a story is published would depend on how much pull a person can develop with the editor, who takes pity on friends. To be an impartial gatekeeper, the ethical editor in a sense has to be without friends— or enemies.

What news of arrests, lawsuits, bankruptcies or other unhappy incidents would be printed if the rule were the desire of editors to have such news left out about themselves and their friends? The publication of most spot news items probably makes someone unhappy, and news organizations would go out of business if they did not seek a higher principle than saving someone's feelings. Sometimes they must publish or broadcast news that hurts individuals. Therefore, they apply a standard of fairness to all.

Notes

1. Andrew Boyd, *Broadcast Journalism: Techniques of Radio and Television News* (Oxford: Focal Press 2002), 20.

2. Mario R. Garcia and Pegie Stark, *Eyes on the News* (St. Petersburg, Fla.: Poynter Institute for Media Studies, 1991).

3. Liz Cox, "Imagine: Sixty-seven Young Journalists and the Newspaper of Their Dreams," *Columbia Journalism Review* (January/February 2003).

4. Pablo J. Boczkowski, *Digitizing the News: Innovation in Online Newspapers* (Cambridge, Mass.: MIT Press, 2004), 185–186

5. Bill Kovach and Tom Rosenstiel, *The Elements of Journalism: What Newspeople Should Know and the Public Should Expect* (New York: Three Rivers Press, 2001), 30.

6. Leonard Downie Jr. and Robert G. Kaiser, *The News About the News: American Journalism in Peril* (New York: Vintage Books, 2002).

CHAPTER 3

The Editor in the Newsroom

In a sense, a newsroom—no matter the medium—is an assembly line, with different workers assigned different tasks as information is gathered and moves toward publication. A news clerk who answers phones receives a tip about a student with a gun on a high school campus. The clerk passes this along to an assignment editor, who tells a reporter to check it out. The reporter gets on the phone to the police, who tell her that something's going on at the school but won't say exactly what. The reporter lets the editor know this and rushes out of the newsroom. The editor alerts the photo desk and the online editor and dispatches several more reporters to the scene.

Fifteen minutes later, the lead reporter calls the editor to report that police have the school cordoned off and that a student with a gun is in a classroom with 15 other students and a teacher. The editor transfers the reporter to a clerk, who dictates a few paragraphs that are quickly edited and sent to the online editor, who posts them to the newspaper's Web site. A half-hour after the initial tip, the news is already out there for readers to learn about. The reporters on the scene continue to gather information, reporting updates to the newsroom for Web site updates. Photographers at the scene digitally process their photographs and send them to the newsroom to put online.

Eventually, authorities talk the student with the gun into giving up. The reporters and photographers head back to the newsroom to begin assembling the package for the next morning's newspaper. The reporters work with the assignment editor and a graphic artist to craft the story and an informational graphic. The photographers work with photo editors to choose the best images. The assignment editor and photo editor then work with a page designer in preparing the overall presentation of the package. A copy editor checks the story for holes and style and grammatical problems, and writes headlines and photo captions. A copy chief checks the copy editor's work and approves the headlines. The page designer puts the final touches on the page and makes a proof. Another copy editor checks the package for errors before the page is sent to the production department to be readied for the press. (See Figure 3.1.)

The computer automatically feeds the story to the newspaper's Web site, where a story is posted immediately and can be revised later when an online editor comes in in the morning.

The next morning, it starts all over again.

Newsroom Structure

No two newsrooms are the same, but the similarities outnumber the differences. Most newsrooms are led by an editor who carries the title of executive editor, editor-in-chief or simply editor. This editor is generally the big picture manager in the newsroom, plotting course and direction for the operation of the editorial department. The top editor usually reports to the publisher and is in charge of the newsroom's budget.

The second ranking editor in the newsroom is the managing editor, who is responsible for the day-to-day operation of the newsroom. This editor works with other editors in the newsroom to plan the day's coverage, make sure resources are adequately deployed, and choose the stories that will be placed on the front page. (See Figure 3.2.)

At the next level are assignment editors, sometimes called line editors, who work directly with reporters, photographers and artists to develop stories, photos and graphics. Each assignment editor has a different area of supervision. Types of assignment editors include but are not limited to: city editors, metro editors, regional editors, state editors, suburban editors, bureau editors, features editors, entertainment editors, sports editors, business editors, projects editors, photo editors and art directors. This level of the newsroom is at the heart of the information-gathering process.

Another set of editors in the newsroom is in charge of production. These include wire editors, news editors, page designers, copy editors and copy desk chiefs, also known as slot editors. The production editors package the material generated by the assignment desks into newspaper and Web pages.

The Assignment Editors

Assignment editors and their assistants supervise staffs that may range from one to 50 or more people, and each is responsible for a certain part of the publication. Although they are supervising the news report for the once-daily print publication, they also keep in mind the 24-hour news cycle of their Web sites and funnel early versions of stories to the online editors.

The best known of these assignment editors is the city editor, who di-

Copy flow at a daily newspaper

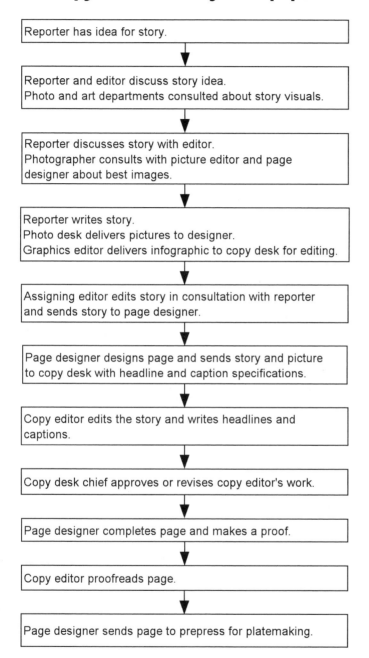

Reporter has idea for story.

Reporter and editor discuss story idea.
Photo and art departments consulted about story visuals.

Reporter discusses story with editor.
Photographer consults with picture editor and page designer about best images.

Reporter writes story.
Photo desk delivers pictures to designer.
Graphics editor delivers infographic to copy desk for editing.

Assigning editor edits story in consultation with reporter and sends story to page designer.

Page designer designs page and sends story and picture to copy desk with headline and caption specifications.

Copy editor edits the story and writes headlines and captions.

Copy desk chief approves or revises copy editor's work.

Page designer completes page and makes a proof.

Copy editor proofreads page.

Page designer sends page to prepress for platemaking.

Figure 3.1.
How a story moves through the reporting and editing process in a newsroom that produces both a newspaper and a Web site.

rects reporters covering the city and, often, its environs. A few papers give this person the title of metro editor, because coverage of the metropolitan area is handled at the same desk. Another assignment editor, the state editor, takes care of a broader area but rarely the whole state because few newspapers sell that widely. "Regional editor" or "county editor" might be a more accurate title than "state editor" because such a person supervises the collection of news in the publication's circulation area out-

Figure 3.2.
Organizational charts for
the *Lodi News-Sentinel*
and the *Sacramento Bee*.
The chart for the *Bee* is
more complex than that
for the smaller *News-
Sentinel*. Each of the
Bee's assistant managing
editors and deputy man-
aging editor, listed in
the left columns, reports
to the managing editor,
who in turn reports to the
executive editor.

Lodi News-Sentinel Newsroom

side the metropolitan area. A suburban editor—in contrast to the city editor—is responsible for coverage outside the core city area. Most big-city papers include strong sections of suburban news because many people in suburbia are more interested in their own towns than in the center city, and because the demographics of the suburbs are more attractive to advertisers. The suburban news often appears in zoned editions, with each edition tailored to readers in a section of the newspaper's circulation area. The *Chicago Tribune* is zoned eight ways, providing different parts of northeastern Illinois news tailored for different regions. The *Sacramento Bee* publishes seven regional sections on Thursdays and four on Sundays. Zoning editions this way also allows advertisers to tailor their messages to specific markets. (See Figure 3.3.)

The sports editor cuts across area lines, collecting sports news from everywhere. The sports editor supervises writers, edits their copy and selects news from the wire services.

The features editor collects softer material for use in lifestyle and entertainment sections. These sections include stories on culture, child care, hobbies, social problems, food preparation and fashions. Stories might be on such subjects as coping with divorce, handling a hyperactive child or dealing with the problems of aging parents. A separate entertainment editor may be responsible for coverage of music, movies, theater and the arts.

The business editor is responsible for the publication's coverage of the economy and financial world. These stories range from profiles of local small business and the daily stock market report to personal finance news that helps readers decide how to invest their money.

Welcome to the editor's chair

It would be ideal if every person had a year or more of experience on a desk before becoming an assignment editor. Preferably, the experience

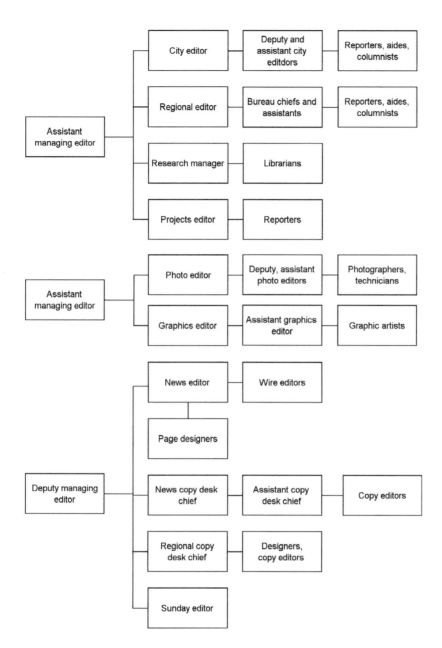

Figure 3.2. *(continued)*

would be as assistant to an assignment editor. But except on the biggest publications, this kind of background is usually impossible. Often a person will be told one day by the managing editor, "You're going to be the sports editor (or city editor or state editor)." The person may have had only sketchy editing experience and no steady experience in writing headlines or in design. No opportunity has existed to learn how to supervise the work of others. How can anyone make the jump gracefully and safely?

A new editor unfamiliar with the job should cram. Pumping other staffers, including predecessors, for information and tips, and even solic-

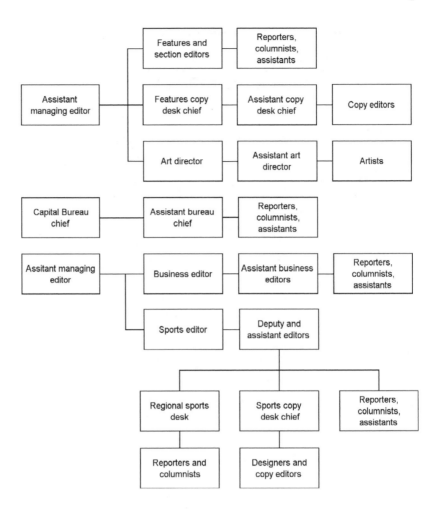

Figure 3.2. *(continued)*

iting criticisms, without indicating a lack of confidence, can help the new editor overcome inexperience.

The assignment editor, if possible, should delegate a certain amount of responsibility. By doing everything, an editor probably will do nothing well. Nor will there be time to do any planning or reflecting on how the job will be affected by changing times. Moreover, by delegating, the assignment editor possibly becomes available to fill in for the news editor or even managing editor during sickness or vacations. Should the editor be promoted or leave the paper, the assignment editor will be prepared to take over.

The assignment editor whose staff can work without constant supervision can set aside a certain time to inspect the territory. The demands of the job can pressure editors into spending the whole work day bent over a desk, while they, especially the city editor, should be out checking community developments once in awhile. Any editor should go occasionally to a meeting on a hot local issue to observe the debates and gain insight into public thinking. Such visits create empathy with staffers, because they sense that their editor has become directly concerned with the events they cover.

www.sacbee.com/elkgrove   The Sacramento Bee

CHURCHILL DOWNS
VINEYARD
COUNTRYSIDE
RANCHO MURIETA
WILTON
ELK GROVE
LAGUNA
GALT
FRANKLIN
THE DELTA

Section
G

ELK GROVE

THURSDAY
September 23, 2004

▶ YOUR SCHOOLS **G2**   ▶ SPORTS **G6–G7**   ▶ COMMUNITY CALENDAR **G8**

GREEK TO THEM

Athina Holland of Elk Grove spoons a ground meat mixture into grape leaves to make stuffed dolmas.

Members of St. Katherine Church are cooking up a storm in preparation for the annual food festival

By Loretta Kalb
BEE STAFF WRITER

So you missed the Acropolis and other scenic treasures in Athens, Greece, last month during the Summer Olympics.

Don't worry. You still can soak up a bit of Greek-style romance starting Saturday in Laguna West, where members of St. Katherine Greek Orthodox Church have labored for weeks to stage "A Weekend in Greece."

Admission is free and will include music, dancing and church tours. But the aroma of Greek foods will compel the hundreds of expected visitors to dig into their pockets and buy the tasty fare made from ingredients donated by Greek-American parishioners.

A Weekend in Greece

When: 11 a.m. to 9 p.m. Saturday and Sunday
Where: St. Katherine Greek Orthodox Church, 9165 Peets St., Laguna West
Admission: Free
A la carte fare: $2 to $4 a serving
Feast to include:
400 cheese pies, four varieties
500 spinach pies
12 pans of moussaka
18 pans of pastitsio
1 lamb on a spit
600 soudlaka
2,000 dolmas
15 pans of baklava

Menu items will include moussaka, that delicate blend of eggplant, flour and cheese; baklava, the famous Greek phyllo pastry treat; Greek twist cookies; and more hearty fare.

"This is an excellent opportunity for those people who weren't able to see the Olympics to enjoy some of the great Greek culture that the people who actually went there enjoyed," said the Rev. Constantine Pappademos, church pastor.

Church members have worked to stage the event, which will help the parish furnish its new $1.5 million church hall – to be known as Tsakopoulos Hall – and help fund its local ministries.

Next year, preparations for the annual event will be far easier. This year, the church's

▶ GREEK, page G5

Helen Rotas of Sacramento grills eggplant to make moussaka, a baked dish made with meat sauce and grated Parmesan cheese, at St. Katherine Greek Orthodox Church for this weekend's festival.

Baklava

1 pound unsalted butter
4 cups walnuts, chopped fine
1/2 cup sugar
1 pound phyllo dough
1 teaspoon cinnamon

Combine walnuts, cinnamon and sugar. Set aside. Melt butter. Brush butter on bottom of 9-by-13-inch pan. Place one sheet of phyllo dough in pan and brush with melted butter. Repeat until you have eight sheets in the pan, one over the other. Sprinkle a little nut mixture over the top sheet. Then top with another sheet phyllo, brush with butter. Continue doing this until all of the nut mixture is used. Then top with remaining sheets of phyllo dough, brushing each with butter. Brush top with butter. Place pan in refrigerator for a few minutes until butter is firm. At this point, the baklava can be frozen. When ready to bake, cut baklava into diamond shapes. Bake for one hour at 300 degrees until golden brown.

Syrup for baklava

Note: When pouring syrup on baklava, syrup must be cool and baklava hot. It is best to make the syrup first.

4 cups sugar
Juice from half a lemon
2 cups water
1/2 cup honey
1 cinnamon stick

Boil sugar and water about 15 minutes until thickened. Add honey and lemon juice. Let cool. Allow baklava to cool and absorb the syrup. Serve warm or completely cooled.

Recipe provided by St. Katherine Greek Orthodox Church

> **"We're being singled out because of one organization's actions, and it's not fair."**
> **Karen Fong Cotton**
> president of the Sacramento Asian Sports Foundation

Projects proceed despite threat

Plans move ahead for a bike path and sports complex, with or without grant money.

By Sandy Louey
BEE STAFF WRITER

City officials say a bike path could help draw people to Old Town Elk Grove – a piece of the larger revitalization effort that Elk Grove is launching for the area.

Across town in Laguna West, the Sacramento Asian Sports Foundation hopes to break ground on a sports and recreation complex next year – the culmination of more than a decade of planning.

Despite learning recently that they might lose grant money from the California Department of Parks and Recreation, officials with the city and the foundation said their projects are moving ahead.

"Despite the fact we may or may not lose this money, we will still proceed forward," foundation President Karen Fong Cotton said.

On Sept. 14, state Controller Steve Westly ordered $15 million in grants from the Department of Parks and Recreation withheld after a

▶ FUNDS, page G2

Quick OK expected for school site

By Gabriel Baird
BEE STAFF WRITER

The Elk Grove Planning Commission is expected to rubber-stamp the location of a school site in the Laguna Ridge area tonight, a routine but necessary step if the facility is to open within the next three years as planned.

Elk Grove Unified School District officials need the OK to secure the state's approval of the nearly 80-acre site under the California Environmental Quality Act.

The district intends to open a combined middle and high school campus by fall 2007 near the middle of the Laguna Ridge Specific Plan area, where Big Horn Boulevard and Laguna Ridge Road eventually will intersect, said Constantine Baranoff, assistant superintendent of facilities and planning.

The Elk Grove City Council approved the Laguna Ridge Specific Plan in June, allowing for

▶ SITE, page G5

School collects coins to buy bench in memory of student

Remembering an angel: A water bottle with a halo sits on the counter of Florence Marketer Elementary. Its wings were taken off, says secretary Tammi Barrett, because the change kept falling between the doilies and the bottle. A little more than $300 has been donated in the "Pennies for Haven" angel. The school is trying to collect $1,400 for a bench, plaque and tree to remember Haven Scarborough, who would have been in third grade this year. The 8-year-old Elk Grove resident drowned in July when her hair got caught in a pool drain. "We felt that there was a need for the students to have some place to go back and remember Haven," Tammi said. She said students have a hard time understanding how someone so young and popular can die. The memorial would be near the play area. Fund-raising Solutions, a company that works with

the school to raise funds, gave $500. It's still not enough. To make more money, the school is selling tickets to the Willow Pumpkin Patch in Wilton. Although the fund-raiser is meant to help pay for assemblies, it will first be used to make up the difference needed for the bench. ...

Drawing straws: Wendy Cevola of Elk Grove got the deal of a lifetime: 25,000 straws for $1.98, plus $40 shipping. Wendy likes straws; she won't drink without one. "Remember when you were a little kid and got down to the last little bit, and the ice whacked you in the nose?" Wendy asked. One day, realizing she spends about $10 a month on straws, Wendy decided there had to be a cheaper way. She turned to eBay.

DIANA LAMBERT

There was an auction for 10,000 straws. "No one bid on it, so I placed a dollar bid," she said. She won. Her bargain-hunting confidence heightened, she plunked down a $1 bid for 5,000 straws in another auction and won. Because no one else bid, she got each for the 99-cent opening bid. "My husband said that no company would send 15,000 straws for $1.98," Wendy said. After three weeks of waiting, Wendy began to believe her husband. She called the company. A few days later, the FedEx man appeared at the door with 20,000 straws – striped and fluorescent, the type that bend at the top. Two days later, another 5,000 straws arrived. They could have been consola-

tion for her wait, but Wendy didn't ask. She figures she has about 12 years' worth of straws. Happy sipping. ...

What's new?: Original Pete's, Port City Java, Aloha Barbeque and a beauty and nail shop have signed leases at Harbour Palms at Elk Grove Boulevard and Harbour Point Drive, says John Wallace of Local Centers, Harbour Palms developer. The 10,000-square-foot center is expected to open near the end of the year. The pizza parlor will take up about a third of that space. Wallace, known for guiding the folks on the Web site Elk Grove Online, says that after talking to residents, it was clear there is a need for more restaurants. All three eateries will be owned by Elk Grove residents. ...

Bus fire blues: Vanessa Garcia, 16, was on her way to the Meadowview area when the Regional Transit bus she was riding in started to beep, beep. Bus 56

had just started its route about 3:15 p.m. Monday, from Third Street and Elk Grove Boulevard to its next stop in Bruceville Road, when an alarm sounded. The driver rounded up the four riders and got them off the bus before activating the fire-extinguishing system, says Michael Zehnder, Elk Grove battalion chief. "I just heard a beeping sound," Garcia said. In the end, everyone was safe, although a little annoyed. Two of the four passengers sat on a bench to await the next bus. Guada Dixon was already there. She had been waiting for more than an hour for Bus 56. An hour later, they continued to wait.

□ □ □

Reach Diana Lambert at (916) 478-2672 or dlambert@sacbee.com. Back columns: www.sacbee.com/lambert. Bee staff writer Loretta Kalb contributed to this column.

Figure 3.3.
The Sacramento Bee publishes regional sections twice a week to serve different parts of its circulation area. Copyright 2004, *The Sacramento Bee*. Used with permission.

Editors must direct the operations of reporters and copy editors, and that job is not simple. Some people cannot give orders without being abrasive. Others swing between joviality and gloom. Some editors demand quality one day and forget it the next.

Supervisors ought to be consistent and reasonable with the staff. When they were reporters or copy editors they certainly wanted congenial surroundings, a competent supervisor and a chance to get an occasional laugh. Supervising editors should at least try to fulfill their own requirements.

But an editor should beware of the tangles of doing favors for staffers. A day off given to one person may, because of circumstances, be denied to another. It must be made clear to these people that they couldn't get the holiday because of a scheduling problem, not a personal one. One solution is to give no favors that can't be given to everyone. Yet an editor creates a sense of well-being if occasionally a staffer can go home early or slip out during a quiet period to run a personal errand. When the editor is both flexible and impartial, staff morale goes up.

Praise and criticism

No editor should overlook the value of praise. Most journalists are immune to ostentatious flattery—they have seen so much that is phony—but they cherish a casual sentence of praise from a colleague. A simple "Good story, Charley," or "Nice headline, Liz!" will do more to spark professionalism than any scroll of merit. For example, at the *Sacramento Bee*, reporters and copy editors are regularly honored for excellence through e-mails that are sent to everyone in the newsroom.

One of the best ways editors can improve morale is to get pay increases for deserving staff members. When requested raises come through, editors can tell staffers quietly, "Your good work of the last several months means an extra $30 a week from now on." Staffers so rewarded will be pleasantly surprised and grateful for a superior who works for the staff as well as the publisher.

But what happens when a staffer fails to measure up? In the old days, the editor probably would bellow, "You're fired!" Such abrupt dismissal is rare today because editors realize that it is cruel and that it often loses a potentially good employee. Furthermore, workers represented by unions such as the Newspaper Guild often work under contracts that bar dismissal without specific cause.

Instead of muttering deprecations about an inadequate staffer, an editor should aim to teach. A few minutes spent every day helping the new staffer correct shortcomings and speaking favorably about strong points will improve both the newcomer's morale and usefulness to the publication. Sometimes the editor assigns another person to go over a novice reporter's copy, sentence by sentence, to show how it can be improved. If all efforts fail in getting improvement, it would be better for the newsroom and the employees if the inadequate employees were urged to look elsewhere for work. Staffers who are not fired outright can more easily find another job that they may handle well. Any such conversation with a staffer, of course, should be private. The wise editor, under these circumstances, refrains from suggesting that a person get into another line of work. Many successful journalists have, at one time or another, had such advice and, fortunately, not taken it. But newspeople who recognize they have no journalistic talent should quit.

Promising reporters and copy editors should be encouraged to attend the increasing number of workshops and study sessions being held throughout the country. They should be urged, also, to take courses at local colleges or universities. Some publications pay the tuition if the person completes them satisfactorily. The courses need not be on journalism; almost any knowledge can be valuable to a journalist.

Opportunities for Training

A searchable database of training available to journalists is at www.journalismtraining.org. Here are some of the many organizations that provide training for journalists:

- The Poynter Institute for Media Studies, www.poynteronline.org
- The American Press Institute, www.americanpressinstitute.org
- Foundation for American Communications, www.facsnet.org
- Society for News Design, www.snd.org
- American Copy Editors Society, www.copydesk.org

Sometimes even a good reporter or copy editor hits a slump, forcing an analysis of the problem in a talk with an editor. Perhaps some personal problem is causing worry, or the job itself has become dull. Talking it out may be just what the staffer needs to regain former enthusiasm and skill. Other times the editor can suggest or even provide solutions to the problem. For example, a person who has worked on the desk for a couple of years and basically likes the work may be getting a little tired of sitting all day. Couldn't a special reporting assignment be made once in a while for a change of pace?

Directing news collection

An assignment editor soon discovers that the efficiency and morale of the staff depend partly on the flow of work. Every journalist knows that news comes in spurts. News may be heavy for a week or more, and then for a few days nothing seems to happen. Some of these quiet periods can be predicted. Summer is the calmest season. Schools and legislatures are out of session, and most community action slacks off as workers prepare for vacations. The Christmas season repeats this lull in those civic affairs that produce most of the nonspectacular news.

In some places local news is heavy a couple of days a week and light on others. The city council may meet Mondays and the school board Tuesdays. Both normally provide several stories. The county board of supervisors, another good news source, also may meet on a Tuesday. If the city planning commission meets Monday night and the zoning board Tuesday, then local government news may well pile up the first of the week. Unless the city editor plans for peaks and slumps, coverage on Thursday, Friday and Saturday will be drab and insignificant—not worth reading—and the staff will suffer from being alternately swamped and idled.

During the dull periods the staff should be scratching for feature stories or digging for important information below the surface of events. If it is obvious that the city council will make news about building codes early one week, why not interview the city engineer the week before on new building techniques or talk to a leading architect on ideas for the city of the future? On the other hand, if the council makes a surprising or especially significant decision on Monday, the rest of the week provides time to follow up on the reasons for the decision and its implications.

The ability to create story ideas is among the editor's greatest assets. The assignment editor must develop this skill if the job requires more than a person who gives routine assignments, edits copy, writes headlines, designs pages and pats a reporter's back once in a while. An editor may do the routine well, but first-rate status will not come without imagination. And since imagination is always in short supply, an editor should encourage it among colleagues. The willingness to stimulate story ideas and the play of stories are characteristics that develop a spirited staff. People get excited on a newspaper whose editors listen to new ideas and are willing to experiment and reward enterprise. Every assignment editor should have a device for soliciting staffers' suggestions. But if suggestions are rejected, the contributor ought to know why. An editor who repeatedly ignores ideas quickly freezes staff initiative. Every suggestion needs acknowledgment and at least a word of thanks.

The city editor

Journalists generally concede that the city editor's job is the most difficult of all the assignment editor positions. The person with this task has to supervise the biggest staff of reporters and fit the talents of these reporters to dozens of jobs. Throughout the workday alterations, suggestions and specific directions must be given. The city editor gives assignments to reporters and photographers, sees that the copy is edited properly and checks the fit of local copy to the available space.

On smaller publications the job may seem easier but often it is not. Although the city editor on a small paper may have only a few reporters to supervise, the task also requires reading all their copy, writing all the headlines and sometimes producing a few stories on the side. Since many reporters on small papers are inexperienced, the city editor must try to make up for their deficiencies with editing and training. This training, because of a lack of time, often must consist of an over-the-shoulder comment from time to time or some brief instructions on how to get the information for a certain story.

City editors on medium-sized papers will have an assistant or two. One assistant may handle the assignment chore, with the city editor suggesting a special story, and another may edit local pictures. The editor and assistants all will edit some local copy. The city editor often designs local news pages. On the biggest papers the city editor has a half-dozen or more assistants, each with a team of reporters.

This supervisory role gives the city editor the flexibility needed to handle the day's little or big emergencies. The gifted city editor manages to keep most emergencies in the newsroom from becoming severe. Adequate preparation allows the staff to move swiftly in any crisis. Preparation means anticipating major stories and having reporters and editors ready to handle all facets of the events. It also means the ability to alter plans swiftly when an unexpected event occurs.

Preparedness is vital to the smooth operation of a city desk. For a coming election, the inept editor fails to prepare for stories that anyone would expect to happen. The well-organized editor plans who will write the story or stories on state legislative races and who will handle city council contests. Preparation means the difference between a confused scramble to write stories and the provision of thorough, balanced coverage.

Though an election obviously needs planning if it is to be covered adequately, the demands of some events are more subtle. As an illustration, a news publication in a city surrounded by prime farmland may become concerned by urban sprawl creeping over those rich and productive fields. The editors may worry about lower food production and the cost of new streets, sewer lines and public transportation. Editors would need a careful but flexible plan if prospective stories on the subject were to be covered. The farm writer might discover how many acres have been taken out of agriculture in the past 10 years. The county government reporter might examine zoning laws and how they have been enforced. Land use experts, developers and farmers could be interviewed. Stories on the broad subject might run from time to time over a year. Every couple of months, the publication might run a story summarizing in a few hundred words what had been discovered.

Almost no publication, of course, has the staff, the facilities or the need to plan for a campaign that would take the energies of half a dozen staffers for six months. But every paper should look down the calendar a few months or even years to make sure that it does not miss a good story. For example, a school board issue may be brewing over whether to build a new school, and the town seems headed for a full-fledged dispute. The education writer should be on top of it, but some help may be required. The city hall reporter might note how the issue spills into city government; a general assignment reporter may visit a neighboring city to see how that town resolved a similar dispute. In another example, a prominent politician may be getting up in years and just might announce his or her retirement an hour before deadline. Good planning would mean that when the announcement comes, stories are almost ready on that person's political life and the jostling by a dozen who will battle to take over the job. A sidebar may be ready on the politician's humble beginnings. These stories could be produced swiftly because reporters could check the publication's library or online archive and recall facts or anecdotes from their own memories. Editors could suggest calling people who have known the official for years.

Even when emergencies force city editors to make quick decisions, they should pause and ponder: "Are we getting the whole story? Are we missing anything? Are we overplaying? Have we got the right pictures? What's the best layout for all these stories? What must we cut or drop in order to print this hot news?"

To do the job properly, the city editor must be able to grasp instantly the value of news, coach young reporters, juggle staff to get the best coverage and inspire respect, if not admiration.

The press of time

The city editor soon finds that the clock becomes the main obstacle to good coverage. Is the information solid enough to post online now? To go to press in the morning? How much time to deadline for the print newspaper, and the pressures of competition online, are the paramount questions as to whether there is time to publish any more than the bare facts of a story and get a picture or two to illustrate it.

To keep from being unduly harassed by the clock, the city editor strives to develop top efficiency. Aides are chosen who can move swiftly to solve the problems that develop. Editors learn the strengths and weaknesses of reporters and give the story needing the swiftest work to the fastest writer. City editors eliminate inefficient habits. Since memos, notes and other newspapers usually surround city editors, they are tempted to set some aside to read later. An excellent city editor once remarked that no one should handle the same piece of paper twice. "Read it and decide what to do with it," was his motto.

The best city editors today keep tabs on more than the city room. In addition to getting around the city themselves, they read up on its history so that they can guide their staffs to write stories that set the social and economic problems of the community in historical context. They will report such things as the changing political power base, local developments in mental health, the deep and often hidden frictions behind violence, or a real critique of the local educational system.

The sports editor

The sports editor has one advantage over other assignment editors: Almost all sports news is expected. The editor knows at the start of the workday that several games or events are scheduled, so plans for the section can be seriously altered only by such things as the cancellation of an event, the death of a famous athlete, the highly unexpected outcome of a contest or the setting of some record.

The sports editor does have some special problems. For one, readers want to know right away how their favorite teams did, so it's doubly important to get stories ready for online publication. For another, because many people find sports and sports stars dramatic and spectacular, sports copy tends to be overly dramatic. The sports editor has to guard against absurdly melodramatic stories. He must keep in mind that victory for the home team really is not the greatest of glories, and defeat is not the greatest of tragedies. The pages should not treat athletes as superpeople, either, for sometimes off the field they are far from heroic.

Sportswriters, often strong on clichés, need a watchful editor. Sometimes a writer attempts to be different and brings forth what amounts to an essay on a game. Although this may be a fine piece of writing, too often the writer gets so wrapped up in unaccustomed rhetoric that the score is omitted. Hyperbole should never replace accuracy and completeness.

Sports publicists, in common with politicians, constantly push reporters and editors to promote their pet topics. Editors have to be sure that they are covering, not promoting, a sport. Long ago, sports pages ran all kinds of stories on professional wrestling even though it was generally known that matches were rigged. Finally, a number of editors, deciding not to promote fraud, quit printing stories and pictures about pro wrestlers.

Minor league baseball is another sport for which almost tearful requests for promotion must be resisted. In dozens of cities around the country, sports editors have been asked to boost the hometown team. If they decline, team supporters scorn them as disloyal. Yet most of the teams are owned by private businesses, the major league clubs. By allowing excessive coverage, the newspaper actually subsidizes private business. Such baseball teams often get more stories than any other group in town. No other public performance—movie, play, concert, or opera—receives the kind of coverage that is given a minor league team that may draw only a few hundred fans a night.

Some sports editors today try to trim coverage of professional and top amateur athletes to make room for unorganized sports. More and more Americans are enjoying sport for its own sake. They sail, ski, surf, hike, bike, camp, fly, shoot and skin-dive. Because most of these sports, though vigorous, are not competitive, the modern sports editor seeks fresh ways to cover them. Usually this is done with feature stories and pictures.

The good editor always has to be attentive to pictures, not only because photography plays an important part in sports but also because today's readers spend more time watching sports on TV, which means that only exceptional pictures are likely to capture their interest. Consistently good photographs are hard to find anywhere, and sports editors usually have the highest proportion of cliché shots. This means an abundance of photos showing someone sliding into second base or taking a basketball jump shot. Even the most attentive sports fan will ignore them.

The sports editor must demand truly extraordinary pictures, illustrating athletic grace, skill and intensity. Any editor who demands good pictures must, of course, meet the demands of a good photographer—adequate time, excellent equipment and the promise of seeing the best pictures in print.

Other assignment editors

The list of assignment editors above is by no means exhaustive. Different newsrooms have different needs. Some large publications, such as the *Los Angeles Times* and the *New York Times*, have national and foreign editors who direct, at a sophisticated level, staffs of national and foreign correspondents. Many publications have Sunday editors in charge of the whole Sunday edition with its magazine and special pages or sections devoted to finance, real estate, books, entertainment, travel, hobbies and television. This editor has a weeklong job assembling articles, reviews and photographs from his or her own staff, as well as other journalists across the newsroom.

A few editors are actually specialized reporters. They cover such areas as the arts, education, religion, business or labor. The title "editor" is perhaps justified for reasons other than status or newspaper promotion, because such a person has more independence than the ordinary writer on general assignment. Science editors or music critics usually direct no staffs. They give themselves assignments. Some other editor, probably the city or features editor, is technically the boss, but one who usually defers to the specialized editor-writer's expert assessment of the news.

The Production Editors

Production at daily newspapers is a dynamic process. Because the news is different every day, the approach that editors take every day is necessarily different. Still, processes are in place to assure, for the most part, the orderly assembly of the newspaper such that the press starts on time around midnight. Late press starts cost money and anger publishers, and editors know this. The editors primarily responsible for the final production of the newspaper include page designers (sometimes called news editors), copy editors (sometimes called rim editors) and slot editors (sometimes called copy desk chiefs).

Page designers are responsible for the look of each day's newspaper, following the newspaper's design style. These pages range from the heavily designed fronts of sections to simple pages inside that can accommodate only a single story. The designers work with the photo and graphics editors to decide on what art to use, decide how and where to place stories, and create headline and caption assignments for copy editors. Page design is discussed in more detail in Chapter 8.

Copy editors are the unsung heroes of the newsroom. Because when they get a story to edit without having been involved in its creation, they provide a fresh eye—the reader's eye—to the story. They look for unanswered questions, lapses of logic and problems with story flow. They look critically for problems with grammar, spelling, style and punctuation. Although they are not expected to check every fact in a story—there just isn't time—they assure a story's accuracy by conducting spot checks and by verifying anything that raises a question.

At most newspapers, after applying this critical eye, copy editors write the headlines to the specifications provided by the page designer. If required, they also write captions to go with pictures, and proofread informational graphics, which must be consistent with the story that they accompany. After the page is completed by the page editor, copy editors proofread the pages before they are sent to plate-making.

It's the job of the slot editor—so-called because before computers came to newsrooms, slot editors sat inside the center of a horseshoe-shaped desk—to check the work of the copy editors and send it back to the page designer for final assembly on the page. Depending on the amount of time available, the slot editor may read the whole story again, or may just give it a quick glance to make sure that the headline is accurate and that the captions are appropriate to the package. In many newsrooms, the slot editor is also the copy desk chief, the newsroom manager responsible for evaluation and development of the copy editors.

The Online Editors

Because online news media are so new, the structure of their operations is less predictable than in the newspaper newsroom. Small operations connected to newsrooms may have only one online employee, whose job includes not only placing content from the print publication online but also preparing advertisements and promotional material and supplying programming help. Larger operations may differentiate between the editors and the advertising function. At Knight Ridder publications nationwide, much of the site maintenance is handled from Knight Ridder Digital headquarters in San Jose, Calif., with liaisons in the newsrooms at the company's print publications.

Other news sites, such SFGate in San Francisco, are operated independently of their sister publications. SFGate's staff includes separate editors responsible for maintaining the home page, the features pages and the sports page. Choosing material from the Associated Press, the *San Francisco Chronicle* and stories and photos created specifically for SFGate, the editors build a successful online news publication that reaches a different demographic from the newspaper. (See Figure 3.4.)

A separate crew of designers and programmers maintains the look and feel of the site. Additional employees process photographs and multimedia presentations for use on the Web site.

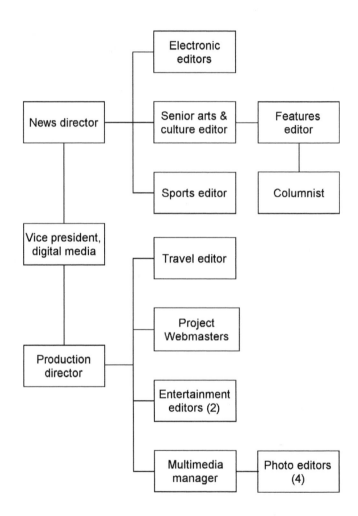

Figure 3.4.
The organizational chart for SFGate, the sister Web site of the *San Francisco Chronicle*.

CHAPTER 4

Editors as Managers

Long gone are the days when curmudgeonly editors bellowed across the newsroom, "WHO WROTE THIS PIECE OF GARBAGE!" In those days, reporters and editors seldom talked about a story as it was being reported or written; the reporter put his words to a typewriter, and as deadline approached, the editor tore the copy from the typewriter in midsentence and started to work on it. Almost all editing was done after-the-fact—and there was little the reporter could do about what was done to his work.

Luckily, today's newsrooms practice more enlightened management. The work of reporters is not only respected but also encouraged along the way. This style of working with reporters is known as coaching, and the approach not only improves story coverage and writing but also helps reporters and editors improve as journalists along the way.

Some news organizations even employ writing coaches or direct an editor to spend at least a couple of days a week helping reporters with their writing. Sometimes the training consists of a coach sitting down with a reporter and carefully going over copy. Each sentence is evaluated and a story's deficiencies are explored. The coach emphasizes getting more information and figuring out ways to make maximum use of all the facts. At other times, the coach might bring a half-dozen reporters together to consider how sentences can be more concise and leads less stereotyped. Before these training sessions start, top editors must determine what kind of writing they want—sprightly or serious, detailed or almost superficial—and encourage the whole staff to aim toward the desired writing style. Editors will not need uniformity, of course, but will strive to avoid excessive variety in styles. But the best coaching comes during the one-on-one daily interactions between reporters and their assigning editors.

The Coaching Process

The coaching process is explained in detail by Roy Peter Clark and Don Fry of the Poynter Institute for Media Studies in their book, *Coaching Writers: Editors and Writers Working Together Across Media Platforms*. Their main advice: Assigning editors should allow reporters to maintain ownership of their stories. They write, "The coaching process speeds things up, investing a little time early to save a lot of time later." Clark and Fry describe six steps in the writing/editing process that editors-as-coaches should employ:

> The coaching editor works in tandem with the reporter. During the **idea** step, the editor **briefs** the reporter, generally a two-minute conversation about the concept, sourcing, photographic and graphic needs, and scope of the projected story. During the **report** step, the editor remains available to **help** if the story changes in the field (as it almost always does), or the reporter needs guidance or simply gets lost. During the **organize** step, the editor **debriefs** the reporter in a short conversation devoted to what the story will say, how and at what length. During the **draft** and **revise** steps, while the reporter types, the editor remains available to **help** if the story changes again, or if the reporter has trouble with the wording, especially the lead. After the reporter files the story, the editor reacts to it and gives it back to the reporter to **finish**, essentially a final revision.[1]

Using this process, the reporter and editor are always in tune on the story; the reporter knows what the editor is expecting, and the editor gets no surprises from the reporter at the end of the process. (See Figure 4.1.)

Helping reporters structure stories

Editors serving as teachers must make clear that instructions for handling simple stories don't quite work for the complex story. The inverted pyramid diagram for a news story quickly breaks down in longer stories.

In his popular English textbook, *The Practical Stylist*, Sheridan Baker argues that the writer should find a thesis to begin a piece. A thesis can be stated as a debate resolution, "Resolved that . . ." When writers thus clarify their aim, they find that the supporting information falls into logical order, into an outline.

This approach has some validity for most news stories, since the beginning states the point of each piece. The concept is most applicable to the work of the editorial writers when they attempt persuasive editorials, but in the newsroom, Baker's thesis on theses is generally valuable. It reminds editors to look for a clear statement of the main point close to the top of a story—the nut graph.

Another rhetorical tradition classifies writing forms, such as the essay, into a natural (and obvious) pattern of three parts—beginning, middle and end, standing like three rectangular blocks piled one on another. The

Figure 4.1.
Jennifer Bonnett, the assistant city editor at the *Lodi-News Sentinel*, shows just how busy editors at small news publications can get. With two mobile phones at the ready, and three stories on her computer at one time, she consults with reporter Ross Farrow about a story.

middle might be subdivided into several paragraphs of development. The bottom block is the conclusion. This plan fits nicely with Baker's if the top contains the statement of thesis, and it leads to more interesting news stories than the inverted pyramid can ever do.

Complex patterns

Analysis of news stories over many decades shows that actually they are not simple inverted triangles. Usually they are a number of triangles on a string, like fish. The story unfolds in two or three paragraphs, then re-caps with more detail, explains at length in a third triangle, and perhaps adds minor detail and color in still another. Consider the story of a major fire in three or four buildings. The first section quickly recounts the deaths and damage. The next section reveals how it started and spread and how firefighting forces were marshaled. The next sections tell who discovered it, what efforts were made to confine it to the first building, and who made a call for outside help. There may be a snippet about two suburbs that sent equipment and firefighters. A block of type may inquire into insurance. Then in more leisurely fashion, the writer may quote the passerby who thought he saw smoke, the watchperson who opened the inner doors and discovered the blaze or the woman who threw her baby into the fire net.

The story may form a more complicated pattern than even a series of triangles. A triangle that tapers off to the inconsequential point would bore a reader. Rather, each triangle becomes blunt bottomed. Some are hardly triangles at all. Can a chronological account be called a triangle, since start, middle and finish are equally essential to the tale? Is a list of injured a triangle? Blocks and wedges are more appropriate to clear portrayal of the way a long story is put together.

The editor who sees news articles in some such schematic fashion will understand better how to help reporters rearrange and tighten them. Perhaps the inner logic requires that a paragraph or two near the end be moved to a higher position, even though these sentences are in themselves almost trivial. Or perhaps killing a minor detail in the heart of the story will strengthen the whole.

An editor able to analyze advanced writing can quickly show reporters where their work is solid and where it is loose or rambling. This analytic skill is especially useful in working with an investigative team. Structuring the long series becomes similar to outlining a lengthy magazine article or a book. Formal logic has to be related to the likelihood that a reader's interest will wane, and to the technical demand that the individual pieces be of a certain length. "Can we shift this block into the first article in the series, and can we give the third piece some punch by building up this anecdote?" an editor might ask. Sometimes these deceptively simple questions lead a writing team into a kind of outline they had hoped to leave in freshman English.

Whatever the pattern, the story needs logic, but not the I, II, III type. It can be chronological or sequential, moving the reader from one point of interest to another. The chief sin is rambling, with the story drifting into subtopics or quotes of little value.

Reporters rarely think of the most effective ways to structure a major story. They tend to turn swiftly to the computer to start writing, as though they were pounding out a routine, three-graf story. As a result, too many potentially excellent stories miss connections with readers. The effective editor-coach must jog writers to strive for patterns that will communicate best.

More should be done at news publications to discover fresh ways to present material related to a central story. Instead of one long story, why not have five short stories, as sidebars to each other? Why not play three or four related stories, perhaps with a box or editor's note to explain their common theme? This can—and should—be done, particularly online, where readers can easily click around the various elements.

Working on Projects

Editors supervising investigations function as any good team leader does: goading, persuading, inspiring and pushing. They guide the collection of information because they usually have more experience and can be more dispassionate than the reporter on the hunt. Furthermore, two or more editorial heads generally are better than a single reporter's. Editors work over story drafts to make sure there are no holes—and no libel. They question the investigators and suggest lines of inquiry that reporters may have missed. They tap their own experience as reporters and editors to make sure the best job is done. Most important, perhaps, they keep telling themselves and the special reporters that there must be no mistakes. They realize that one error in a story may cause the whole investigation to collapse. The people being investigated will shout, "See, the paper's making up the whole thing!"

Editors advise investigators to start by asking seemingly innocuous questions at low levels. Underlings, unaccustomed to dealing with the press, often spill facts that higher-level people would keep to themselves. As the story forms a pattern, reporters move to quiz more informed people and seek more crucial documents. The best human sources are the disgruntled, the idealists or those who relish a kind of conspiracy role. The disgruntled often seek revenge; the idealists seek justice; the "conspirators" hope to be anonymous sources of information. Each type may be overly zealous and may give false or distorted details. This is why investigators often insist on corroboration of a fact before it is printed. If reporters cannot sift their information for truth, the editor should.

In the search, it is not enough to get oral accusations. Documents are essential—letters, memos, canceled checks and official reports. All may be crucial. Editors and reporters should realize that their greatest ally here is the copying machine, for it will duplicate evidence in seconds. That evidence often makes previously silent people decide to tell reporters their whole story.

In the enthusiasm of cracking a big story, journalists may forget a sense of ethical conduct. Theft, lies, fakery or threats may be precisely what is being investigated. A journalist either should not use these shabby practices or should use them only after full soul searching. Some reporters and editors have wrapped themselves in the flag of "public interest" and dashed off to commit shady or even criminal acts.

Editors should realize, too, that many investigations do not look for scandalous or illegal conduct. What may be sought is evidence of ineptitude or incompetence. This is why editors and reporters should take care to avoid accusations and strident language in their stories.

Sometimes editors must use a firm hand to get the news the community deserves. In one middle-sized city the social welfare reporter got the go-ahead to do a series on black employment in local business and industry. He was so thorough that he conducted scores of interviews over several weeks. As time passed, the information in the early interviews began to get stale. The paper's interest flagged, perhaps in part because the lengthy investigation brought worried inquiries from industrial leaders. When the brief series finally appeared, it was weak—much weaker than if it had been done with more dispatch. Perhaps the city editor should have assigned a second reporter to help collect information. Perhaps the editor should have told the reporter at a certain point: "You've got enough material. Write it!" In any event, firm editorial leadership was missing.

Newsroom Management

In addition to working with other journalists in the newsroom, some editors also take on administrative duties. Increasingly, this means keeping close tabs on the news department's budget. They know that quality does not come cheap, but at the same time they also are aware of corporate pressures to maintain profit margins, so they must learn to balance the demands of quality journalism against the profit motive of the publication's owner.

They also must strive to make maximum use of the staff's talents. For example, it is foolish to let a $700-a-week reporter spend an hour typing figures into a computer when a $300-a-week clerk could do it. Managers might try also to stagger copy editors' work hours so that they are likely to stay busy most of the day.

Management style

Every editor-manager inevitably develops a style of administration and so puts a personal stamp on procedure. Some editors are authoritarian, barking orders and pulling rank. The better ones are more democratic, discussing rather than dictating and encouraging consensus among the staff.

Modern management stresses evaluation of people to understand how they can be motivated to work best for a common goal. Many publishers in recent years have grasped that fact and have sent some managers to conferences on learning how to handle their jobs better.

Too many editors, however, have taken key positions with no consideration of how to deal with people. As in other fields, a fair number of martinets or neurotics get into high editorial positions. A few others have tried the super-friendly approach, always forgiving blunders and incompetence. They can't, when needed, become firm and demanding. They stumble badly, too.

A newsroom manager ought to keep in mind that proud, educated and talented reporters, editors, artists and photographers resent being treated like drones. They want to share in the decisions and want to be allowed to argue for specific change. The publication then becomes "our newspaper" or "our Web site," not merely "the paper" or "the site."

Newsroom executives must try to be open and flexible. They should take pains to review their policies frequently. Some rules perhaps never were wise or workable; now they hamstring and stultify. It is not unusual for a new staffer, hearing of a newsroom taboo, to mutter, "Who thought up that stupid rule?" If there is a good reason for the policy, it ought to be explained. Editors also must avoid defending outmoded standards with the cliché, "We've always done it that way."

Flexibility and imagination also help in the editorial managing of money. It is one thing to be economical and another to be parsimonious. Few things annoy a reporter or an assigning editor more than having the management pinch pennies on travel expenses or ordinary newsroom supplies. In newsrooms across the country money questions generate most of the headaches among managing editors. They are not trained as accountants, and their rise through the news ranks probably indicates that figuring budgets is one of their least favorite tasks.

If supervising editors represent all the editorial underlings, they also represent management. Reporters and subeditors may feel that such editors front for the publisher just as university deans are accused of fronting for administrations to hold down faculty salaries or throttle students. They have a delicate role to play as they interpret the realities of publishing to staffs no more enthusiastic about budgeting than top editors are. At the same time, the chief editors must convince everyone, above and below, that they are honest and fair.

Evaluating Staff

Effective management of workers requires constant and constructive evaluation of their work. Most organizations require a formal evaluation once a year, but feedback to reporters, editors, photographers, artists, Web designers and the like should never be relegated to just that. It should be a continuing process. William G. Connolly, a retired senior editor at the *New York Times*, explains:

> Improperly used, performance evaluations are dangerous. They create distrust between management and staff, encouraging a sort of "climate of fear." But when they're properly used (that is, when they're complete, detailed, thoughtful, balanced and fair; when they cite the good as well as the bad; when they lay out ways in which an editor might grow; when they promise how the management will support that growth; when they give the editor an opportunity to have his or her say), well, when they do all that they're a wonderful communications device.
>
> It's extremely difficult and time consuming to write good evaluations. Supervisors and managers naturally resist that obligation. (They're only human, after all.)
>
> But when evaluations are done well, they give copy editors (and reporters and designers and photographers) accurate messages about how they're doing, in management's view. That's a powerful thing for both sides in this exchange. Management can make its message clear. Staff members can learn what it will take to progress in this place and (maybe more important) whether this is a place where they want to stay and progress.
>
> If evaluations are always viewed as critical, they'll never be effective for anyone, sender or recipient. But if they're fair and honest, and viewed that way, they will make any newspaper better and a better place to work.[2]

Staff members should never have to wait a year to hear that they're doing a great job, or worse, that their work is not meeting the publication's standards. Good work needs to be praised right away, and this praise can be as simple as a public, passing comment to a reporter that "I really liked that story on the boy with leukemia" to a more formal awarding of a "headline of the week" or "staff member of the month."

Workers whose performance does not meet a publication's standards need to be told so right away and coached on how to improve so that they can meet those standards. Often, this is a formal process that states in writing what corrections in performance need to be made and what the consequences are if standards cannot be met. Many underperforming workers will improve once problems are pointed out, but those who do not should be dismissed.

Salaries and the Guild

The wicket is especially sticky in bargaining with the journalists' union, The Newspaper Guild. The Guild's job is to persuade all levels of management to give editors, reporters and photographers a better break in pay and fringe benefits. Steps to organize this union were taken in 1933, in the depths of the Great Depression, by the newspaper columnist Heywood Broun. Since it is organized on industrial trade union principles, the Guild includes not only those employees in editorial but also those in advertising, business, circulation, maintenance and promotion. It is now part of the Communications Workers of America. Membership hovers around 34,000.

Union locals for papers in more than a hundred cities in the United States, Canada and Puerto Rico now have agreements with publishers. Major magazines and the Associated Press also have Guild contracts. Even though managing editors may have been members on their way up, they often have to take management's part in union negotiations.

The Guild is continuing pressure to raise the minimum pay for experienced reporters, photographers and copy editors. The so-called top minimum of $200 a week was first adopted at the *Washington Post* in 1964. That figure has at least quadrupled since, and it is not unusual these days for metro staffers below top management to make $52,000 a year or more.

The Guild, of course, also aims for cost-of-living increases, medical insurance payments, more vacations and holidays, and a shorter work week. Most Guild members now work a 37.5-hour week, with overtime payment for extra hours.

In the dickering—and sometimes bickering—with the Guild, managing editors can be crushed between the stones of management and staff. But if they are strong, and if they maintain good humor, they can often mediate differences. Editors of integrity will be trusted when the staff is told frankly about how far the publisher can go on salaries and fringe benefits. At the same time, they can press management to re-member that not only the news organization's reputation but also its financial strength rests on quality, which in turn depends upon compet-itive salaries.

Managing editors may not fret if they cannot get the money they want for stenographers and editorial assistants. But they can bleed if they see their best staffers leave for higher pay at other publications. If they need two new reporters and they persuade the publisher to give them $60,000 for salaries, they know they won't lure real talent with $30,000 apiece. If they can get $75,000, however, they might pay one $40,000 and another $35,000 and attract seasoned reporters. More than money is required, however. Reportorial freedom, good assignments and praise for good work are essential, too. The editor with clear goals and drive can attract writers who admire sharp leadership, but in the end, even that editor needs dollars in the budget.

Budgeting the Space

The budgeting of news space in a newspaper is, like the budgeting of money, a source of cooperation—and friction—between business man-agement and editors. The news hole (the amount of space devoted to material other than advertising) varies from day to day. The reading pub-lic may not appreciate the need to expand or contract the amount of ed-itorial material as advertising sales go up or down, but all editors recog-nize this fact of publishing life.

To be fair to readers, editors want some stability in news hole size. Publishers have cause to scream if the percentage of advertising drops to, say, 50 percent. They will go bankrupt if the news hole widens. But it is the managing editor who should scream if advertising goes up to 75 or 80 percent. There is no set proportion suitable for all papers, but the managing editor should get nervous about quality when the news hole drops much below a third. It takes planning and discussion day in and day out to maintain a satisfactory balance.

It wastes time and talent—and demoralizes staffers—to have many stories that never are printed. Managing editors can control space by careful planning. They usually accomplish this by adjusting the news hole each day. For example, on Monday and Tuesday, when advertising is light, the news hole may be 110 columns. The space for news may jump to 140 on Wednesday and Thursday and drop to 120 on Friday.

Proper use of the news hole demands consultation with assignment editors to see whether a few columns in one department can be shifted on certain days to another section. For example, sports demand a lot of space on most weekends, while lifestyle might be able to give up a little space if it can be returned early in the week. Such consultations eventu-ally must bring in the advertising manager so that the ad placement can reflect these planned adjustments each day. The good editor, naturally, will aim to fill the paper with quality news and features even when the space jumps 20 percent. Readers can become irritated if much of what is called news only fills space around all those ads.

Budgeting of People

More important for editors than allotment of dollars and space is the budgeting of time, for both their staffs and themselves. It is best if, from the start, editors consider this budget question not in terms of hours and minutes but of people who work for them. What are their wants and needs? What will satisfy and stimulate them as employees and as human beings working together?

Journalists believe they work on something important, and wise editors run their shops so that employees keep sight of this. Their feelings of significance ultimately give them job satisfaction. Good feelings cannot replace good pay, but they do contribute to a quality paper. Editors find ways to help staffers express themselves, such as letting a photographer get that special art shot or a reporter dig into an exposé without fear of losing editorial support.

The good editor operates as democratically as possible, turning decisions over to groups or committees. Such procedure introduces all the well-known shortcomings of democracy—delays, circumventions, slowness. But it also sparks spirit and creativity. One newspaper editor, reminded that the newsroom was shabby, let the Guild unit form a committee to recommend plans for redecoration. The committee members, excited about the task, suggested inexpensive changes that made the place attractive and convenient. The newsroom's workers felt that they had done well on a job normally considered management's baby.

Supervising the Team

Newsroom managers easily can be saddled with all kinds of pesky details, such as time cards, overtime slips and expense accounts. Unless they are careful, they will spend hours each day handling clerical duties. A competent secretary can handle most of these chores, plus writing most letters, and give the editor time to manage. All editors must set priorities so that they can do the best with the abilities they have. This may mean giving away one task while taking on another, possibly shedding a job they aren't good at to allow time to do another task better. The managing editor might find, for example, that hiring a clerk could relieve several staffers of routine work. The newsroom may be clumsily arranged so that each staffer wastes several minutes each day dodging equipment. A minor shift of the furniture may smooth operations.

Perhaps the staffer writing lifestyle stories would bolster the city feature staff, or be ready to come onto the copy desk. Maybe a sportswriter has tired of the job and would like a crack at general assignment under the city editor. The managing editor must ponder such changes if the staff is to be kept alert and stimulated.

Many changes will result from conferences with other editors in the newsroom. But not just any kind of conference will do. A weekly meeting for which no one has prepared criticisms or suggestions ends up in a long, tedious bull session, filled with gripes and half-baked ideas. A one-hour session, however, during which each assignment editor reports on plans for the next month or offers concrete suggestions for change, can yield all kinds of ideas and a sense of cooperative management.

The managing editor also will confer with the advertising manager so that the two may gain an appreciation of each other's difficulties and perhaps solve at least some minor production problems. A talk with the circulation manager may result in a slightly earlier deadline for the first edition or a decision to trim coverage in a nearby town because there is no hope of increasing circulation there.

The managing editor must be wary of associating almost exclusively with six or eight assignment editors and executives in the business department. Reporters are important, too, and a few chats with them can strengthen relationships and give the ME ideas from other staffers. The editor can contribute to staff enthusiasm in little ways, too, such as taking a reporter to lunch, financing a newsroom picnic or having pizza and soda brought in when much of the staff is on overtime to handle some major event, such as an election.

Most of all, perhaps, the managing editor needs to sense when to do nothing and keep still. Sometimes the best change is no change. Certainly an arrogant, all-knowing editor who constantly juggles and shifts will irritate and even enrage a staff, particularly those members who have spent months learning a part of the craft.

Looking for Improvement

The managing editor should continually review the editorial operation for improvement. What new spot would excite and hold one of the better staffers? Which weak links need replacement? Is a basic reorganization needed?

Editorial hiring is still one of the soft spots of newsroom management. Too often it is hit or miss. An opening goes to a person who happens to drop into the office or to one who persists, rather than to the best journalist available for the salary. Well-organized managing editors watch bylines at news operations they can raid. They get acquainted with reporters at professional meetings and on university campuses. When they lose a specialist in urban affairs or agriculture, they are able to pick knowledgeably from the best.

Some editors recruit in journalism schools, of course, but sometimes they seek only a list of people who might be considered for jobs in a couple of years, when the young reporters have gathered experience at smaller organizations.

The editor may promote from within, and morale rises when staffers see that the editor looks around the newsroom to pick someone when a job opens. It may be that the would-be expert on education or the environment is now writing obituaries or society notes. If managing editors take the time to chat with their staff, they will know what their interests and talents are.

Home-grown specialists

Editors with tight budgets rarely can go scouting about the country to snap up one of the four or five best writers in a particular field. They need to develop their own skilled staffers. This can be done outright by asking staffers what they would like to cover if they had the chance. Then the staffer could be given a little time to read in that field, to attend a workshop, or to study at a local college at the publication's expense.

Almost no reporter starts out in a specialized field. Young people get out of college, take a general assignment reporting job and sometimes by luck stumble into a specialty that fascinates them. They learn on and off the job until they are genuine experts. Young staffers can, of course, prepare for the break when it comes. They can study and observe—and tell the managing editor, for example, "If the courthouse beat is ever open, I'd like a crack at it."

In improving their editorial staffs, imaginative editors may want to particularly emphasize this development of specialists. Here they might take a tip from competing media in shaping goals and the staff to reach them. Recently, magazines devoted to specialized topics—travel, electronics or boating, for example—have made the biggest circulation gains. Editors need not feel that every story must interest everyone. Some writers could well devote at least part of their time to cover medicine or psychology or other specialized topics of great interest to an important segment of readers.

The Editor's Attitude

To supervise and reorganize effectively, top editors must have the standards or goals of the news organization clearly in mind, for they are not merely managing but also managing to a purpose. If perfection is impossible, then their target can be at least improvement. The approach of the late Lester Markel, long-time Sunday editor of the *New York Times*, was not "Is it good?" but "What can I do to make it better?" Editors must know where they want their publication to go and have the courage to drive it there.

Establishing priorities

Editors must establish priorities. No publication can be all they would like, or even close to it. Something has to give way; something has to be advanced. Editors must have the courage to focus on unpopular social issues but also to decide that no money or energy is available to ride out on this or that hobby horse, though important and influential and even highly moral forces press for it. How well editors succeed depends first on how clearly they see and enforce the priorities that will take the publication to its goal.

As they clarify those priorities, editors communicate not only facts or instructions but also policies and standards. Then they check how well the communications are heeded. At the end of the workday, many an editor sighs at simply seeing the miracle of getting the publication out again. That sigh is both a confession and a profound self-criticism. Top editors somehow have to organize themselves and their staffs so that they have the time to evaluate as well as marvel at the daily miracle. They must reflect and contemplate on what values are coming across. Only as they seriously ask such questions, day after day, and strive to get them answered right are editors really dealing effectively with goals and standards. Perhaps the best title for top editorial administrators would not be executive or managing editors but evaluation editors.

Notes

1. Roy Peter Clark and Don Fry, *Coaching Writers: Editors and Reporters Working Together Across Media Platforms*, 2nd ed. (Boston: Bedford/St. Martin's, 2003), 85–86. Used with permission.

2. Posted on the American Copy Editors Society discussion board, www.copydesk.org. Used with permission.

CHAPTER 5

Working With Stories

Deciding what stories to cover and working with reporters to develop them are just two parts of the editing process. Sooner or later, it's time to sit down with the copy and go to work. This part of the process is necessarily the same whether the story was reported for print, online or broadcast: Writing must be clear, concise, relevant and grammatically correct. Words and names must be spelled correctly. The facts must be straight. The narrative should flow seamlessly. The problems editors will encounter vary from the mundane (fixing a typo) to the large (the need for wholesale restructuring). It's here where quality control begins to be an important part of the newsgathering process.

Assignment editors and copy editors will typically take different approaches to a story. The assignment editor, as discussed in earlier chapters, has worked with the reporter from the story's inception and thus has a good idea of what the story is about. The assignment editor may edit the story initially on his own and then consult with the reporter, or he may sit down with the reporter and together work through the story. One editor at the *St. Petersburg Times* simply placed asterisks in stories and then discussed with reporters what changes she thought needed to be made at these places. The reporters were responsible for making the changes—and learning what mistakes to avoid in the future.[1]

Editors on the copy desk take a different, yet just-as-important, view of the story. They haven't been involved in the development of the story and are able to look at the story as a reader would—without any preconceptions of what it should be. This step back from the story helps prevent presentations that play too much to insiders or are missing information. As described in Chapter 3, the copy desk is the last step before the story goes out to the public. It's the last chance to make sure everything is set to go.

Good Catches

When somebody in the newsroom finds a mistake that saves a newsroom from public embarrassment, it's known as a good catch. Editors on the American Copy Editors Society Internet mailing list reported some catches they had made:

- Direct accusations of crime.
- Plagiarism of other publications.
- Numbers that didn't add up on a real estate story.
- Problems with the way surveys were reported.
- Pie charts that didn't add up to 100 percent.
- A story that identified the AARP as the American Association of Retarded Persons.
- A story that said two veterans for whom a building was named would attend a ceremony there—except that the veterans were long dead.

Know the Community, and More

That editors need to be familiar with their communities cannot be over-emphasized. Even the smallest errors—for example, a story that refers to Grant Street, when it's Grant Avenue—can draw scorn from long-time residents who know better. Not knowing that a prominent business-woman was mayor 10 years ago can hobble a publication's presentation about her business and political aspirations.

Editors new to a community should come up to speed quickly. They should find books on local history and read up. If they're new to the state, they should learn that state's history, its governmental structure and the current problems the state faces. Editors should browse the publication's archives to become familiar with the issues facing the community. They need to know who the community's leaders are and what those leaders' alliances are. They should be well-read; at the minimum, they need to read their own publication every day. Ideally, they also should check regional and national publications as well.

The Meanings of Style

Style is used by news editors in at least two senses. The uniform system of spelling, capitalization and usage is called style, but the form and presentation of news writing are also style.

Good journalistic style is not florid, ornate or rhetorical. The late journalism dean Frank Luther Mott used to say the best journalism is also good literature, as clearly demonstrated in the reporting of Ben Franklin, Stephen Crane and Ernest Hemingway. English professors have long contended that good prose is usually plain and straightforward and therefore clear. "The approach to style is by way of plainness, simplicity, orderliness, sincerity," says William Strunk Jr. and E. B. White's *The Elements of Style*. The same goes for good news style, too.

Effective prose communicates ideas and information. It might be argued that some writing is used to convey an ambiance or feeling without presenting much fact. But such usage in news reports is rare. Journalistic style has to be functional. The need to convey ideas quickly from one

Standard copy editing and proofreading marks

headed for for approval	delete word
weapons of masss destruction	delete character
Courtney Cox Arquette	insert character
the plumber, Joe Smith said	insert comma
Dr. Alexander Baker	insert period
the vice president left for vacation	insert word
raised taxes 20 percent	insert space
gas prices are higher	insert space (alternate)
went to Reids house	insert apostrophe
the 30 year-old man	insert hyphen
CHICAGO Fourteen people died	insert dash
"I am not a crook, he said.	insert quotation marks
down town arena	close up space
off the scrap heap	retain
Bedford Falls city council	capitalize (make uppercase)
the Mayor vetoed	make lowercase
Doctor Bill Gonzalez	abbreviate
the W.Va. native	don't abbreviate
forty miles from town	make figures
lost in Atlanta	transpose characters
wrong order word	transpose words
In the beginning,	indent paragraph
From one place you want	connect undeleted material
to go to the next	

Figure 5.1.

Many news organizations still proof pages on paper, so it's still necessary for editors to know proofreader's marks.

mind to other minds underlies the need for simple, clear writing. What language scholars call standard English is appropriate to news writing. Neither the formal English of the academic book nor the nonstandard or colloquial dialect of folksy talk has much place in newspapers or in on-line news publication. For most purposes, reporters and editors should choose their words from the broad range of language understood by most moderately educated people.

Standard English is threatened on the one side by jargon and gobbledygook. Reporters close to many professions may fall into legalese or bureaucratic gibberish. On the other side is a threat from what has traditionally been known as slang—faddish talk. The young and academics, for example, sometimes aim to have their own secret language. The young use their special slang whereas academics develop obscure words and terms that have meaning only to a specialized few. News writing must avoid both kinds of fringe English if they are to communicate with a diverse readership.

Advocates of plain, simple style sometimes face the objection that this kind of writing is dull and lifeless. It need not be. Concrete nouns and strong verbs close to human experience can make a simple sentence vivid and lively. Yet sometimes even a good writer will fill a story with the stereotyped and obvious until it shrivels and dies.

Some editors, aware that too many stories jam one fact upon another, try to get some personal touches into copy. They seek a few quotes that show sources as human beings who laugh and cry. They introduce a bit of levity—or passionate concern—over some issues. As so often happens, some editors overdo it, saturating stories with personal details. But the best editors get stories with dashes of warmth and humor among the cold facts.

An examination of style by editors comes down to their analysis of the grammatical ingredients of the story—paragraphs, sentences and words. There is a mystic quality in the overall effect of writing. The sources for the finished story somehow turn out to be greater than the sum of the parts. Still, some of the mystery can be penetrated by seeing how individual blocks fit together.

Paragraphs

In most writing, the paragraph is an obvious block. The formal outline of an essay or a book divides into topics, subtopics and sub-subtopics; each sub-subtopic may be treated as a paragraph, which might run various lengths. In type, long blocks look forbidding, so journalists use shorter paragraphs, often only one or two sentences long.

Copy is not effectively formed into short paragraphs by haphazard chopping, as some reporters and copy readers apparently suppose. The best procedure is to search the "normal" paragraph of the topic-sentence variety for the clusters of ideas within it. Thus a 12-sentence unit may prove to be made up of four to six smaller pieces. Each piece then may become a news article-type paragraph, and each may run one or two, perhaps three, sentences, but rarely more. If writers see the relation of these shorter paragraphs to the overall pattern, they are able to write in a more logical style.

Sentences

A paragraph rarely should run more than 50 words. If such a paragraph has even two or three sentences, they must obviously be short—perhaps an average of 15 words, though no such limit should be imposed arbitrarily. Length is thus one criterion of the good sentence, and news story sentences are usually short compared with those in books or scholarly magazines.

Sentences also should be straight: clear and to the point. Good examples of such sentences can be found in nearly every news publication. The editor's job, of course, is to make sure that all sentences are straight. Although grammatically most straight sentences are simple, with a few compound and even fewer complex, journalists might pay more attention to what is known in English classes as the periodic sentence, building from beginning to end, so the last element is the climax. For example, "Mayor Jones paused over the document, frowned, and then, as his face reddened, shouted, 'Never!'" Of course, putting an idea at the start of a sentence also can have impact: "Cut taxes."

Writers sometimes try to pack too much information into a short space, making stories opaque. The antidote in each case is to lighten the load of each sentence. Even the most intelligent readers need frequent periods to catch their breath.

A fruitful suggestion for better writing is summarized in the slogan "One idea, one sentence." The main idea of each sentence stands out so that the reader can grasp it quickly.

Words

The strength of sentences depends ultimately on the choice and arrangement of words. Good editors become expert on these basic blocks. Instead of the vague, the abstract and the unusual, they seek words that are direct, concrete and familiar—words that build vivid and accurate pictures for most readers.

Accuracy and strength, as well as commonness, should guide word choice, and vitality in verbs is especially important. Forms of "to be" are generally static, so editors prefer strong, specific verbs. For example, "He crept to the door" has much more meaning than "He went to the door." One-syllable words often generate the most power. Reducing the sentence usually adds strength. Pare weak or unnecessary adjectives and adverbs.

A final word on jargon

As noted, jargon confuses more than clarifies. In medicine or law, to be sure, a specialized word may add precision. But even there problems exist, for lawyers may rattle off *en banc* or *nol prosse* and only confuse other people.

"When you get your degree you can't wear it around your neck to prove you're educated," the late urban reformer Saul Alinsky wrote in *Harper's* magazine, "so instead you use a lot of three- and four-syllable words. Of course, they aren't any use at all if you really want to communicate with people. You have to talk straight English, using a small word every time you can instead of a big one."[2] Such advice is good not only for educators, economists and sociologists, for example, but also for reporters and editors.

Approaching the Story

Editors should give story leads particular attention, for a lead makes or breaks the story's interest. If the lead seems clumsy, lacks facts or misses the point, the editor certainly should revise it, in consultation with the writer and assignment editor.

Good editors, unless squeezed by a deadline, read each story at least twice. The first read should focus on the content of the story. Are all the questions answered? Does the story flow logically? Are transitions smooth? Does the writer use proper attribution? What else will the reader want to know? Are there any factual errors? If the writer has used a feature-style lead, is the nut paragraph high enough to let the reader know the essence of the story?

Editors should check to see whether the story rambles on for 10 or 11 paragraphs of details without placing essential information close to the top. This shortcoming often mars stories of strikes. The beginning usually reports who says what and how long the strike has been going on, but what the strike is all about may be buried or ignored.

The second read then looks for mechanical errors, such as grammar, spelling, punctuation and style. Editors who make changes should read those changes two or three times to make sure that they have not altered the meaning or introduced errors themselves.

The editor should make necessary changes and quit. This means hands off clear and accurate writing. Editors should resist the temptation to make changes just because it's the way they would have done it; each writer has his or her own style, which should be not only respected but also encouraged. The job of editors is to go over copy to correct grammar, to oust waste words and sentences, and to make language more graceful. Every effort should be made to produce rhythm in language so that anyone reading a sentence aloud will not stumble.

Here's a simple example:

"The women's basketball team plays well in the first half but bogs down badly in the second," said the coach, Wilma Andersen, Friday.

Smooth the last part by making it "Coach Wilma Andersen said Friday."

Editors should throttle clichés such as "run like a deer," "a dream come true" and "boggles the mind." A good list of clichés to avoid is at http://clichesite.com. Editors also should hunt down ambiguous phrases and errors in syntax. Editors must have been dozing when one story referred to an "insecure computer" or another referred to how funds would be "dispersed." (The writers meant "unsecured" and "disbursed.") One editor in a hurry heard, somewhat embarrassed, from the production department that a vulgarity had been typeset in the sports scoreboard. Apparently, the newspaper's spelling checker recognized the swear word that should have been "shot." One story about prison building in California made reference to the "foreseeable future"—what it meant was the "near future"; nobody can foresee the future.

The Probing Editor

Editors need a quizzical, skeptical approach if they are to catch errors. They must keep asking as they read, "Can this be right?" With this in mind, they will question whether a certain rock star was born in California or whether the University of Michigan is in Kalamazoo.

Editors must check to see whether needed information is omitted. To do this, they have to think like the audience: What will people reading or hearing this want to know? What information is vital to their understanding of the story? One publication ran a story about prostitution problems along a main boulevard that runs the length of the city, but didn't say what part of the boulevard was affected. It should have listed cross streets to give readers a frame of reference.

If there is any doubt about the accuracy of changes in a story, the editor should check with the best authority—the writer of the story. The reporter might be asked, "Does this improve the meaning of the story? Have I made it clearer, or have I muddled the facts?" Reporters will be furious, and they have a right to be, if editors revise a story in error. It makes them look like fools to news sources, not to mention the embarrassment it causes the publication.

Where a reporter has used an inappropriate word, the editor should find the right one. This requires familiarity with semantics to be sure that the words convey the intended meaning. For example, where the reporter has written "dignitaries," the word "politicians" might be better.

Editors must always look out for libel. Every story that defames anyone—and many stories do—should be checked to see whether the defamatory phrases can be used safely under law. Chapter 13 discusses in detail the legal pitfalls that always lurk near even the most diligent editors.

Beware of hoaxes. A naive reporter may write a story that sounds like a dandy. The more experienced editor, however, may recall that the same story ran a decade ago and was exposed as a fake. This story needs to be killed.

Useful References for Editors

Every newsroom should have an ample supply of reference materials for editors to check facts, and the Internet has reduced the time it takes for this part of the job. Here are some useful books and Web sites for checking facts.

Books

- A dictionary. Publications may designate a specific dictionary as the one for use by its journalists. (For publications that follow Associated Press style, this is *Webster's New World College Dictionary*.) The newsroom also should have an unabridged dictionary to check for words that didn't make the abridged version.
- An almanac gives editors quick access to thousands of facts on recent history, dates, biographies and records. A desk encyclopedia can save an editor a trip to the library.
- A book on American usage. One version popular with copy editors is *Garner's Modern American Usage*, by Bryan Garner.
- A thesaurus.
- *A Dictionary of American Idioms*, by Adam Makkai, M. T. Boatner and J. E. Gates.
- Congressional Directory.
- Area telephone books.
- Various kinds of Who's Who.
- State government rosters.
- *Cambridge Dictionary of American Biography*.
- A complete, modern atlas, such as the *National Geographic Atlas of the World*.
- A geographical dictionary, such as *Merriam-Webster's Geographical Dictionary*.
- The Bible.
- *Editor & Publisher International Yearbook*.
- *Bartlett's Familiar Quotations*.
- Various sports record books and military directories.

Web Sites

- Internet Movie Database, www.imdb.com
- U.S. Census Bureau, www.census.gov
- Google, www.google.com
- CIA World Fact Book, www.cia.gov/cia/publications/factbook/index.html
- Bartleby.com, for various literary information, www.bartleby.com
- Maps at maps.yahoo.com or **www.mapquest.com**

- U.S. Centers for Disease Control, www.cdc.gov
- The Slot, a spot for copy editors, www.theslot.com
- For finding people or phone numbers, www.reversephonedirectory.com or www.anywho.com
- The White House, www.whitehouse.gov
- Thomas, federal legislative information, www.thomas.loc.gov
- The Federal Register, www.gpoaccess.gov/fr/index.html
- Securities and Exchange Commission filing information, www.gpoaccess. gov/fr/index.html
- Merriam-Webster, www.m-w.com/home.htm

Some publications have been known to run the same story twice, causing merriment among readers but not among top editors. It is doubly amusing if the same stories get into the paper the same day. Occasionally, different reporters will write essentially the same story a few days apart. Although the writer of the second story should have read the paper more carefully, such an oversight is no excuse for editors to repeat the error. Alert editors, for both print and online, must likewise kill outdated stories. A story announcing last night's event as "tonight" is bad news for the participants, the frustrated audience and the publication.

Editors also have to watch for advertising that masquerades as news. Since news organizations sell advertising, news stories should mention advertisers only when they make news. For example, if a meeting is scheduled at a hotel, the reporter has to say which hotel. This "advertising" is unavoidable and therefore permissible. After the event, it is safe to say only that the event was held "in a hotel."

It is even harder but more important to eliminate propaganda. Many people try to sneak their points of view into the paper under the guise of news. This is most apparent during election campaigns, when events are staged to attract attention. Political candidates give the same stump speech from town to town; the tendency to report it as news each time must be resisted. Government officials often stage-manage events to get maximum exposure. The editor should sift through all the propaganda and stick to a factual report.

Sometimes an inexperienced reporter will quote a news source too much and let the source misuse the news columns to further an individual or a cause. The editor gives this material its proper weight, which sometimes is nothing.

Problems to Look For

The same types of errors in stories come up time and time again. Diligent editors will be on the lookout for problems that involve names, attribution, redundancy, euphemisms and language.

Check names

Double-check names. Any time an editor has any doubt about the spelling of a name, she should look it up. Sometimes this is as easy as checking databases that the publications maintain. The *Los Angeles Times* maintains lists of names that frequently appear in the news and how they should appear in the *Times*.

San Jose Mercury News Style Sheet

The *San Jose Mercury News* keeps a running reference file for the events of Sept. 11, 2001, and the subsequent wars in Afghanistan and Iraq. The purpose of the file is make sure that the newspaper and its Web site spell names consistently and use agreed-upon figures. It also contains chronologies and background information about various organizations. The actual style file is much longer, but here some excerpts:

SEPT. 11 CASUALTIES, IN BRIEF

TOTAL: [1/24/04 update] The official Sept. 11 toll at all three crash locations is 2,982. Note that New York counts its toll a different way, so you may be obliged to use these numbers in different configurations.

NEW YORK: [1/23/04 update] New York City's official count of Sept. 11 dead and missing in the city is 2,749. The city reduced its toll several times to account for people who could not be proven to have died . . . or, in some cases, even to have existed. The official list of people missing in the attacks now matches the number of death certificates issued. Note that New York has chosen to include in its total the people on the ground; crew members of the two hijacked planes that hit the twin towers; and all the passengers on both planes but not the 10 hijackers. [See detailed breakdown further in this file]

PENTAGON: In the building, 125 dead or unaccounted for. 64 died on American Airlines Flight 77 (five hijackers, 59 other crew/passengers), for a total of 189 dead and missing. Final count.

PENNSYLVANIA: 44 dead, all of them aboard United Airlines Flight 93. There were four hijackers and 40 other crew/passengers. Final count.

SPELLINGS AND STYLE

Abdullah Abdullah . . . A key figure in the Northern Alliance, in late December 2001, he was sworn in as foreign minister in a new coalition government led by Hamid Karzai. On June 19, 2002, after Karzai was selected to lead Afghanistan, Abdullah was appointed to continue as foreign minister.

Al-Jazeera . . . Qatar-based satellite television station. Its name is Arabic
for "the Island."

Al-Qaida . . . Not Al Qaeda, Al-Qaeda or al-Qaida. The name of Osama
bin Laden's organization, it means "the Base." Don't drop the definite
article "Al-" in any uses. See BINLADENSTYLE for more information.

ground zero . . . Lowercase the zone of destruction in Manhattan where
the World Trade Center once stood.

Hamid Karzai . . . Chosen in early December 2001, by Afghan factions
meeting in Germany, to be Afghanistan's interim leader. A Pashtun
tribal leader with six siblings living in the United States, Karzai took
over as head of a coalition government Dec. 22, 2001.

On June 13, 2002, he was overwhelmingly elected in a *loya jirga* (ital-
icized, lowercase) . . . a traditional grand assembly . . . to serve as Afghanistan's president for 18 months. He was inaugurated June 19,
2002.

Moslem. Never use this spelling. Use Muslim.

Muhammad . . . Always use this spelling (not "Mohammed," "Mohamed,"
etc.) when mentioning the prophet of Islam. Capitalize "prophet" in
references like the Prophet Muhammad or "Muhammad, our Prophet" (parallel: "the Lord Jesus Christ"). But the spelling of this name
among individuals other than the prophet of Islam varies widely; it
depends on individual preference, regional variation and publication
style.

Be sure that a name is spelled correctly throughout a story; a person
should not be Whelan in the first paragraph and Whalen in the second.
The editor should watch for a common lapse associated with names: The
reporter uses a person's full name in the lead but mistakenly substitutes
the first or middle name for the last in the rest of the story. For example,
the lead may refer to a university president as William Carson McDuff.
From then on, however, he is Carson, instead of McDuff. Editors should
catch this blunder.

Another common error to watch for is no first reference for a name.
An editor will be reading a story and come across somebody referred to
by last name who hasn't been referred to before. This typically happens
when a story is trimmed or rearranged, and the person making the fixes
forgot to change first and subsequent references, too.

Attribute facts

Attribution refers to telling audiences where the information came from.
Attribute facts properly. Almost anything that was not witnessed by the
reporter should be attributed to some person or other source. The "almost" is essential to remember because often stories contain facts neither
observed by reporters nor found through records, and yet there is no at-

tribution. Attribution is unnecessary when the source obviously is telling the truth. It is silly, for example, to attribute to a university president the employment of every single new faculty member. The university is not going to announce an appointment in a news release and then back out of it, so phrases like "the president announced" are unnecessary.

Additionally, facts considered to be general knowledge—such as those found in almanacs and encyclopedias—usually do not require attribution.

"Write around it"

Sometimes an editor spots what appears to be a minor misstatement in a story and the reporter is not around for verification. Any other check might take 15 minutes. The item is not worth that much time, so the editor "writes around it." A story may say, "Jones, who moved here in 1988, has served on the county board for 17 years." The copy editor may trust "17 years" but doubt "1988." How could Jones have won an election so soon? So the editor writes around the problem by changing the sentence to "Jones has served on the county board for 17 years."

Simplify the language

News reports are not written for morons but for people who want easily read news and comment. Simpler words should replace involved ones such as *inextricable*, *dichotomy* and *tangential*. Language even for an intellectual audience should be precise and readable, not pretentious.

Reporters often get caught up in the special language or jargon of the fields they cover. Court reporters, for instance, may write "filed a demurrer," "stayed the execution" or "granted a continuance." Such terms may be hard for a nonlawyer to grasp, and the editor who thinks the story should interest ordinary people will either change the wording or send it back to the reporter for translation.

Recognize your own prejudices

Editors need to double-check themselves to be sure that they do not make decisions to chop one story and inflate another because of personal prejudice. Some editors who control news content favor stories that concern their personal hobbies. A person who loves to sail may run an unusual number of stories about boats and the sea. Such prejudices are basically harmless, although they could make the paper look amateurish. Sometimes, however, an editor may intensely dislike a senator or fear that the nation is moving rapidly on the wrong course. This person may edit the news to make the senator look foolish or to emphasize personal political views. This kind of editing is harmful and unprofessional. Editors must develop an attitude of detachment in handling news.

Don't trust your memory

Editors are often tempted to drop a fact into a story as a way to improve the article. These facts should be inserted, however, only when necessary and the editor is absolutely sure of them. If one isn't certain, it is essential to verify the information.

Fairness and taste

Copy should be fair and tasteful. Balancing objective reporting and interpretation is a continual problem, but even if a story is primarily interpretative it should be fair. Snide, belittling comments should be removed.

People criticized in stories should have an opportunity to respond. Copy also should remain in good taste. Taste is difficult to assess, but most editors have a rule of thumb: Stories read by all kinds of people, including children, should soften or eliminate the most brutal or intimate details.

Beware of doublespeak and euphemisms

The practice of using language to deceive has swollen so much that the term doublespeak has been adapted from George Orwell's newspeak. Much of this deception may be unintentional—the speaker or writer was plain sloppy, as in the case of the senator who said, "We might ventilate the structure of campaigning." But much of the deception is deliberate. The military announces a *protective strike*, to avoid saying bombing. Presidents talk often of *national security*. Diplomats rattle off *balance of power*.

A journalist learns on the first workday that people *die*, they don't *pass away*. The State Department doesn't *terminate* people, it *fires* them. In euphemistic writing, *poor* gets replaced by *low-income* or *culturally deprived*; *slums* become *inner city*; *dumps* become *sanitary landfills*; *prisons* become *correctional facilities*; *chemical*, *biological* and *nuclear arms* become *weapons of mass destruction*; American soldiers are killed by *friendly fire*; dead civilians are *collateral damage*. These terms either lack meaning or are intended to fool the public. The editor should oust such phrases and encourage reporters to challenge sources who spout doublespeak or euphemism. Editors should translate.

Check the facts

Checking facts is a traditional function on most copy desks. Editors should view facts in stories skeptically and verify information when questions arise. One copy editor noted that a recent "Today in History" feature listing the anniversary of the Emancipation Proclamation misstated what the proclamation did. An editor at another publication noted that a reference to the same proclamation had the incorrect year. Facts like these are now easily checked using Internet resources.

If a reporter quotes someone as saying, "Crime costs the nation $100 billion a year," editors should be concerned. Who can have anything but a wild guess on what crime costs? Editors, always skeptical, should ask frequently, "Who said so? Where did the source get this information? How would anyone know that?"

Avoid fad words

Americans race from one fad to another in clothing styles, entertainment, food—and word usage. A word or phrase will pop into everyone's vocabulary, and the meaning often is obscure. Words or phrases such as "bottom line," "in the wake of," "unveil," "arguably," "linkage," "parameters," "back to square one," "scenario" and "paranoid" are misused or quickly become tedious. Editors should delete such overworked or misused words.

Stay alert

Sometimes while working with stories, editors become distracted or start to daydream, allowing ridiculous errors to slip by. One publication used the word *gentile* when it meant *genteel.* Another once noted that a judge had granted a *change of revenue* when it meant a *change of venue.* It's also easy to miss *disperse* when the writer meant *disburse,* or to give somebody *free reign* when really they have *free rein.* Editors need to stay on task and focused. Sometimes it's a good idea to stand up and take a short stroll around the building as a refresher. See Chapter 6 for a list of commonly misused words.

Look for holes

Reporters occasionally omit an essential detail, causing a hole in a story. One reporter wrote a story about a cut in library hours and why the cut was necessary but never said what the new hours were. Another reported that a city had produced a special directory but didn't tell where it could be obtained.

Editors should approach stories with the assumption that the reader doesn't know anything about the subject, even if it involves an ongoing issue in the news. Editors should make sure that reporters provide sufficient background so that a reader new to the piece can quickly come up to speed on the topic.

Check the arithmetic

There's an old joke that people go into journalism because they're bad with math. But much of journalism involves numbers, and editors must know what they mean and how to use them. Editors need to run figures through their heads—or calculators—to see whether they make sense. For example, a story once said the value of Argentine currency had dropped 100 percent. That would make the money worthless; 50 percent was the proper figure. Editors should always double-check numbers to make sure they make sense. Some of the problem areas include averages, medians and percentages.

Averages

The average, also known as the mean, is one typical measure of central tendency. An average is calculated by adding all the values and dividing by the number of values. But editors should be wary of using averages if values at either end of the range of values are extreme. In such cases, it's more meaningful to report the median.

Medians

Another typical measure of central tendency is the median. Exactly half of all the values fall under the median and half over the median. If you have an even number of values, the middle two values are averaged to calculate the median. One typical use of the median is to report home sale prices in a community.

Percentages

When a school board votes to spend more money next year than this year, the additional spending is often reported as a percentage of change from the previous year. Editors should always check the calculation of a percentage of change, as this is an area in which reporters sometimes make mistakes. To arrive at the percentage of change, subtract the original value from the new value, divide by the original value and multiply by 100:

(New number − old number) ÷ old number × 100

For example, if this year's budget is $22 million and next year's budget is $23.5 million, use this calculation:

(23.5 − 22) ÷ 22 × 100 = 6.8 percent

Percentages also are used to illustrate what portion of a whole a figure represents. To calculate this, just divide the portion by the whole and multiply by 100. For example, in the above school district, the reporter might want to report how much teacher salaries account for in the new budget. If teacher salaries are $17 million, the calculation is:

$$17 \div 23.5 \times 100 = 72 \text{ percent of the total budget}$$

Avoid redundancy

Redundancies are harder to spot than quotes or identification tags and are more worrisome. They waste space and elicit snickers from readers. Obvious ones like "killed to death" rarely creep into copy, but ones like "widow of the late John Smith" are unsettlingly common. "Autopsy of the body" suggests that autopsies are performed on things other than bodies. "Graves of dead soldiers will be decorated" indicates that some soldiers are buried alive. Houses cannot be *completely destroyed* (they are either destroyed or damaged) and something cannot be the *most unique* (unique means one of the kind; there are no degrees of uniqueness).

Watch out for double meanings

There is always someone around who will spot the secondary—and possibly racy or bawdy—meaning of a phrase. These double meanings amuse readers but detract from professionalism. Examples of these appear in the back of *Columbia Journalism Review*. A recent issue noted the following headlines that could be read more than one way:

Bush planning Mars trip

2 in apparent shooting plot to stay in custody

Scouts can drive

A headline on Yahoo News read, "Man who vanished heading to North Carolina base."

Eliminate editorializing

Any trace of personal opinion or a value judgment should be eliminated unless the story is an interpretative feature or news analysis. Opinions belong in the opinion section, not in news stories.

Problems with Mechanics

Problems with structure aren't all that editors must correct when working copy. They must also make sure that stories follow the rules of grammar, punctuation and usage. As with the structural problems discussed previously, certain mechanical problems frequently arise in reporters' work.

Pronoun agreement

It is not unusual to see a story that says something like, "The council went to their meeting." The singular subject, council, requires a singular pronoun, its. "The group will take cars to their hotels," however, is correct because each member is acting independently and not as a collective.

Unclear antecedents

Editors should check *he*, *she*, *it* or *they* to see whether the right person or thing is identified. If there is doubt, a suitable noun, not a pronoun, should be used. For example, in the sentence, "Martinez and Sokoloff decided to drive his car across the country on vacation," it's unclear whether *his* refers to Martinez or Sokoloff. Replace it with the person's name: "Martinez and Sokoloff decided to drive Sokoloff's car across the country on vacation."

Dangling or unnecessary modifiers

An introductory phrase or clause in a sentence should modify the subject of the sentence; otherwise, it risks being nonsensical. A sentence such as "While mowing the lawn, the squirrel scurried off," says that a squirrel is mowing the lawn. "While giving his campaign speech outside City Hall, a bird landed on the bench" has a bird giving a speech. Such sentences need rewriting.

Similarly, watch out for unnecessary or unrelated phrases and clauses. "A graduate of Harvard, he is the father of eight children." Being a father has nothing to do with attending Harvard.

Parallel construction

The following sentence illustrates a failure to use parallel construction in a series: "As a compromise, the county supervisors voted to raise taxes, cut welfare payments, and the streets will no longer be swept." The last part of the series needs to grammatically follow the first two parts: "As a compromise, the county supervisors voted to raise taxes, cut welfare payments and eliminate street sweeping."

Punctuation

Commas, quotation marks, hyphens, semicolons and apostrophes need special attention. *Its* and *it's* always require a third look, and every possessive ought to get an extra glance to make sure the apostrophe is in the right place. Hyphens are needed occasionally. There's a difference between a short story writer and a short-story writer. The *Associated Press Stylebook* devotes an entire chapter to punctuation; editors should be familiar with its contents.

Spelling and homonyms

Everybody who touches a story should run a spelling check on it, but even spelling checkers are not fool-proof, so it's necessary to keep a critical eye. A spelling program may think "their" is correct when the writer meant "there," or "reign" when the correct word was "rein," or "canvas" when the correct one is "canvass," or "peddle" when the writer meant "pedal." Editors must know the differences in word meanings. Whenever you are in the slightest doubt, consult a dictionary. A list of commonly misspelled words appears in Chapter 6.

Localizing Stories

Local angles should be placed high in stories because readers tend to pay attention to stories that mention local issues or people. A wire story about a ranking of cities for desirability should put the local city in the lead, no matter where in the list it fell.

Localization can be taken to absurdity, of course. Here is an example from an Oshkosh, Wis., newspaper:

> The brother-in-law of a man who lived in Oshkosh in 1962 was arrested today in Dallas on a charge of panhandling.

But if an Oshkosh native wins a Nobel Prize, the Oshkosh paper had better have his birthplace in the lead, not in the ninth paragraph, where it probably would be when it comes over the wire.

Localizing often requires some juggling of paragraphs. Sometimes it requires only a phrase inserted high in the story (noted here by the underscore):

> Fifteen cities, <u>including Tulsa,</u> have lost federal grants aimed at reducing poverty.

Restructuring Stories

Other stories will require considerable restructuring, perhaps rewriting the lead or inserting paragraph seven after paragraph one. Feature writers have a habit of writing long introductions before getting to the heart of the story. Often an editor can chop whole paragraphs at the beginning of such pieces and trim the tail end of many news stories.

Whenever possible, stories should be organized to pinpoint the significance for the reader. Most of us read stories, as the communications researcher Wilbur Schramm has pointed out, because we want to be rewarded. We want to know what will affect our pocketbooks, to know what has happened to our friends and acquaintances, to know what might please us or upset us. The reporter writes stories with these ideas in mind, and the editor fixes the reporter's oversights (noted by the underscore):

> School <u>property</u> taxes will go up $1.5 million next year, the board of education decided Tuesday. <u>The new rate means that a resident who paid $300 in school taxes this year will pay $324 next year.</u>

Because editors know that every reader or listener has certain areas of ignorance, they often explain what the reporter thought obvious. "Died of nephritis" needs an addition: "a kidney disease." If the story mentions District IV schools, tell the reader at least roughly what area District IV covers. If the story mentions Theodore Roosevelt, add an identifying phrase. The story must remind as well as inform readers, and even the brightest of them have knowledge gaps.

Balancing the Reporter's Judgment

The reporter is the eyes, ears, hands, nose and tongue of the public. If the reporter does not describe the look, sound, feel, smell or taste of something that needs these descriptions, the editor should get this information in the story if possible. But the editor occasionally thinks that a reporter, striving for vividness, has given an incorrect tone. Perhaps the reporter unconsciously chose the words the editor thinks will sound snide, superior or patronizing to the reader. Words like *intellectual, wealthy, radical, foreigner, dropout* or *uneducated,* if used in certain contexts, may alter the story tone. For example, a story may start, "Militant environmentalists picketed City Hall on Thursday, demanding an end to toxic waste dumping in the landfill." *Militant* is a loaded word, often evoking an emotional response. *Demanding* possibly exaggerates the pickets' position.

On the other hand, a reporter may turn in a biographical story filled with syrupy phrases that make a rather ordinary person appear saintly.

The deletion of a half-dozen adjectives in these cases usually makes the tone ring true. No one should assume, however, that the tone of stories need always be coldly factual. A funny incident should be reported in a funny way. A story on a political session may be irreverent. And a story on a funeral generally should be dignified and restrained.

Editors should encourage reporters to write extraordinary leads, even for ordinary stories. Consider these fine examples:

> They say that Lockwood Vogeli was as true to his colors as he was to his customers. (From an obituary of a paint store owner in the *Sacramento Bee*.)

> The man told police he broke in looking for jewelry or money, but his 73-year-old victim disarmed him with a glass of milk, some family photos and prayer. (From a crime story in the *Contra Costa Times*.)

> The crowd abandoned all traces of Zen and grace at the door.
> Buddhists and Christians screamed at and shoved one another Wednesday at the entrance to the building where the Los Angeles County Regional Planning Commission was about to hold a hearing on a proposed Buddhist temple and retreat center in Rowland Heights. (*Los Angeles Times*)

Of course, every story should have the essential facts as well as the right tone. Audiences are interested in the overall view of an event, but they also expect the story to answer reasonable questions. If the reporter doesn't have the answer, the story should say why: "Petersen's age was not learned."

Polishing a Story

It's best to send a story that need wholesale restructuring back to the writer with advice on how to improve it, but sometimes time won't allow this. In that case, the editor should work together with the writer to make the necessary changes.

Quotes in stories are the seasoning, not the meat, and should be used judiciously. They should not be used for straight factual materials but rather to provide elaboration or to convey the emotion of the event. Quotations that look brief in a word processor can take up an alarming amount of space when squeezed into a column width or on a Web page. The editor can boil down long-winded quotations by combining material, omitting by ellipsis or using partial quotes:

> "The dam, which is designed to bring vast blessings to the people of Central Nebraska and which will avoid terrifying floods, will cost $8 million and be built within two years," the governor said.

The quote could be paraphrased:

The dam will cost $8 million and take two years to build, the governor said.

Another possibility would be:

"The dam . . . will cost $8 million and be built within two years," the governor said.

Quotation marks suggest authenticity, but too many of them make the report look patched together. The paraphrase above works best for this quote.

Reporters who keep interrupting their own stories with unnecessary information put the reader in a coma with the comma. An involved sentence that stitches facts together with commas needs editing (deleted material is stricken through):

The Tobiason boy, 8 years old and a fourth-grader at the new Leal school, said that his mother, ~~who was Miss America 14 years ago,~~ had planned to pick him up at 4 p.m. at the school.

The reference to her former title, if essential, can be inserted elsewhere.

Other reporters string identifications of people throughout a story, particularly on the sports page. In the first paragraph the football player is simply "a halfback," in the second he is "the native of Florida," in the third "the 205-pounder," in the fourth "the Big Ten's leading ground gainer" and in the fifth "the junior economics major." Such detailed identification, if used at all, should form a separate short paragraph of background information.

The correct use of words can raise interesting problems. A dictionary, of course, is a good guide, but sometimes a correctly used word will convey the wrong sense. An editorial writer once referred to a major religious denomination as a "sect." If connotation is ignored, this is a correct use of the word. But many readers were incensed, for they viewed the word as a term for little flocks that convene in abandoned stores.

Trimming Stories

For print publications, editors often have to trim stories to fit the space allotted. Editing to space means applying the scalpel, not the meat ax. Some copy butchers would merely whack off six inches from the story's end, but most stories these days are crafted with endings, and such hacking wrecks those endings. Skillful editors, however, recreate, take off the last two paragraphs, remove the fourth, combine two rather long sentences into one of moderate length, take a phrase from two or three different sentences, and make a long quotation into a short one.

Polishing pointers

- In architecture we may speak of "gingerbread," meaning excessive decoration. Language, too, can be loaded with grand words and opulent sentences. Editors in most cases should eliminate the fancy in favor of the plain.
- Sometimes reporters fall into the bad habit of making verbs out of nouns. Impact is a common noun misused as a verb, as in *the campaign impacted upon the voters*. A secretary of state once said, "I'll caveat that," perhaps making the most startling switch of noun to verb.
- A noted columnist used *conglomerating*, and *concertize* slips into entertainment stories—as though someone can "concert." Someone even concocted *strategize*.
- Editors should watch also for preposition pad, in which a stream of prepositional phrases fills a sentence, as in *He ran into the store in the early morning after a quick breakfast during a rain shower, and in his haste in ordering overpaid*. Prepositional phrases often can be dropped by using the possessive: Instead of *the main points of the platform*, try *the platform's main points*. *One of the students* can become *a student*.
- Copy is improved, too, by reducing the number of words ending in -ize. The word *use* does nicely in place of *utilize* and *set priorities* is an improvement over *prioritize*. Only a few words should end with -wise, so that rule should oust such creations as *moneywise, weatherwise* and *transportwise*.
- Politicians often try to obfuscate fact with passive voice ("Mistakes were made"), but editors should allow their reporters to use it only sparingly ("Administrators made mistakes"). In most instances, use the more vigorous active voice:

> *The building was destroyed by fire* becomes *Fire destroyed the building.*
> *Fifteen hot dogs were eaten by the boy* becomes *The boy ate 15 hot dogs.*

An example

Here are two examples of an editor's finished work (added material is underscored; deleted material is stricken through):

> Three area villages—Homer, Chatsworth and Hansonville—will get special federal grants totaling $2.5 million to finance sewer reconstruction. The grants will amount to 2,500,000 dollars. The villages are Homer, Chatsworth and Hansonville.
>
> The grants will pay for construction costs of a total of 14 miles of new sewer lines replacement in the towns. Some of the sewers are 60 years old.

Mayor Florence Stegeman of Homer said ~~she had conferred with~~ the mayors of the other villages ~~and they~~ agreed that the work could be ~~finnished~~ in two years.

She ~~averred~~said that the three towns will aim to let contracts within four months. She assumed contractors will start work about ~~6~~six weeks later.

The grant money is not divided evenly between the towns. Homer and Hansonville will get $900,000~~,000~~ each and Chatsworth will get $700,000.

The school board ~~at its meeting~~ Monday night voted ~~by~~7 to ~~_~~4 ~~margin~~ to raise ~~the~~ property tax~~es~~ ~~by two~~2 percent.

The new levy is expected to produce $700,000 ~~in new revenue~~ and will help the board grant teachers a 9 percent pay increase ~~in the coming year.~~

~~The tax will be assessed on property beginning in July but t~~The extra tax ~~payments~~ will not be billed until October.

Charles C. Bogart, the school board president~~of the school board~~, said the increase should ~~give the board~~ produce a balanced budget in the next fiscal year.

~~The four dissenters were divided in their opposition to the tax increase.~~ Two dissenters wanted to raise taxes ~~three~~3 percent and two wanted ~~the~~a 1 percent increase~~limited to one percent~~.

The ~~school~~ board taxes only property~~to raise its revenue~~. The rest of its income comes from state and federal aid~~, calculated basically on the number of pupils~~. The property tax yields ~~only~~ 31 percent of the ~~school~~ budget.

The cutting may not seem like much, but in the second story it removed about six lines of copy. In print, this means that the story in type will be about an inch shorter—but even online, a tighter story is a better story.

Stylebooks

Every news publication should have a stylebook describing how capitalization, abbreviation and punctuation are handled. Many use the *Associated Press Stylebook* and then create supplements that address local concerns, such as special abbreviations specific to their audiences. The consistency established by the stylebook prevents the reader from being annoyed when a story spells a proper name two or three different ways in as many paragraphs or abbreviates a word one time and spells it out the next.

Reporters are supposed to follow these sets of rules, or *style*, but sometimes they don't. The editor, to correct their errors, needs to be thoroughly familiar with the stylebook but willing to look up an obscure point whenever there is any doubt or argument.

Notes

1. Roy Peter Clark and Don Fry, *Coaching Writers: Editors and Reporters Working Together Across Media Platforms*, 2nd ed. (Boston: Bedford/St. Martin's, 2003), 92.

2. Saul Alinsky, "The Professional Radical," *Harper's* (June 1965), 39.

CHAPTER 6

Word Watching

Top editors tell their reporters and editors to "use words correctly." Good advice, of course, but hard to follow. What is correct? Who said so? What about new words not yet in dictionaries? Which dictionary is correct? Not only are new words constantly added to the language, but old words take on new meaning, as with *gay*, *turkey* and *tight*.

News organizations use a standard for the meanings of words. If they did not, readers would be confused frequently by jargon, slang and malapropism. The dictionary of first reference for news organizations that follow Associated Press style is the current edition of *Webster's New World College Dictionary*, published by Wiley. Editors who cannot find the word they need in that dictionary should consult *Webster's Third New International Dictionary of the English Language, Unabridged*, published by Merriam-Webster. Editors should take care to avoid words or meanings that they think will appear for a short time and then pass into obscurity even as they are being listed in a new dictionary. A good guide to word usage for newsrooms would be to cling to the old so that the meaning of language does not change every generation, but adapt to the new if it brings freshness and vividness to the language.

Editors should not only be alert to changing usage but also spot redundancies, grammatical errors and misleading language. The following tips on usage, grammar and spelling should be valuable.

Words and Phrases Often Mistakenly Used

Actual fact or *true fact*. A *fact* is by definition *true*.

Advance planning. Planning implies advance work or thought. *Advance reservations* also is redundant.

Advise, inform. "He was *informed* (not *advised*) of his wife's illness and *advised* to call her doctor immediately."

Allusion. A reference, as in "Her *allusion* to Hamlet. . ."

Alternative, for *alternate.* "He had an *alternate* (not *alternative*) plan. It gave the voter a choice of *alternatives.*"

Alumna, alumnus, alumnae, alumni. One female graduate is an alumna; more than one, *alumnae.* One male graduate is an alumnus; more than one, *alumni,* which also is the plural for a group including both men and women.

Amateur, novice, professional. A *novice* is a beginner; an *amateur* is one who works or plays for fun, not money; a *professional* works or plays for money. Because the professional usually is highly skilled, an amateur sometimes is complimented by being called "professional."

Amused. See *bemused.*

Ancestor. A person from whom one is descended.

And etc. Etc. stands for *et cetera,* which means "and the rest" in Latin, so the *and* is redundant.

Anxious, for *eager.* To be eager means to look forward to; to be anxious is to feel anxiety: "He was *eager* (not *anxious*) to try, but his mother was *anxious* for his safety."

Ask. In its various forms it can often be dropped. *"Asked* what he thought about the game, he said he thought it was good" can be simply "He said he thought the game was good."

At the present time. Use *now* instead.

Author, as a verb. "He *authored* a novel" should be "He wrote a novel."

Baby girl (or boy) *is born.* Redundant, as no one is born fully grown.

Badly injured. No injury is good; say *severely injured.*

Balding. A person is either bald or getting bald.

Beautiful. The word involves a value judgment, and some crank is bound to disagree, especially over a *"beautiful* woman."

Bemused, for *amused. Bemused* means "dazed," "preoccupied," or "confused."

Boat, for *ship.* Technically, *boats* are carried on *ships;* generally, a *boat* is a small vessel.

Bridegroom. See *groom.*

Britain. See *Great Britain.*

Broadcasted. The past participle of *broadcast* is *broadcast.* "The program was *broadcast* daily."

Brutal beating. No *beating* is gentle.

Burglar. A person who breaks into a building with intent to steal something.

Calvary. The hill on which Jesus was crucified.

Cavalry. A military unit, originally riding on horses.

Celebrant, celebrator. A *celebrant* takes part in a religious rite. A *celebrator* whoops it up.

Collide. This verb refers to a bumping of two moving objects. If one object was stationary, they did not collide. "The car hit (not *collided with*) a telephone pole and then *collided* with another car."

Combine. Do not use as a noun, unless it refers to a piece of harvesting equipment.

Complected or *complexioned*. The noun *complexion* has no adjective form. "She is fair *complected* (or *complexioned*)" should be "She has a fair *complexion*."

Completely destroyed. The *completely* is redundant.

Comprise. Means "contain," "embrace" or "include." The whole *comprises* the parts.

Consensus of opinion. *Of opinion* is redundant, as a *consensus* is a collective opinion.

Controversial usually is a waste word. "The crowd shouted down the *controversial* proposal" can be simply "The crowd shouted down the proposal."

Contusion. See *laceration*.

Convince, persuade. To get people to overcome doubt and believe something is to *convince* them; to cause them to do something is to *persuade* them.

Crescendo. Means "rising" or "increasing," not "loud."

Critical, for *critical condition*. A sick person in *critical condition* is seldom *critical*.

Debark. Use only for those getting off ships or out of boats.

Decimate. To destroy one-tenth.

Descendant. An offspring, perhaps remote, of an ancestor.

Devout, for *religious*. *Devout* is an exceptionally high degree of devotion—too high for the layman to measure.

Diagnose. Conditions are *diagnosed*; patients are not.

Different than, for *different from*. "Each house is *different from* (not *different than*) the one next to it."

Disburse, disperse. To *disburse* is to pay out; to *disperse* is to scatter.

Disinterested, uninterested. To be *disinterested* is to be impartial or unbiased. *Uninterested* means without interest.

Dove, for *dived*. *Dove* is the colloquial, not the written, past tense of *dive*. "He *dived* (not *dove*) from the side of the boat."

Due to, for *because*. "The schools were closed *because of* (not *due to*) the snowstorm. He had been *due to* meet us at noon."

Eager. See *anxious, eager*.

Elderly. Be cautious about this word, because even people of 75 may be sensitive about being called *elderly*.

Enormity, enormous. *Enormity* implies evil. *Enormous* means "large."

Esquire, the honorable, and other undefinable titles should be omitted.

Etc. See *and etc.*

Fewer. See *less*.

Finalize. Try *complete, end*, or *finish*.

Flaunt. Means "to disregard rules" or "make a boastful display."

Flout. Means to "treat with contempt."

Foreseeable future. Who can see into the future?

Forgotten. See *gotten*.

For the purpose of can be simply *for*.

Fortuitous. By chance, not by good fortune.

Freak accident is a cliché. Let the facts show that the accident is unusual.

Fulsome. Overfull or excessive because of insincerity.

Gauntlet, gantlet. A *gauntlet* is a glove that can be thrown down; a *gantlet* is a form of punishment that can be run.

Gender, sex. Gender is a grammatical distinction; *sex* refers to physiological differences.

Gotten, for *got. Gotten* is the colloquial past participle of *get,* but *forgotten* is the regular past participle of *forget.* "He had *got* the man's address but had *forgotten* to get his age."

Great Britain, United Kingdom. Great Britain, or simply Britain, encompasses England, Wales and Scotland. A *subject,* not a *citizen,* of the country is a *Briton.* The *United Kingdom* includes Great Britain and Northern Ireland.

Groom, for *bridegroom.* "The *bridegroom* had recently been employed as a *groom* with Smith Stables."

Ground rules. Except in reference to baseball games, skip the *ground.*

Half mast. Flags may fly at *half mast* on ships or naval installations, but ashore they fly at *half staff.*

Hanged, hung. "Spectators *hung* over the wall to see the murderer *hanged.*"

Harebrained. Compares somebody's intellect to that of a rabbit; *hairbrained* is incorrect.

Heart condition. Everyone has one; some have heart *disease* or heart *ailments.*

If and when. Just *when* will do.

Inform. See *advise.*

Intrigue. As a verb, it means "to plot," not "to interest" or "to mystify."

Jewish rabbi. Rabbi is Jewish by definition.

Kin. Means "relatives," not "one relative."

Knot. A nautical mile an hour. *Knots an hour* is redundant.

Laceration, contusion. A *laceration* is a cut; a *contusion* is a bruise.

Ladies, for *women.* All *ladies* are women, but not all *women* are ladies. So call all women *women.*

Lawmen. A vague term, and sexist to boot. Use *police, deputies, prosecutors.*

Less for *fewer. Less* refers to a general quantity; *fewer* refers to the specific items that make it up. *Fewer* dollars earned mean *less* money to spend.

Like. Don't confuse with *such as;* for example, not "cities *like* Chicago" but "cities *such as* Chicago."

Litany. A prayer, not a list.

Litmus test. Use it only for stories about chemistry.

Livid. Black and blue or the color of lead; not flushed or red.

Located, for *situated. Located* means "found," and *situated* means "placed at." "He *located* the school, which was *situated* five miles from town." As in this example, even *situated* can often be dropped without loss of meaning.

Majority, for *plurality.* In an election, a *majority* is more than half the votes, and the *plurality* is the margin of victory. "Jones was elected by a clear *majority* (64 percent), rolling up a *plurality* of 115,000 votes."

Masterly, masterful. Masterly means skillful; *masterful* means "imperious or domineering."

Matinee performance. A *matinee* is a *performance.*

Media, medium. Media is the plural of *medium.* "Television is an important *medium.*" And, *"Media* are a good source of information."

Menial. The word has degrading overtones; avoid using it to describe workers.

Militant, for *protester* or for *rowdy.* A *militant* is a vigorous fighter for a cause and may be nonviolent; a *rowdy* fights for selfish reasons. A *protester* may be against violence.

Money, monies. Money is collective, so the plural is unnecessary.

More unique, or *most unique. Unique* means one of a kind, so it cannot be modified.

Mourning dove. Not *morning dove,* for the sound is mournful.

New record. When a *record* is set it is *new.*

Novice. See *amateur.*

Orientated, for *oriented. Oriented* is the preferred past tense of *orient.*

Panic, riot, disaster, and so on should not be used unless the facts clearly indicate the need for strong words.

Per (in *per year, per day,* and so on). Skip the Latin; use *a* year, *a* day. *Per annum* is doubly unfortunate.

Personal friend. No one is called an *impersonal friend.*

Persuade. See *convince, persuade.*

Plurality. See *majority.*

Presently. Presently is a long word meaning "soon." It does not mean "now."

Prior to should be simply *before.*

Professional. See *amateur.*

Protester. See *militant.*

Query. A question, not an inquiry.

Raised, reared. Children are *reared;* animals are *raised.*

Ravage, ravish. Ravage means destroy. *Ravish* means "to carry away with force" or "to rape."

Reason why. The *why* is redundant.

Refute. To prove to be wrong. It does not mean "debate."

Religious. See *devout.*

Remand back. Skip the *back.*

Resides is a fancy way of saying *lives.*

Revert back. The *back* is redundant.

Robber. A person who threatens another in the act of stealing. An *armed robber,* of course, has a weapon.

Row. (Rhymes with *plow.)* An argument or to have an argument. Avoid, for readers easily confuse it with other meanings.

Sex. See *gender.*

Ship. See *boat.*

Situated. See *located.*

Snow. It is not *white stuff.*

Soldiers. See *troops.*

Sudden explosion is redundant.

Superlatives (such as *eldest, fastest, biggest*) should be handled with care. Often someone will be challenged to find something that surpasses your example.

The before a plural noun is often, but not always, unnecessary. "*The* voters filled the polling booths" could be simply "Voters filled the polling booths." Let your ear be your guide.

Thief. A person who steals, but without threatening others and without breaking into buildings.

Thusly should be *thus.*

To death is often redundant, as in *strangled to death* or *drowned to death.*

Troop. A group of soldiers. Do not use it to mean a single serviceman or servicewoman.

Unaware of the fact that should be simply *unaware that.*

Uninterested. See *disinterested.*

United Kingdom. See *Great Britain.*

Unknown. Use sparingly, for usually someone knows what is labeled *unknown*: for example, "her age was *unknown.*"

Utterly, flatly, sheerly, categorically, definitely and many other such adverbs are padding most of the time.

Very should be used very seldom.

Watershed. Not to be used as a synonym for *high point* or *landmark.*

Whether or not, for *whether.* Because it implies an alternative, *whether* rarely needs to be followed by *or not.*

-wise. A bad suffix for general use. *Otherwise* is fine, but *healthwise, automobilewise, taxwise* and so on smack too much of advertising shoptalk.

Journalists Should Review These Grammatical Points Often

About may indicate approximation; *around* implies motion. "He weighs *about* 150 pounds and runs two miles *around* the track each day."

Adjective phrases should be hyphenated. "The *2-year-old* boy ran to the *sad-looking* man."

Adjective-noun agreement. This kind, not *these* kind.

Adjectives for adverbs. An adverb modifies verbs, so "She hits *good*" and "He plays *good*" are incorrect; for *good* here modifies verbs. Change the *good* to *well.*

Adjectives referring to health or emotion. See *feel.*

Affect is a verb that means "to have influence." *Effect,* as a noun, refers to a result. "His speech *affected* the audience deeply; the *effect* was a silence so profound one could hear the crickets outside the tent." As a verb, *effect* means "to bring about or accomplish." "His work *effected* a cure." Note that as a verb *effect* is usually unnecessary. "His work cured her."

Agreement. A subject and its predicate, and a noun and its pronoun, should agree in number. "The *group* of boys *was* trying to break down the door. The *girls* inside *were* screaming in panic. The *group* lost *its* steam when the dean appeared and told the *boys* he had called *their* parents."

Among. See *between.*

Apostrophe (to indicate possession). See *possessives.*

Around. See *about.*

As. See *like.*

Beside refers to nearness; *besides* means "in addition to." "*Besides* being sheriff he was dogcatcher, so he built the dog pound *beside* the jail."

Between refers to two persons or things; *among* refers to three or more. "The power of government is divided *among* the legislative, judicial and executive branches. The legislative power is divided *between* the Senate and the House."

Capitalization (in quotations). See *quotations.*

Commas that set off appositives or interrupters come in pairs. "John Smith, senator from Vermont will speak today" should be "John Smith, senator from Vermont, will speak today." And "The meeting, surprisingly enough went off on schedule" needs a comma after *enough.*

Complement means "to accompany" or "enhance." *Compliment* means "to praise."

Contrary-to-fact statements. See *subjunctive mood.*

Double negatives. Can't hardly and *can't scarcely* are examples of redundant negatives.

Doubt, statements of. See *subjunctive mood.*

Effect. See *affect.*

Either pairs with *or; neither* pairs with *nor.* "*Either* he *or* I is at fault, but *neither* he *nor* I admits guilt." Note that both *either* and *neither* require singular verbs.

Farther refers to distance; *further* refers to thoroughness. "He wanted to check *further* on the flood damage, so he walked *farther* onto the bridge."

Feel, when it refers to health or emotion, requires an adjective, not an adverb. "I feel *bad* about not calling him back." "I feel *badly*" would imply an impaired sense of touch. The same rule applies to *look, sound, smell* and *taste.*

Gerunds coupled with a pronoun require the possessive. "I could watch *his dancing* for hours."

Hyphenation, of adjective phrases. See *adjective phrases.*

It's and *its. It's* is a contraction of *it is; its* is a possessive pronoun. "*It's* too bad the store lost *its* lease."

Lay and *lie. To lay* is a transitive verb and therefore takes an object; *to lie* is intransitive and thus takes no object. Transitive: He *lays* bricks for a living. He is *laying* the box on the counter. *Lay* the box on the counter. He *laid* the box down. Intransitive: He *lies* in bed till noon. He is *lying* in the sun. *Lie* down for an hour or so. He *lay* down to rest. His head *lay* on the pillow. He has *lain* there long enough. The *Associated Press Stylebook* is a good resource on lay and lie; it's best to check it every time you come across one of these troublesome words.

Like is a preposition and requires an object; *as* is a conjunction and requires a following clause. "She looks *like* her mother, just *as* (not *like*) we thought." *Like* may be used as a conjunction in a simile. "He performed *like* Peter Serkin."

Look, when referring to health. See *feel*.

Neither. See *either*.

Nor. See *either*.

Or. See *either*.

Parallel construction. Don't shift the form of construction in a sentence, as in 'John was *tall and heavy and had a fair complexion.*" Instead, use "John was *tall, heavy and fair.*"

Plurals. Generally, you need only add -s or -es to make nouns plural. Watch out for writers who want to make plurals by adding apostrophe-s; the only time that is permissible is when making single letters plural: "He received all A's on his report card." Also, be careful of plurals for compound subjects when the second word is the modifier, such as *courts martial, attorneys general, fathers-in-law*. For a more extensive discussion, see *The Associated Press Stylebook*.

Possessives. To form the singular possessive, in most cases, add an apostrophe and an *s*. "The dog's coat is glossy." To form a plural possessive, in most cases, just add the apostrophe. "The dogs' coats are wet." For singular proper nouns that end in s, add just an apostrophe. "The Bible tells of Jesus' life." A number of exceptions to these rules apply; consult *The Associated Press Stylebook*, which provides an extensive discussion.

Prepositional object. When a pronoun is the object of a preposition, it should be in the objective case. "The decision was between *him* and *me.*"

Pronouns. They should match the case of the nouns to which they refer, as "we students are leaving" and "she told *us students.*" Pronouns must be used with care to assure clearness. This sentence is confusing: "Deborah told *her* mother *her* purse was stolen." Whose purse?

Quotations. A quoted sentence needs only one capital: "It is a difficult problem," Smith said, "but we can solve it."

Two quoted sentences require two capitals: "The well is dry," she said. "We must get water elsewhere."

A quote within a quote takes single quotation marks: "New devices let people 'hear' atomic explosions thousands of miles away," he said.

When quoted material continues for more than one paragraph, save the *ending* quotation marks for the end of the quoted material: "The well is dry," she said, "so we must get it elsewhere.

"Maybe we can get it at the next farm."

Set and *sit*. *To set* is a transitive verb and thereby takes an object; *to sit* is intransitive and thus takes no object. Transitive: He *sets* tile for a living. He is *setting* plants in the garden. *Set* the box on the table. He *set* the box down. Intransitive: He *sits* here regularly. She was *sitting* in the chair. *Sit* down, please. He *sat* in front. Have you *sat* there before?

Smell. See *feel*.

Sound. See *feel*.

Subjunctive mood. The subjunctive mood expresses wishes, doubts or things contrary to fact. It requires a plural verb. "If he *were* 7 feet tall, he would be on the basketball team for sure" (contrary to fact). "I wish I *were* old enough to be president" (wish). "He acts as if he *were* unable to speak" (doubt).

Taste. See *feel*.

That, which. A restrictive clause (essential to the meaning of a sentence) is introduced by *that* and does *not* take a comma. "Police found the gun that was used in the slaying." (Crucial to the meaning.)

A nonrestrictive clause (not essential to the meaning of the sentence) is introduced by *which* and takes a comma: "Police found the gun, which was an antique Colt 45." (Incidental information is added about the gun, but it's not essential to the meaning of the sentence.)

Touch. See *feel*.

Try. Make it *try to*, not *try and*.

Voice. Don't shift voices in the same sentence, as in "He *will travel* to Maine (active), and *will be traded* (passive) to New Orleans."

Were. See *subjunctive mood*.

Which. See *that, which*.

Who, whom. *Who* should be used as the subject of a sentence or a clause, as in "*Who* will come? *Whom* is used when the objective case is required, as in "They wondered *whom* she would choose." A good rule of thumb in trying to figure which to use is to substitute other pronouns. For instance, if you would use "he," then the correct pronoun is "who"; for "him," use "whom."

Commonly Misspelled or Misused Words

abbot
abscess
absence
accidentally
accommodate
accumulate
across
advice, advise, adviser
advisory
allege
all right

allotted
amateur
arctic
appellate
apologize
ascend
athlete
baptize
believe
benefited
breath, breathe

bridal, bridle
Britain, Briton
calendar
canceled
canvas, canvass
capital, capitol
category
cellar
cemetery
changeable
cite, site, sight
compliment, complement
conscious
consensus
coroner
corps, corpse
council, counsel
defendant
desert, dessert
develop
discreet, discrete
dyeing, dying
emigrate, immigrate
embarrass
endurance
envelop, envelope
equivalent
existence
exorbitant
extravagance
eyeing
familiar
flew, flu, flue
gauge
guerrilla
guillotine
height
hemorrhage
hypocrisy
inaugurate
independent
innocuous
irrelevant
judgment
knowledgeable
lessen, lesson
libel, liable

loose, lose
lovable
lying
mantel, mantle
marshal
mileage
missile
misspell
necessary
Niagara
nickel
obscene
occasion
occurred
omitted
ordinance, ordnance
paid
peaceable
penitentiary
personal, personnel
Philippines
picnicked
plaque
potatoes
prairie
precede, proceed
preventive
principal, principle
privilege
questionnaire
rein, reign
rhyme
rhythm
ricochet
salable
sauerkraut
scion
scissors
seize
separate
sergeant
sheriff
siege
sizable
soccer
sophomore
stationary, stationery

straitjacket

superintendent

supersede

there, their, they're

tomatoes

traveled

truly

unnecessary

vaccinate

vane, vain, vein

varicose

weird

wholly

wield

your, you're

CHAPTER 7

Writing Headlines

A story may have the greatest lead ever written but that will be for naught if it isn't accompanied by a headline that draws the reader to it in the first place. The best headlines both "tell and sell," that is, they tell the reader quickly what the news is and persuade the reader that the story is worth reading.

The first notion, the "telling," is the headline's most important function. The well-written headline—"head" or "hed" for short—immediately tells them the gist of the accompanying story. For better or worse, most Web site and newspaper readers are skimmers; what they know of the world, they get from headlines. Skimming makes possible rapid news comprehension because no one can read all the stories processed each day. If the heads do their most important job—rapid summary—the careful skimmer will get the general drift of events and slow down for a story that may be worth careful reading.

The second important goal of headlines is related to their billboard function. Headlines must sell. On news racks in competitive cities, front-page headlines tend to sell one paper instead of another. On the Internet and the inside pages of newspapers, headlines lure the reader into a story.

A third function of headlines is ranking the news. One head shouts that this story is important. Another suggests quietly that this one might be of some interest as well—but not of the same importance. The size and style of type help communicate to the reader the importance and quality of the news—whether it is a cataclysm or a pleasant afternoon tea. A more extensive explanation of how the editor evaluates the news appears in Chapter 2.

A final purpose of headlines is to stimulate the reader's artistic sense. Dull heads make a dull page. But graphic artistry is much more complex than merely replacing dullness with brightness. Headlines may add to the clutter of ugly or confusing pages. But when heads are well-written and well-placed with styles that are attractive, the print or Web pages are clean and good-looking. The personality of a publication, in part, is set by the consistent use of heads day after day, and a sudden, drastic change in heads may make a reader feel that a familiar friend has moved away.

Although headlines for the World Wide Web differ in some respects from newspaper heads, for the most part the process of writing them is the same. This discussion looks at the similarities first and then examines how online headline-writing differs.

Heads of Quality

Figure 7.1.
The home page of MSNBC.com shows serviceable headlines at work. Copyright, 2004 Microsoft Corp. Used with permission.

Most headline writers do a good job, day in, day out. They may often compose routine or dull heads, but they are accurate. Nothing better illustrates such good, ordinary headlines—unimaginative, perhaps, but fair—than the latest news headline on a news Web site. (See Figure 7.1.)

Praise for head writing usually goes to the writers who have a flair for saying the difficult with style. The head that draws the envy of other professionals usually displays unique imagery or wit. Neophytes who want to distinguish themselves as head writers should try to develop a colorful way of putting things in a few words; sometimes they will falter, but they may develop a valuable talent. The head writer should probe nearly every story for something amusing or clever that can be brought up to a headline. In some instances, as in an obituary, it would be in bad taste. So would heads that make puns out of a person's name. But some real effort to be droll or even funny will produce an occasional gem. (See Figure 7.2.)

The Sacramento Bee honors exceptional headlines in a general e-mail to the newsroom staff. This headline appeared on a story about California Gov. Arnold Schwarzenegger's fight against an unauthorized product bearing his image:

**Bobbleheads will roll,
governor's lawyers say**

This headline drew readers to a story about improvements in math education:

Algebra success adds up at last

A story about the sale of fireworks had this headline:

They'll be gone in a flash

This headline ran above a story about the controversy of the phrase "under God" in the Pledge of Allegiance:

Does 'under God' do justice for all?

*Loaded for Bear:
Is It Sporting to Lure
Prey With Pastries?*

*   *   *

**In Two Big Hunting States,
Banning Bait Is on Ballot;
Maine Fears Bruin Boom**

Gift Wrap Goes Over the Top

*Pearls, Silk, Chenille—All Are
Fit to Be Tied Onto Presents
From Style-Conscious Givers*

Figure 7.2.
Editors at *The Wall Street Journal* continually write headlines that both entertain and inform.

Basic Rules for Heads

Unlike those in other parts of the world, news publications in the United States prefer vivid, dramatic, summary headlines. American readers have come to expect headlines written in the present tense, using active voice and omitting articles. Imagine coming across this on a news site:

The congressmen were in a disagreement on the housing legislation

Three things are wrong: It's past tense; it has no active verb; and it has several articles. Furthermore, most of the words are too long for a conventional head.

A better headline would be:

Lawmakers split on home bill

This head is in the present tense; a concrete noun is followed by a strong, active verb; and articles have been sliced out. This same example, however, has some head-writing weaknesses. "Split" may be read here as a verb in the past tense or an adjective, and it doubtless overstates the debate the reporter discussed. And although "home bill" has punch, it introduces an oversimplification and perhaps even connotations that the more complex language avoids.

Boiling it to the essence

How do copy editors decide what to put in the headline's abbreviated key sentence?

As reporters try to get the gist of the story into a lead that summarizes the event, head writers boil that sentence to fit the publication's specifications. At its simplest, copy editors switch the sentence into the present or future tense and eliminate articles and time-place references. The remaining skeleton is typically subject, verb and, perhaps, direct or indirect object.

Assume that the wire carries this lead:

WASHINGTON—The House launched into a bitter debate Thursday on a bill to set up a new version of the Job Corps.

An editor might write a two-line head:

**Job Corps bill
debated in House**

The second line is a little long, so it can be altered easily to make it fit:

**House debates
Job Corps bill**

Some slot editor may argue that this does not reflect the ire the bill has produced—and it starts with a flat word: "House." Another might do the job:

**Job Corps fight
erupts in House**

But maybe this one is too strong. A calmer head might be tried:

**Job Corps bill
debate fiery**

This one only implies the verb *is,* so another one is tried:

**House wrangles
over Job Corps**

This starts with "House" but may indicate the intensity of the debate without exaggeration. It would fit and tell the story.

Headline writing guidelines

Different publications set rules for how headlines should be written, but most news publications follow these general rules.

Be accurate.   If necessary, sacrifice color and drama in a headline to avoid leaving an erroneous impression.

Accuracy may force the copy editor to sift the story for the kernel of the news. Of course, if the lead is buried, the good editor revises the story, putting the major news at the top and then drawing the head from the revised lead. But an interpretative news story may properly start with an anecdotal lead. Then the head writer has to grasp the full meaning of the story and try to summarize it accurately.

Here, for example, is the lead of a story in the *Sacramento Bee:*

> LAST CHANCE CREEK, Plumas County—High in the northern Sierra Nevada, meadowlarks and red-winged black birds flit among the reeds at the edge of two small ponds that are a part of an effort to protect the Sacramento River Delta.

The story proceeds for two more paragraphs before getting to the nut graph:

> Ten watershed restoration projects have turned nearly 2,000 acres along Last Chance Creek, a major tributary to the Feather River, into functioning meadows, including the wetlands around this pair of ponds near Artray Creek.

The *Bee's* headline writer summarized the whole piece with this head:

Rehab projects turn dry flats into wetlands

Be specific and concrete.   *One-eyed thief* is better than *robber* or *man*; *3,000 bales* is better than *cotton*; *killed* is better than *died*. Increasingly, it is difficult to write heads that tell the story on complicated economic issues, international tensions or environmental legislation. A single word such as *economy, accord* or *nature* rarely gets across what the subject is about. Vague, abstract words make headlines without punch. But blunt words that fit may mislead.

Use strong verbs.   Avoid jelly words such as *discuss* and *indicate*; also avoid forms of *to be*. As in good news story style, use strong verbs in the active voice—*slash, pinpoint, reveal, assail, hit, kill*. Some otherwise good words have been used so much that good editors avoid or ban their use; these include *rap, sift, probe* and *blast*. Remember that verbs must be accurate as well as active. So perhaps *assail* should be replaced by *criticize* or *denounce* by *chide*.

Start with the news.   The first line of the head should tell readers what they want to know immediately. A short noun followed by a short, active verb will usually do:

Senator upset . . .
Workers strike . . .
Majority found . . .

Of the five W's used in the lead, the top line of the head almost always summarizes the *who* and *what*.

But sometimes the *who* is less important and newsworthy, at least in a label word, than is the body acted upon. So, as indicated already, *Congress* and *legislature* as the first word of a head probably will have less pulling power than the tag for the legislation passed, as with *pollution bill* or *jobs program*. Though such a subject forces the verb into the weaker passive form, you can still give it strength, as with *debated, argued* or *killed*.

Punctuate correctly.   To save space in headlines, editors bend some punctuation rules. For one, headlines rarely use periods at the end. Commas are used in place of the word "and," and semicolons are used to join independent clauses. Single quotation marks are used instead of double quotation marks. The dash has many good head uses, but since words are not split at the end of the line in the heads, hyphens appear only between words. Some examples:

School board OKs budget,
adopts new code of conduct

President starts vacation;
city braces for bad traffic

Whether periods mark a head abbreviation is a question of the paper's style; it may be Y.W.C.A. or YWCA. Sometimes a publication will use periods in one group of initials but not in another, according to a tradition that the editor must learn. Similarly, abbreviation is according to style. *Prof.* without the name and *Dept.* are typical abbreviations that many newspapers would ban. But *Dr.* and *Rev.* and *Co.* (with appropriate names) or *FBI* or *U.N.* would be used without hesitation.

Don't repeat.   A good headline, as with a good sentence, avoids simple-minded repetition. **Club manager tells plans for club** obviously is awkward. Editors also should skip awkward repetition of sounds, as in **Legislators eye new racing legislation.**

One of the greatest temptations is to repeat a word from a main headline in a secondary headline, commonly called a deck. Even use of a synonym sounds strained, so the deck should usually reveal a second angle.

Don't overpack.   It is good advice to try to get many ideas into a head; good practice avoids padding and thinning. Yet one can cross a line and cause the head to become so packed with ideas that the reader has trouble translating it. Piling up nouns as modifiers makes awkward heads. **State Police investigators** is clear to most. **State Police traffic toll investigators** is more difficult, **but State Police major highway traffic toll investigators** is impossible.

Don't use headlinese.   Good English is best. Headlinese is the language of overworked words. They may be the short, punchy verbs, so some editors object to even *hit* and *gut* as headlinese. Certain nouns, such as *cops* and *tryst*, are overworked and slangy. Stay alert to usage; when a word becomes a cliché, avoid it. Homely words become headlinese when used for their size and not their sense. One of the most infelicitous of such uses is *said* for *termed, called* or *described as.* Those who employ this poor English can argue that it is short for "is said to be," but the mind swirls at fitting in the missing words, as in this head:

**Bilateral
trade said
valuable**

Called is nearly the same width as *said* and in this instance would have fit. (Words such as *called* or *labeled* are considered attributive words. They indicate to the reader that someone is making a statement. Without such words the headline would become a flat statement, such as **Bilateral trade valuable,** which would be appropriate on an opinion piece but not over news stories.)

Don't be ambiguous.   Mushy words leave mushy meanings. The many legitimate meanings of a single English word make the writer's job difficult. The verb *will*, in faulty context, may appear to be a noun, which one reader may mistake for *determination*, another for *legal document*. Humor sometimes results from unexpected double meanings:

**Roberts will suit
stalls over horses**

Precision is essential in heads.

Avoid lazy techniques.   Some headline writers will snap off anything that will fit, even if the reader is puzzled, as in these outrages:

Pimples good for you: Study

Panel: Chemical waste harmless

Don't repeat the wording in the lead.   A story may begin: "Despite $75 tickets, business is booming among Broadway theaters." But readers hear an echo if the head reads:

Despite $75 prices, Broadway theaters booming

Specificity counts.   Beginning headline writers, as with beginning news writers, tend to produce vague copy. They appear to be reluctant to get to the meat of the story. For a story of a crash that killed 15 people in Los Angeles, for example, they may produce heads that say:

Plane crashes at airport

Jet crashes on runway

These obviously won't get much news across to the reader. The head writer might turn to the story lead and write a digest of that paragraph:

15 killed in L.A. air crash

This way the reader knows immediately the seriousness of the accident, what kind of accident it was and where it was.

Headline writers should say to themselves as they tackle a head: What's the real news? How can I tell it in a few words? How can I squeeze in more information? Is it essential to tell where something took place? If headlines only skirt basic facts, readers sense that the publication is bland and dull.

Headlines Are Easy, Aren't They?

By Wayne Countryman

Headline writing is easy. Edit story, check whether cutline is needed, make sure coding is correct, convey hed information concisely and accurately, send to slot.

Oh, you want good headlines? That's difficult.

It gets easier with experience, except when repetition makes it more difficult.

"C'mon, this ain't brain surgery. It's not rocket science," barks your newsroom's enforcer of deadlines. True: Brain surgeons and rocket scientists don't have to put clever, enticing labels on their work while struggling with daily/nightly deadlines.

Ten basic rules I've been taught for writing headlines:

1. Always use active tense.
2. It is not necessary to use active tense.
3. Use clever punctuation.
4. Don't get clever with punctuation.
5. Read your work aloud. Bounce ideas off your co-workers.
6. Shut up, we're trying to work here.
7. Use the most vivid image in the story.
8. Write it from the lede. And don't steal the reporter's thunder.
9. Use the hed to draw the reader into the story.
10. Write the hed so that the reader doesn't need to read the story.

Hmmmmm, it's a wonder that I ever write a decent hed.

Let's try again. Most of us began as reporters; what did we learn then?

1. Keep it tight (as if headline writers have a choice).
2. Get it right (that includes facts and spelling). Spell check, if you work on a computer with that function. Keep a dictionary and other reference books nearby.
3. Know your publication's style. Follow it, unless you have a reason that you can put into words that a harried slot editor might heed.
4. Write for the reader (not your ex-professors, contest judges, competitors or co-workers).
5. Eschew obfuscation. For example, "buy," a short word, often is the best. "Infrastructure," popular with bureaucrats, means little without elaboration. With the elaboration, "infrastructure" might not be needed.
6. If you're not sure what a word or term means, ask someone who does or look it up. Or use something else.
7. You have no idea what approach to take: Do you understand your subject? Is the problem with your source material? Fix.
8. Rewrite, so that others need not reread.
9. Read the work of others, especially those who do good work. This includes non-news publications, and even fiction. (Don't imitate

James Joyce or Harlequin romances often, though.) But don't plagiarize.

10. Listen to suggestions and criticism. Apply or reject as appropriate.

11. Don't lock yourself into a gimmick, such as keeping a list to 10.

Other ways in which I cope with my weaknesses:

1. If a great headline idea hits me, I write it at the top before I forget it,
   even if I haven't finished reading the story. If the idea no longer seems
   great after the story is edited, I look for another idea.

2. Trying to force too much information into a tight headline does no
   one a favor.

3. Banging your head on your desk merely delays the inevitable—
   writing the headline.

4. Running a headline past the reporter or assigning editor can help, but
   don't lead them to expect it. (I do this about once a year.)

5. Negotiate with the layout editor. A drophead, please? Smaller point
   size, perhaps?

6. Deep breaths and chocolate.

Go get 'em!

Wayne Countryman has worked as a copy editor at five newspapers, including
The Baltimore Sun *and* The Roanoke Times. *This piece appears on the Web site*
of the American Copy Editors Society, www.copydesk.org. Used with permission.

Newspaper Headlines

Not only does a newspaper headline need to sell and tell and pay attention to some of the foregoing guidelines, it also has to fit, often in extremely tight space—putting an additional challenge on print editors.
Print editors need to be familiar with typography and different styles of
headlines and additional headline writing rules.

Typography

Knowledge of basic typography—the use of type—is essential for headline writing for print publications. Editors must know about the differences between typefaces and fonts, what a point represents, how wide a
pica is, and how all these things work together in the presentation of
body text, headlines, captions and other display type.

Measuring type

Points and picas are the two main printing measures. In general, points
are used as a vertical measure. One point equals 1/72 inch. Seventy-

two-point type, then, is 1 inch high, measured from the top of an ascender—such as a capital letter—to the bottom of a descender, such as the bottom of the letter "g." Thirty-six-point is a half-inch. Twenty-four-point is a quarter-inch. Most *body type*—the type used for news stories—is 8- to 10-point. (See Figure 7.3.)

The measure for horizontal distance is the *pica*, which measures one-sixth of an inch. The width of columns is usually expressed in picas, and fractions of picas in points. A column that is set 12 picas is 2 inches wide; a column set 10p2 is 10 picas, 2 points wide. A column set 15p10 is 15 picas, 10 points wide.

Points, picas

Points and picas are measures used in typography. Picas are used for widths, while points are used for depths. Six picas or 72 points constitute an inch.

Points

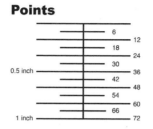

Picas

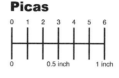

Figure 7.3.
Measuring type.

Space between lines is called leading, a term that dates to hand composition of type, when printers would insert thin pieces of lead between lines. Depending on the look the publication is seeking, body text may be set with no leading or up to a point or more. Space between lines of a headline may be several points, depending on the look the publication wants.

Although computers can now set type at any size, many news designers still use traditional headline sizes that date to the days when printers set type in lead. Generally, these come in six-point increments: 18, 24, 30, 36, 42, 48, 54, 60 and 72. Sticking with these numbers helps to guarantee headline size variation, as discussed on Chapter 8.

Types of type

The typefaces that a news publication uses are part of its personality; organizations put great effort into developing the look they want to convey to their audiences. Readers become accustomed to these appearances and often express alarm when they are changed.

Typefaces come in families that generally fall into two categories, serif and sans serif. Serifs are the ornamentations and curly-cues and the like on type that might be considered more old-fashioned. Sans serif typefaces are more modern-looking, possessing more uniform character widths and lacking the ornamentations that characterize serif typefaces. Some examples are in Figure 7.4.

Type families contain various weights and styles, such as lights, boldfaces, utlrabolds, italics and so forth. The term *font*, while becoming synonymous with typeface, more traditionally refers to all the characters of a given typeface's style and size. For example, 9-point Times Roman italic would be a font of the Times Roman typeface family.

Know your typefaces

Sans serif

Helvetica is an example of a *sans-serif* typeface. Note the uniformity of the character widths and the lack of ornamentations, known as serifs. Sans-serif typefaces are generally reserved for display type such as headlines and captions, although some publications also use them for body text. This column is set in 10-point type with 1 point of *leading*, or space, between the lines. Also note that it is set *flush left*, with the lines breaking unevenly. Other styles within the Helvetica family include:

Helvetica bold.
Helvetica italic.
Helvetica bold italic.

Other examples of sans-serif typefaces include:

Gill Sans
Optima
Lucida Grande

Serif

Times is an example of a *serif* typeface. Note that the width of the characters varies, and the presence of ornamentations, known as serifs. This column is set 9.5 points, with a half-point of *leading*, or space, between the lines. Most news publications use a 9- to 10-point serif typeface for body text. This column is *justified*, with both edges straightly aligned. Other styles within the Times family include:

Times bold.
Times italic.
Times bold italic.

Computers can manipulate the look of type as well, condensing letters like this, or stretching them out like this.

Other examples of of serif typefaces include:

Courier
New York
Didot
Palatino

Figure 7.4.
Typeface examples.

Making heads fit

In paper-and-pencil editing days, editors had to know which letters were fat and which were thin. On a computer, you can see right away whether a headline will fit. Still, it helps headline writers to understand that different characters carry different widths. One line a little short? Come up with a word with a "w" in it!

In headline counting, each small letter counts one character, except that *l, i, f, t* and usually *j* and spaces are thin and count as only one-half character. Also, *m* and *w* are fat and count as 1.5 characters. So do all capital letters, except *M* and *W*, which count as two characters. A headline starting with *Simple Simon* counts as 12, and the text will fit nicely if the column can accommodate 13 characters.

Some headline terminology

Banner—A headline that runs at the top of the page, the full width of the page. At most publications, banners are used only for very important news events. Some editors call these *streamers* or *lines*. (See Figure 7.5.)

Iraq car bomb kills dozens
Attack is deadliest since sovereignty hand-over

Figure 7.5.
A banner headline from across the top of the *Chicago Tribune.*

Deck—Also sometimes called a *summary deck* or just a *summary*, this is a secondary headline that follows a main headline. Some publications call these headlines *readouts*. (See Figure 7.6.)

Motorola, Turkey chase family for missing billions

The Uzans owe the Turkish government and the U.S. cell phone maker large sums, but collecting assets and finding the suspects prove difficult

Figure 7.6.
A two-column headline with a two-column deck from the *Chicago Tribune.*

Kicker—A short, smaller headline that runs atop a main headline and is usually underlined. Although generally out of vogue, some publications still use them, including *The Wall Street Journal*. (See Figure 7.7.)

Vulnerable System
Behind Flu-Vaccine Shortage: Struggle to Police Drugs Globally

Figure 7.7.
A kicker headline from the *Wall Street Journal.*

Hammer—A large headline of a few words, used for dramatic effect. A hammer is always accompanied by a deck head. (See Figure 7.8.)

Figure 7.8.
A hammer headline with deck from the *Dallas Morning News.*

Devastation in Iran

Death estimates from earthquake start at 5,000

Subhead—A small headline placed within the text of a story, used to break up sections of long pieces and as a design device to help break up gray areas on news pages.

Jump head—When a news story continues on another page, it takes a new headline with the portion that "jumps."

Sidesaddle—When space is tight at the top of a page, editors will sometimes call for a headline to run next to, rather than above, the story, hence the term *sidesaddle.*

Tripod—A headline that runs one or two large words followed by a colon and then two lines of deck that run next to it.

Upstyle—A few publications, including the *New York Times* and the *Los Angeles Times*, still use *upstyle* headlines, capitalizing all nouns and verbs in the style of a title, but most now use *downstyle,* capitalizing only the first word and proper nouns. (See Figure 7.9.)

Figure 7.9.
The *New York Times* is one of the few papers in the United States that still uses upstyle headlines.

N.B.A. Hands Tough Penalties To Players Involved in Brawl

Head calls

Newspaper pages are built on grids, typically six columns wide (see Chapter 8 for a discussion of page design). Headlines may be just one column wide or a full six columns wide, or any width in between. A standard protocol for referring to a headline's size (known as a *head call* or *head order* or simply *spex*, for specifications) is to put the width first, followed by the size of the type and then the number of lines. So, an order of 2/42/3 would yield a headline that is two columns wide, uses 42-point type and occupies three lines. If the width of the headline is not a standard column width, the width is reported in picas: 18p/42/4 would be a headline that's 18 picas wide, uses 42-point type, and goes four lines deep.

Depending on the computer system in use, the headline writer may write a headline in WYSIWYG (what you see is what you get) or may use a key that will tell how close the headline comes to fitting. Publications have different requirements regarding how close to full each line must be; a good rule of thumb is that they should come up short no more than two picas. But editors should be wary of placing form over function— what the headline says should not be sacrificed for the sake of filling out every line.

Print headline writers should be careful not to use bad breaks in headlines, also known as *splitting* a headline. Splitting a head means dividing a natural grouping of words by the end of a line. This can involve splitting a modifier from its noun or verb, a title from a name, or, the most egregious split, putting the "to" of an infinitive at the end of one line and the verb on the next:

Teacher wants to
revise curriculum

Other bad splits include separating prepositional phrases and breaking up a compound verb between lines. (To keep headline writers sane, editors usually allow splits between the second and third lines of a three-line head.)

Subheads and jump heads

Rules for subheads are somewhat more flexible than for regular heads; although active voice is preferred, labels (heads that lack a verb) are acceptable for subheads.

Stories continued inside the paper need some heading for the continuation, or *jump*. At some publications, the *jump head* repeats basically the front page head. Some papers now use a smaller head for the jump. It typically has a better count than the one on the front page, and the editor may be able to get ideas and precision here that were abandoned in writing the main head. Other publications require that the jump head refer to information that is introduced in the jumped part of the story.

The jump word is often a single key word. It may be employed with a jump head, or it may stand alone. As with the slug, this word should distinguish the story from all others that day. The jump word is set in larger type or caps, and a box, rules or white space should make it easy to spot.

Writing Headlines for the Internet

News publication on the Internet has the potential to reach a much wider audience, and online headline writers need to keep that in mind. For the most part, headlines should follow the same guidelines for print publication, using present tense and active words, eliminating articles and such. But online headline writers don't face the same space constraints that print headline writers face. So the potential is less for awkward heads caused by space limitations, although many will limit a headline to one line at a standard screen width. (Because a Web page is scalable, a head may break depending on how wide a user sets the window.) There's no need to replace a slightly less-desirable synonym to make a head fit; editors should just use the best word.

Online editors have differing philosophies about crafting online heads. One editor reported that he tries to give online heads a little more of an edge than his organization's print counterpart would allow. An online producer says she tries to get people's names into online headlines as much as possible so that they can be picked up by Google or another Internet search engine. Conversely, an online editor at a small newspaper *removes* names from headlines when they move from the print publication to online. He argues that readers across the country are more likely to relate to "mayor" than the name of somebody they don't know.

Developing the Knack

Some headlines come easily and naturally and fit the first time, but often editors have to ponder several possibilities. They should try to put the whole head together at one time and make space adjustments afterward. If they tinker to make the first line perfect before going on to the rest, they will likely find it impossible to fit other lines to the first line.

Flexibility is most important. The editor should try not to get the mind locked in on a particular wording. If a pet phrase doesn't work after a bit of trying, the head writer should stop wasting time with it and use a new approach. The key statement of the lead may have to be abandoned and the writer may need to rethink what the story is trying to say. Sometimes stepping away from the computer for a few minutes will help refresh the headline writer's mind.

Three pointers

Here are three tips on developing a knack for writing heads.

1. Try for good short synonyms when the head doesn't fit. Because English has many short verbs, these can probably be juggled more easily than others: for example, *assails, slaps, raps, quits.* Sometimes a slight loss in clarity is unavoidable when substituting, as when "School superintendent" becomes "School chief." You can use initials and nicknames, though good desk procedure requires that they be immediately clear to readers and not become too numerous. (Such means may be the only feasible way to distinguish among news figures with the same name; in a city with a mayor named Rudolph

Hammerhill, head writers may use "Rudy," "Ham," "mayor" and other such codes to communicate the right name quickly.)

2. Reverse the head if the first subject-verb pattern doesn't fit.

**British expecting
military cuts**

will fit if changed to

**Military cuts
seen in Britain**

3. Look for a new angle. If the one on the left won't do, perhaps the one on the right will:

Job declines worry nation, poll reveals	**Nation found anxious over loss of jobs**

Hazards of Headlines

Just as headlines are important in drawing attention to a news publication, they are also among an organization's vulnerable points. Readers may grumble about the way an organization covers the news, but often their complaint boils down to dislike of the heads. Simple inattention can make heads read two ways, sometimes ludicrously. Such headlines that made it into print are featured in "The Lower Case" in *Columbia Journalism Review*. Here are two examples:

Teen can't talk about sex with mom
(San Francisco Chronicle, 3/24/04)

Legislators hold forum on electric grid
(Nantucket Inquirer & Mirror, 9/25/03)

Often reporters complain that their stories were all right, but the heads were distorted. Reporters often have to explain to sources that they had nothing to do with the headline. When the head doesn't quite match the story, the reporter is embarrassed and sources are irritated or even angry.

Let's say, for example, that a governor named Rogers is caught up in an emotional campaign to weaken the state's water pollution law. The governor may want the law strengthened, if it is changed at all, but powerful people in and out of the legislature want the law virtually repealed. The issue rages in the news media for weeks, with much of the public choosing sides in the argument. The governor, eager to cool the debate, suggests in a speech that a minor compromise might satisfy reasonable people in both camps.

In such a case the headline should be something like one of these:

Rogers proposes   **Rogers suggests**
step to soothe   **three changes**
pollution debate   **in water law**

Instead, some papers may come up with these:

Rogers concedes   **Rogers relents**
to opposition   **in his battle**
on water law   **on water law**

The inaccurate headlines could cause a storm. Those favoring strong anti-pollution laws would think at first glance that the governor had betrayed them. Those wanting weaker laws would rejoice—and later perhaps feel that the governor had tricked *them.*

The governor would be furious because the inaccurate headline further snarled a difficult political task. He might be so angry that in a press conference a few days later he would charge the news media with distorting his position.

Such attacks by prominent figures erode the public's confidence in news organizations. Admittedly, some head writers do distort the news, or they editorialize. Even careful editors face built-in dangers. They have to struggle with the limitations of both space and brief words to convey a fair and accurate impression.

Perhaps oversimplification is the greatest threat in headlines. When the news is complex, the reporter often oversimplifies in writing a tight lead. The editor's job is to polish and tighten that more, if possible. Then the task requires further condensation into a half-dozen words or fewer for the headline. The subtleties inevitably get squeezed out. The honest editor should change the headline angle if necessary to keep from oversimplifying.

A second danger in headlines is emphasis on a minor angle of a story. A common complaint of speakers is that a reporter takes some minor point, even an aside, and builds a big story around it. The fault is compounded if the head plays up this angle, perhaps in oversimplified form. What the speaker and audience both understood as almost a joke may, for example, be blazoned:

Rogers denounces bleeding hearts

Readers who were there—and perhaps the speaker's future audiences—will be re-convinced that news organizations distort and sensationalize.

Another danger in headlines is overplay. Too much emphasis on a story usually results from a bad choice of type, but vivid headline words also may overdramatize. Another factor is news flow. A story that would deserve a small one-column head inside on an ordinary day may be over-played under several columns on the front page when news is dull. A few newspapers run a full-width banner head across the front page every day. This tradition inevitably overplays some stories.

Underplay is also a threat. Admitting that there is no universal stan-dard of correct play, fair-minded editors nevertheless acknowledge that some papers do not give certain stories the space or heads they deserve. This may be policy or ignorance—maybe the desk person does not real-ize that the coup in such-and-such a country really affects local readers. Some editors knowingly order small heads on racial strife in other com-munities, on the theory that large heads would stir things up at home.

CHAPTER 8

Editors and Design

Good news coverage, news selection, editing and headline writing are four of the five essentials of an excellent news site or newspaper. The remaining element of excellence is good design: the choices of type and the placement of type, photos and graphics on a page and the way multimedia are used on a Web page. Good design attracts audiences and makes reading easier. Readers will find that they need not squint to read the material and that photos, graphics, audio and video enhance storytelling.

Functions of Design

Although design aims primarily at making news easy to read, it has several other functions. One is to reflect a newspaper's personality. The *New York Times,* a serious paper, would be unwise to adopt a frivolous design. Its makeup has been modernized but the paper still radiates a no-nonsense approach. Much of this serious impression stems from typography, for the type and the layout indicate tradition and formality. On the other hand, the design of the *New York Post* suggests not a "paper of record" but a paper that clings to the policies of love, lust and lucre, with headlines and pictures that scream for attention. The same can be seen in the design of the competing newspapers' Web sites.

Another function of design is to tell the reader what editors consider the day's most significant stories. As noted in Chapter 7, headline size does part of this job. Usually, the bigger the head, the more important the story. But not always. A short story on page one with a small but special headline tells the reader that the story is short but important. The size of pictures, use of color and length of stories also indicate news value.

WED: Write-Edit-Design

Previous chapters have discussed how reporters, editors and designers come together to tell a story. This concept, pioneered by newspaper and magazine designer Mario Garcia, is known as WED, for write-edit-design. The best packages come out of this collaboration, serving as a true representation of the cliché that the whole is greater than the sum of its parts.

The use of WED is particularly important in the planning of feature packages. It's far better to involve the photographer and the designer at the start of the process rather than just hand the designer the pieces later. The photographer may have ideas for how to illustrate the story that would never have occurred to the editor—and will always come back with better pictures when he feels he has been made part of the creative process. The designer may think of other ways to illustrate the package with graphics and typography, something she might not have had time for if not involved in the story from the outset. Garcia argues that writing, editing and design "can never be separated."[1]

Where the Eye Goes

The Poynter Institute for Media Studies in St. Petersburg, Fla., has conducted several studies about how users read newspapers and online news by tracking the movement of their eyes. Understanding how readers approach publications is critical for effective page design. The Poynter findings were surprisingly different for each medium.

Newspaper eye tracking

In the early 1990s, as newspapers struggled with the decision of whether to invest in color printing technology, the Poynter Institute commissioned a study to see what effects color had on the way audiences read the newspaper. Using a head-mounted machine, researchers were able to track where readers' eyes went—and stopped—on newspaper pages. Among the team's findings:

- Readers' eyes are drawn first to photos and artwork.
- Devices that refer to inside stories are generally noticed.
- Readers' eyes move from the dominant image on the page to the dominant headline or the next most-dominant image.[2]

Online eye tracking

With the advent of the delivery of news online, the Poynter Institute returned to eye tracking to assess how readers received their news online.

Using a similar head-mounted machine, the researchers were able to track readers' eye movements as they navigated the Internet in search of news. In contrast to the earlier study about newspapers, the researchers found that Internet readers' eyes first went to text, not to a photograph or graphic, and usually to either a brief story or a photo caption. The study also found that readers tended to read "shallow but wide," but they stopped to read longer stories on selected topics.[3]

Poynter conducted a second eye-tracking study in 2004 that confirmed the findings of the first: Web site users' eyes first fixated on text rather than an image. The study also found that:

- Smaller type is more likely to be read closely than larger type.
- Headline writing is critical to drawing readers into a story.
- It's possible to get readers to scan the lower parts of a page by scrolling down "below the fold."
- Navigation tools across the top of a home page are better than other placements.
- Shorter paragraphs—two or three sentences—are desirable.
- Reader recall of information is enhanced with use of multimedia graphics.
- Larger images hold attention longer than smaller ones.[4]

In the first online study, the researchers speculated that because images are slower to load on the Internet, the eyes move to the text first, but designer Mario Garcia believes that the real reason is that photographs are ineffectively used on the Internet; images on home pages are too small to draw the eye.[5]

Newspaper Design

The dominant design in use at newspapers is *modular,* a system that uses modules, or rectangles, to form blocks that, pieced together properly, form a pleasing combination of type and art (see Figure 8.1). Each rectangle acts as a container for all the pieces that fit together: the headline, the story, the photograph, the caption and anything else that may be used to help tell the story. Modular design borrows heavily from contemporary architecture and other modern art forms. One main advantage of modular style is the way the whole story fits into one compact unit, instead of starting in one column and continuing in a longer one elsewhere. In modular design, the eye is less likely to be diverted from the module than it is from any other design form.

A few newspapers still use a design format that allows pieces to wrap around one another—known as dog-legging—and others, such as the *Wall Street Journal,* use a vertical format that runs stories the length of the page. But a browse through the front pages of most newspapers across the country shows that the modular approach dominates.

Figure 8.1.

In modular design, each news story and its components fill a rectangle. At a minimum, each rectangle contains a story and a headline. Other elements can include photographs, captions, graphics, pull quotes and column logos. Page copyright 2004, *Sacramento Bee.* Used with permission.

Placement cues the reader. A story on page one rates high. On the first page of another section, it also rates high. But if it is three paragraphs long and deep inside a section, the reader realizes that the editor considers the item little more than a filler.

Good design provides other aids for the reader. The various sections—editorial page, comics, sports, and others—should be in about the same place every day so that the reader isn't forced to hunt for them. Related stories, such as news from around the state, should be grouped. If this is not possible, a *reference* or *refer* (pronounced "reefer") can be inserted in the story:

State unemployment rate drops from 7.7 to 7.6 percent. Story on A9

News before beauty

It is easy for editors to get so enthusiastic about design that they let it overshadow content. They concentrate on how the paper looks, not on what the words or pictures tell. Their newspaper makes a good first impression. Readers eagerly pick it up because it looks so appealing. But their eagerness changes to disgust if they find the news play clumsy, the stories disjointed and important items buried or even omitted. Editors infatuated with appearance may refuse to change one day's makeup when a breaking news story demands it. They are so smitten with page design that alteration cannot be tolerated.

Newspaper design should always enhance storytelling, not overwhelm it. Editors must first consider the news. They must select it, weigh its merits and decide what stories are most important. Then they will decide the typographical display of the most important stories and pictures. No matter how clever the makeup, the editor must be willing to scrap or revise it whenever news events demand.

Dummying

Before computer page composition came about, editors designed pages in a process known as *dummying*—drawing fairly precise diagrams of pages that served to instruct printers where to place the various elements of the page. Although computer pagination has negated the need for dummying, some editors still find it helpful to sketch on paper what a page will look like—even if only a rough estimate—before they start on the page on the computer.

Dummy sheets provide a representation of the space available on a news page. Most newspapers today are built on grids of six columns by 21 to 21.5 inches. Each rectangle on a dummy sheet represents a column inch—the width of one column, 1 inch deep. So, a story that measures

9 column inches will fill nine rectangles on a dummy sheet. Headline space is easy to tabulate. If a headline is 24-point, three lines equal 1 inch. The editor simply provides the equivalent space on the dummy. (See Figure 8.2.)

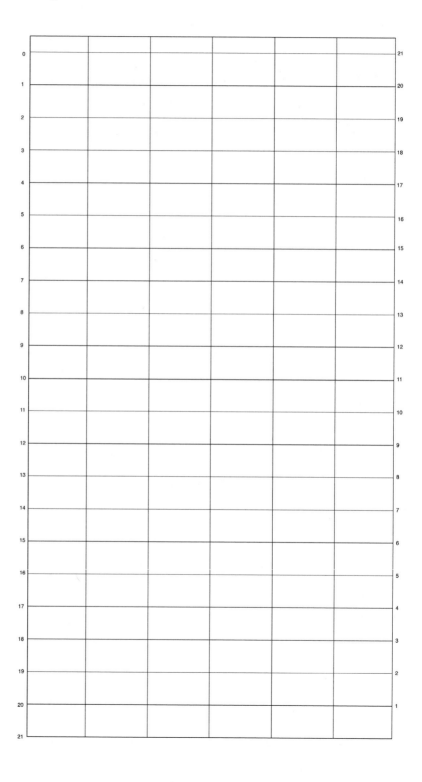

Figure 8.2.
Before computer pagination, editors used dummy sheets to design pages. Some editors still use them to make a preliminary sketch before using the computer to build the page.

Designing the page

Newspaper pages today are, for the most part, built on computers by newsroom editors using pagination software. A number of stand-alone applications and fully integrated systems are available, including packages from Quark, Adobe, Atex, CCI, Unisys and others. Some newsrooms looking to hire editors ask for experience in QuarkXPress, a widely used program, but others will train designers on the job. Experience in one program can help designers more quickly adapt to others. (Page templates in QuarkXPress and Adobe InDesign are available on this book's CD-ROM.) (See Figure 8.3.)

Before starting on a page, a design editor must know what all the elements will be. Generally, it's inadvisable to start designing a page without seeing the photo or graphic that's scheduled for it. The only time editors should design a page without seeing the photo is when it's being shot late and must be "dropped into" the space allocated just before deadline.

Designers use four basic building blocks: stories, headlines, photographs and captions.[6] Depending on the need, other supplementary building blocks include pull quotes, refers and informational graphics. But at a minimum, most pages will have at least one story, one headline, a photograph and caption (also called a cutline).

When designing a page, editors need to keep a few things in mind:

- Each page needs a dominant image. The reader's eye goes first to the dominant image on the page—so make sure that the page has one. A page with two photos the same size is not as effective.
- A big headline should appear at or near the top of the page. Many newspapers still follow an outdated rule that the lead story must be in the upper-right position on the page, but the eye-tracking studies have debunked this notion.
- Use headline hierarchy on the page, gradually reducing the point sizes on the headline while moving down the page, generally in 6-point increments. A headline hierarchy serves to tell readers which stories on the page are more important than others.
- The start of a story should almost always be directly below either a main headline or a deck headline.
- Keep all related elements within rectangles to maintain modular design.
- Stories can wrap beneath photographs but should not wrap on top of them.

Examples of how dummies would look for two pages appear in Figures 8.4 and 8.5.

Page designers who become daunted at the prospect of filling pages should first look at each package that will appear on the page. For example, if a designer has a page budget that calls for three stories, one of which has a photo, she should envision what the most effective pack-

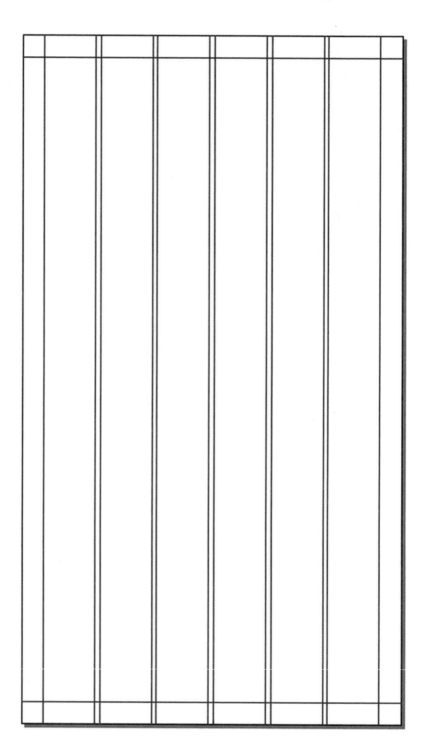

Figure 8.3.
Page designers using QuarkXpress for pagination start with a standard grid prepared for their publications. This is a 6-column grid.

aging will be for the story with the art and then build the page around that package. (See Figure 8.6) Notice that stories never wrap *on top* of photographs.

Some typographical devices

Editors can use a variety of typographic devices to enhance their pages, keeping in mind the publication's style rules and the necessity that design enhances the presentation of the news but does not overtake it. Some of these devices include:

1. **Boxes.** Borders can be placed around stories to form a box. Boxes can consist of single columns, double columns or even six columns.
2. **Wide measure.** This is type set wider than the standard column wide; for example, a designer could choose to make story two columns wide across three standard columns, beneath a three-column headline. This is sometimes called a bastard measure.
3. **Alternative headline styles.** Refer to those discussed in Chapter 7.
4. **Centered headline.** A centered headline in a page of heads set flush left makes an effective contrast.
5. **Pull quotes.** Interesting quotations taken from stories are displayed in large type inset in the body text.
6. **Logos.** These are styles or designs that call attention to recurring features, such as columns or a political campaign.
7. **Highlights boxes.** These are graphical text boxes that tell readers important details at a glance.

In the following front pages, note how the designers used modular design, dominant images, headline hierarchy and other typographic devices to present the news. (Figures 8.7–8.11)

Fitting stories to space

Page design would be easier if there were an endless number of good stories of various lengths. Then the editor could readily choose the right one to fit a certain hole. The story desired for a specific place, however, is almost invariably too long or too short. Four choices remain: Select another story; shorten or lengthen the one in hand; shorten an adjoining story to make room for the one that didn't fit; or adjust the size of adjacent art. Editors usually don't have the time to lengthen stories, so they keep shortening, choosing and juggling until the page is filled.

The job of fitting copy to available space in a limited time requires a system. Most papers work the system something like this: Various editors are assigned to fill a certain number of pages. They then review stories as they become available and note the stories expected by deadline. As-

Figure 8.4.

Here's how a dummy would look for this section front from the *Sacramento Bee*. Used with permission.

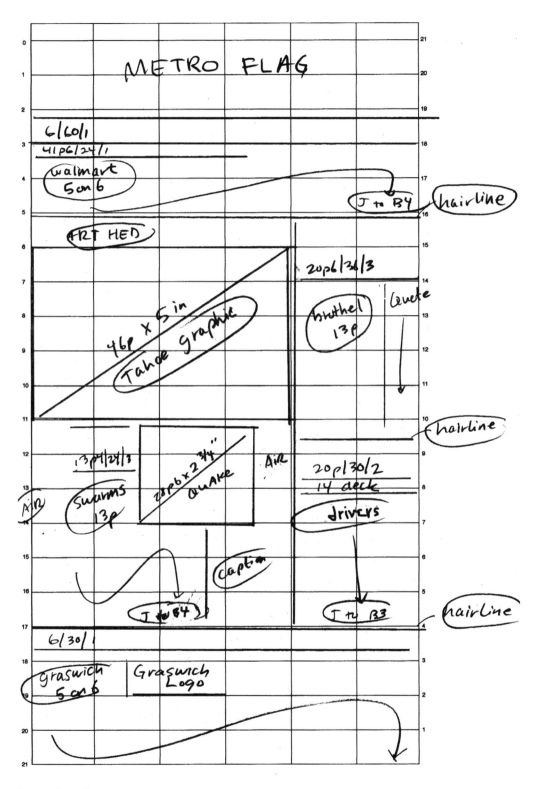

Figure 8.4. *(continued)*

Figure 8.5.

Here's how a dummy would look for this inside page from the *Sacramento Bee*. Used with permission.

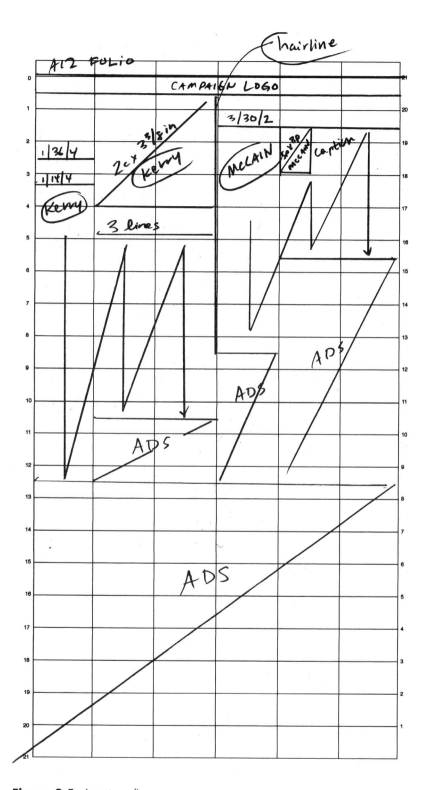

Figure 8.5. *(continued)*

Xgxgxg xgxgxg xgxgxgxg

Lorem ipsum dolor sit amet, consectetuer adipiscing elit.

Sed et felis at diam iaculis viverra. Suspendisse at felis ut mi aliquet congue. Nulla dictum vehicula mi.

Phasellus non tortor. Vivamus sem. Praesent rhoncus. Vestibulum a orci at eros accumsan fringilla. Praesent fringilla. In id elit. Quisque gravida. Duis feugiat mattis purus.

Aliquam tristique semper orci. Nam eros ante, dignissim in, iaculis sed, mattis at, quam. Vivamus euismod magna at enim. Phasellus sodales nunc

Lorem ipsum dolor sit amet, consectetuer adipiscing elit.

luctus erat.

Vestibulum ante ipsum primis in faucibus orci luctus et ultrices posuere cubilia Curae; Sed elementum posuere dui. In vitae metus. Fusce rhoncus dui in ligula.

Phasellus nec nisl at pede pretium mattis. Donec ligula lorem, sagittis sit amet, vulputate ac, egestas nec, nulla. Curabitur eget velit. Suspendisse at nulla consequat ipsum ullamcorper

molestie. Sed vestibulum wisi ac erat. Pellentesque vitae orci. Mauris laoreet mauris at diam. Pellentesque id nibh nec dolor dapibus facilisis. In scelerisque porttitor augue. Maecenas eleifend, est nec accumsan accumsan, arcu tellus consectetuer purus, ac tempor lectus libero vel elit. Curabitur semper enim ut leo. Nam non velit sed orci scelerisque elementum.

Phasellus commodo lobortis sem. Donec suscipit cursus metus. Phasellus nonummy adipiscing nulla. Ut suscipit. Sed eros tor-

Lorem ipsum dolor sit amet, consectetuer adipiscing elit.

Xgxgxg xgxgxg xgxgxgxg

Lorem ipsum dolor sit amet, consectetuer adipiscing elit.

Sed et felis at diam iaculis viverra. Suspendisse at felis ut mi aliquet congue. Nulla dictum vehicula mi.

Phasellus non tortor. Vivamus sem. Praesent rhoncus. Vestibulum a orci at eros accumsan fringilla. Praesent fringilla. In id elit. Quisque gravida. Duis feugiat mattis purus.

Aliquam tristique semper orci. Nam eros ante, dignissim in, iaculis sed, mattis at, quam. Vivamus euismod magna at enim. Phasellus sodales nunc

luctus erat.

Vestibulum ante ipsum primis in faucibus orci luctus et ultrices posuere cubilia Curae; Sed elementum posuere dui. In vitae metus. Fusce rhoncus dui in ligula. Phasellus nec nisl at pede pretium mattis. Donec ligula lorem, sagittis sit amet, vulputate ac, egestas nec, nulla. Curabitur eget velit. Suspendisse at nulla consequat ipsum ullamcorper molestie. Sed vestibulum wisi ac erat. Pellentesque vitae orci. Mauris laoreet mauris at diam. Pellentesque id nibh nec dolor dapibus

Lorem ipsum dolor sit amet, consectetuer adipiscing elit.

facilisis. In scelerisque porttitor augue. Maecenas eleifend, est nec accumsan accumsan, arcu tellus consectetuer purus, ac tempor lectus libero vel elit. Curabitur semper enim ut leo.

Nam non velit sed orci scelerisque elementum.

Phasellus commodo lobortis sem. Donec suscipit cursus metus. Phasellus nonummy adipiscing nulla. Ut suscipit.

Xgxgxg xgx xgxg xgxgx

Lorem ipsum dolor sit amet, consectetuer adipiscing elit.

Sed et felis at diam iaculis viverra. Suspendisse at felis ut mi aliquet congue. Nulla dictum vehicula mi.

Phasellus non tortor. Vivamus sem. Praesent rhoncus. Vestibulum a orci at eros accumsan fringilla. Praesent fringilla. In id elit. Quisque gravida. Duis feugiat mattis purus.

Aliquam tristique semper orci. Nam eros ante, dignissim in, iaculis sed, mattis at, quam. Vivamus euismod magna at enim. Phasellus sodales nunc luctus erat.

Vestibulum ante

ipsum primis in faucibus orci luctus et ultrices posuere cubilia Curae; Sed elementum posuere dui. In vitae metus. Fusce rhoncus dui in ligula. Phasellus nec nisl at pede pretium mattis. Donec ligula lorem, sagittis sit amet, vulputate ac, egestas nec, nulla. Curabitur eget velit. Suspendisse at nulla consequat ipsum ullamcorper molestie. Sed vestibulum wisi ac erat. Pellentesque vitae orci. Mauris laoreet mauris at diam. Pellentesque id nibh nec dolor dapibus facilisis. In scelerisque porttitor augue. Maecenas eleifend, est nec accumsan.

Xgxgxg xgx xgxg xgxgx

Lorem ipsum dolor sit amet, consectetuer adipiscing elit.

Sed et felis at diam iaculis viverra. Suspendisse at felis ut mi aliquet congue. Nulla dictum vehicula mi.

Phasellus non tortor. Vivamus sem. Praesent rhoncus. Vestibulum a orci at eros accumsan fringilla. Praesent fringilla. In id elit. Quisque gravida. Duis feugiat mattis purus.

Aliquam tristique semper orci. Nam eros ante, dignissim in, iaculis sed, mattis at, quam. Vivamus euismod magna at enim.

Phasellus sodales nunc luctus erat.

Vestibulum ante ipsum primis in faucibus orci luctus et ultrices posuere cubilia Curae; Sed elementum posuere dui. In vitae metus. Fusce rhoncus dui in ligula. Phasellus nec nisl at pede pretium mattis. Donec ligula lorem, sagittis sit amet, vulputate ac, egestas nec, nulla. Curabitur eget velit. Suspendisse at nulla consequat ipsum ullamcorper molestie. Sed vestibulum wisi ac erat. Pellentesque vitae orci. Mauris laoreet mauris at diam.

Lorem ipsum dolor sit amet, consectetuer adipiscing elit.

Figure 8.6.

Here are various ways a package that includes a photograph can be designed.

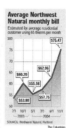

Figure 8.7.
Copyright 2004, *The* (Vancouver, Wash.) *Columbian*. Used with permission.

Figure 8.8.
Copyright 2004, the *Great Falls* (Mont.) *Tribune.* Used with permission.

Rapid City Journal

Saturday, September 25, 2004

© 2004 Rapid City Journal, 507 Main St., Rapid City, South Dakota 57701   www.rapidcityjournal.com

INSIDE

Fall's beauty
Mother Nature puts on a show, Page B1

RVers
Retired Christians lend a helping hand, Page D2

Summit
Indian leaders meet today, Page C2

Good morning

Sunday special

Talking about the food tax

Among the issues on the Nov. 2 general election ballot in South Dakota will be Initiated Measure 1, which will ask voters whether the 4 percent state sales tax on food should be retained or repealed.

Those who want to keep the sales tax argue that the state cannot afford to lose the $41.5 million the Rounds administration says the tax brings in each year.

Those who favor a repeal argue that the tax cut would be easily affordable and say state officials have a series of options when it comes to dealing with the loss.

Sunday's Journal will contain the first installment of reporter Denise Ross' three-part series about the food tax repeal/retention efforts.

Inside

5 sections
Annie's Mailbox, D5
Black Hills Journal, C3
Bridge, B9
Classified ads, B1-16
Comics, D4, 6
Crossword puzzle, D4
Dr. Donohue, D4
Hints from Heloise, D5
Horoscope, D4
Jumble, B10
Local, C1
Markets, D6
Movies, D7
Obituaries, C2
Opinion, A4, 5
Outdoors, D1
People, A2
Religion, D2, 3
Sports, E1-6
Television, TV Journal
Weather, D8

Quote

"What we went through last year is simply unprecedented. I'm very happy we're having a lighter year this year."

— Lon Kightlinger, state epidemiologist, talking about West Nile virus. See story on Page C1.

Outside

High, 82 — low, 48
Sunny skies with a light breeze.
Page D8

Rapid City Journal: 394-8300, 1-800-843-2300   Circulation: 394-8359   Classified: 394-6383   News: 394-8400   Northern Hills: 642-8822, 1-800-542-4455

Plague found in prairie dog

A state official says the disease discovery shouldn't immediately affect management plans.

By Steve Miller
Journal Staff Writer

A prairie dog infected with plague has been found in western Custer County, the first confirmed case of plague in South Dakota wildlife in recent history, state veterinarian Sam Holland said Friday.

A rancher who lives near the Wyoming border found the ill prairie dog last week and submitted it for testing. On Wednesday, tests confirmed plague in the animal.

Humans and pets can get plague from prairie dogs, but the risk to humans is very low, Holland said. However, people should use caution when working with wild animals and make sure their pets don't go onto prairie dog towns, he said. Domestic cats are particularly susceptible to plague.

Anyone who gets ill after coming into contact with either a sick cat, wild animal or rodent should seek immediate medical attention, state epidemiologist Lon Kightlinger said. (See box.)

Plague is highly contagious and has caused massive prairie dog die-offs in eastern Wyoming, Montana, Colorado and other states, Holland said. South Dakota Agriculture Secretary Larry Gabriel said the discovery of plague in South Dakota should not have an immediate effect on state and federal plans to manage prairie dogs in western South Dakota. The plans include a new state-federal effort to poison and shoot prairie dogs in Conata Basin and Fall River County and a soon-to-be-released state prairie dog management plan.

See **Plague**, Page A2

Sylvatic plague profile

Sylvatic plague is a bacterial infection of rodents such as prairie dogs. It is the same organism as bubonic plague, the "Black Death" that killed more than 25 million people in the Middle Ages.

Transmission: From animal to animal and to humans through flea bites. Less frequently, plague bacteria enter through a break in the skin by direct contact with tissue or body fluids of an infected animal, according to state veterinarian Sam Holland.

Plague can also be transmitted by inhaling infected droplets expelled by coughing, by a person or animal, especially domestic cats. Transmission from human to human is uncommon.

Pet owners: Be cautious with any cat that has abscesses under its chin or neck or that is ill and coughing.

Plague in humans can be treated with antibiotics.

Symptoms in humans: headache, high fever and swollen lymph nodes, especially in the armpit or groin.

Effects: If untreated, plague can cause fatal pneumonia and blood poisoning.

Library network running

System returns after almost a week offline.

By Andrea J. Cook
Journal Staff Writer

Library routines gradually returned to normal Friday for 15 libraries on the South Dakota Library Network's new computer system.

The libraries lost access to their online circulation records and card catalogs after a computer server at SDLN's Spearfish site crashed last Sunday.

"Everything is up," SDLN network operations supervisor Gary Johnson said Friday.

"The good news is, we had a serious problem but no loss of data. Sometimes when computers crash, you lose things. This was not that kind of event."

The system was restored Friday morning. Card catalogs were the first services functioning in the libraries. By 2:30 p.m., circulation systems were operating normally.

"We're really looking forward to getting back on the system," Jennifer Irwin, circulation supervisor for Rapid City Public Library, said only minutes before the system was restored.

Irwin said library employees should be caught up with the backlog of books and audio materials still waiting to be checked in. Irwin said the check-ins should be completed by the weekend.

"We're back-dating so people won't end up with fines during the period the computers were down," Irwin said.

Johnson said SDLN will continue phasing additional libraries on to the new system through mid-November. More than 70 libraries across the state are connected through SDLN.

After all SDLN's member libraries are transferred to the new system, a back-up server should prevent a repeat of this week's interruption of services, he said. The system was designed with a second server to handle problems like Sunday's crash.

"If one server goes down, the other can take its place," Johnson said.

All of the library data is kept on a separate data storage unit that is accessible by either server, he said.

During the transition, the second server was used to handle some of the conversion activities, Johnson said.

"With limited resources, we have to do what you have to do. We put that server to good use during our cut-over period, instead of having it sit idle," he said. "We certainly designed, long term, to have a better answer than to have our libraries and patrons endure a significant down time."

Contact Andrea Cook at 394-8423 or andrea.cook@rapidcityjournal.com

---

> 'Troy doesn't have to suffer anymore ... but those people (who are responsible) are going to have to suffer.'
> — Joyce Klug, mother of missing Rapid City man Troy Klug

Joyce Klug took this photo of her son Troy on Skyline Drive last winter.   Courtesy

A mother holds onto memories of missing son

Joyce Klug prays every day for some closure in the case of missing Rapid City man.

By Heidi Bell Gease
Journal Staff Writer

Troy Klug wasn't embarrassed to tell his mom he loved her.

He was also a ladies' man who used to like to date high school students at prom time so he could dress up in a tuxedo.

More recently, he enjoyed spending time with his girlfriend and her young son, camping and rock hunting.

Klug, 26, hasn't been heard from since July 12. And to people following court proceedings against three people accused of kidnapping him, Klug is merely a man who disappeared after going to a St. Cloud Street home to get drugs.

Klug's mother, Joyce Klug, wants people to know there was more to her son.

"I want them to know the good side," Joyce Klug, who doesn't expect to see her son alive again, said. "Because there's good and bad in everybody."

Klug, a retired nurse, had never heard of Troy Teigen, Cynthia Kindall or Teli Cook, the three charged in Troy's kidnapping, before they were arrested. And she didn't know anything about her son using drugs.

"A mother's love is blind," she said. "I didn't see that other side of Troy, what he was involved with."

Troy wouldn't have wanted her to see that side. Born to Joyce later in life — after

See **Missing**, Page A2

Driver pleads

Kyle Martin guilty of manslaughter

By Heidi Bell Gease
Journal Staff Writer

Relatives of three teenage siblings killed in a high-speed car crash in June are worried that a plea agreement with the car's driver, Kyle Martin, will result in a light sentence.

"I'm afraid that he'll walk away with a slap on the hand," Tracey Celhoff, the aunt of the late Brittany, Miguel and Donovan Morales, said Friday.

Celhoff would like to see the court "make as example" of Martin, who had been drinking before the accident. But, she added, "The punishment in this case can never — no matter what he's sentenced to — fit the crime."

Kyle Martin

Martin, 19, on Friday pleaded guilty to three counts of second-degree manslaughter in the deaths of the Morales siblings. In exchange, prosecutors dropped three counts of vehicular homicide, plus a charge of vehicular battery.

Each homicide charge carried a maximum penalty of 15 years in prison and a $15,000 fine upon conviction, and the battery charge was punishable by 10 years in prison. Each count of manslaughter is punishable by 10 years in prison and a $10,000 fine.

As part of the plea deal, prosecutors will ask 7th Circuit Judge John "Jack" Delaney to order that the sentence for the third manslaughter count be served concurrently with the first two counts. In other words, the Pennington County State's Attorney's Office will ask that Martin serve a maximum of 20 years in prison, although Delaney could sentence him to 30 years.

Friday, when Delaney asked Martin what happened on

See **Martin**, Page A2

Curious squirrels spark trouble for utilities

By Tom Mooney
The Providence Journal and Journal Staff

In this season of ripening nuts, a biological weapon of mass destruction is scurrying rampant across the nation.

In the past few weeks alone, thousands of people in Clay, N.Y., Melbourne, Fla., and students at the University of Tennessee in Knoxville, have been driven into darkness by the fidgety antagonist.

The squirrel is on its annual foraging ritual, much to the chagrin of utility companies everywhere.

Not only do gray squirrels create power failures, "they create public relations headaches for utilities," a utility company spokesman said.

Last Sunday, one squirrel traversed the high voltage wires of a Providence, R.I., substation, triggering an electrical failure at Rhode Island Hospital.

"We refer to them as rats with good public relations," said Chris Riley, spokesman for Connecticut Light & Power, which serves 1.2 million customers. "Everyone thinks squirrels are cute, furry and pleasant, when in fact, they are evil rodents."

According to Barb Thirstrup, spokeswoman for Black Hills Power in Rapid

See **Squirrels**, Page A3

Prep football
Local and area teams slog it out in the mud · SPORTS, 1C

Size don't mean a thing
Pee wee football teams play the game just like the big boys · BOSSIER, 2B

The Times

shreveporttimes.com

SHREVEPORT ■ BOSSIER CITY ■ ARK-LA-TEX

SATURDAY, SEPTEMBER 25, 2004

INSIDE THE TIMES

Food shortage in Haiti severe
U.N. troops fired smoke grenades to disperse a crowd of flood victims who broke into a food distribution site.
AP **PAGE 9A**

Police chief takes drug test
Mike Hulphen joins other officers in procedure after police shooting Thursday in shopping center parking lot.
PAGE 1B

Students learn about etiquette
A formal dance concluded a week of learning lessons in courtesy and respect for Cope Middle School students.
Jim Hudelson/The Times **PAGE 1B**

LSU faces hard choice on QBs
Tigers signal-callers Marcus Randall and JaMarcus Russell will likely split time today against Mississippi State.
PAGE 1C

Jim Hudelson/The Times
Students take a test Friday at Southern University-Shreveport. Southern's preliminary numbers show 119 more students.

Super Derby today

By Scott Ferrell
sferrell@gannett.com

The horse racing world's attention turns to Harrah's Louisiana Downs today for the Grade II, $500,000 Super Derby XXV.

The Super Derby is the biggest race nationally this weekend as the only Grade II race run. There are no Grade I races run this weekend.

Imperialism, the third-place finisher in the Kentucky Derby, heads a field of nine horses entered in today's event as the 8-5 morning line favorite.

Imperialism owner Steve Taub has an entry for the first time, despite being familiar with the race.

"I've been in the business about 20 years, about the same as this race," Taub said. "The thing that always interested me was the name."

Another horse to watch today is Borrego, a Kentucky Derby and Preakness contestant. Borrego carried 5-2 morning line odds. The field also includes a couple of horses from prominent local trainers Cole Norman and Bobby Barrett. Norman will send South Africa and Barrett will send Fantastical to post.

"I think it's going to be a competitive race, a very balanced race," Louisiana Downs Vice President of Racing Operations Ray Tromba said. "We're pretty excited about what you'll see from a betting standpoint."

Race essentials

WHEN: 5:05 p.m. post time.
WHERE: Harrah's Louisiana Downs.
MORNING LINE FAVORITE: Imperialism, 8-5.

Soak it up, Ivan's not done yet

A pedestrian walks through an expansive puddle on the side of Texas Street in Shreveport on Friday. The soggy weather was associated with the remnants of tropical storm Ivan, which moved up through Texas.
Callie Reames/The Times

By Cristina Rodriguez
crodriguez@gannett.com

North Louisiana is having a rainy weekend courtesy of Ivan — something it hasn't seen for weeks.

Since the beginning of September, the area has seen a mere 0.6 inches of rain, said Mike Berry, a meteorologist with the National Weather Service in Shreveport. That's about one-fourth of what's normal for the period, he said.

But the former Hurricane Ivan, downgraded to a tropical depression on Friday, was pushed back to the Gulf of Mexico by a high-pressure system that had been keeping storms out of the region this summer.

"We had a blocking ridge of high pressure across the central United

Weekend forecast

Today: Mostly cloudy, scattered showers and thunderstorms. Highs in lower 80s. Chance of rain 50 percent, diminishing to 30 percent by tonight.
Sunday: Partly cloudy with a slight chance of showers and thunderstorms. Highs in the mid-80s. Chance of rain 20 percent.
Source: National Weather Service

States," Berry said. "That kept any weak fronts from moving into this area. It also kept any kind of shower or thunderstorm activity from moving north."

The weather service predicts the sporadic showers will leave the area on Sunday as Ivan weakens and heads northwest through Texas.

A cool front keeping highs in the lower 80s is expected to follow and last through the later part of next week, Berry said.

■ See **RAIN** 2A

■ **Jeanne takes aim at Florida's east coast**
PAGE 8A

Rolls grow at state colleges

By Mike Hasten
mhasten@gannett.com
and Melody Brumble
mbrumble@gannett.com

BATON ROUGE — About 3,500 more students are enrolled in Louisiana's colleges and universities than a year ago and officials are predicting the count could climb as final enrollment head counts come in.

Preliminary figures from the Board of Regents show that about 2,000 additional students are enrolled in four-year universities. The figures compare preliminary head counts from the first 15 days of class this school year to actual enrollment figures last fall.

Community college enrollment is up 1,333 students, but Walter Bumphus, head of the Community and Technical College System, said the figure could be off because it shows a drop of 175 students at Sowela Technical Community College in Lake Charles. The college is still enrolling

students.

"Our greatest increases are in the new two-year schools," said Jimmy Clarke, deputy commissioner of higher education, "and there are realistic explanations for the change."

Shreveport-Bossier colleges and universities saw steady enrollment increases this year.

Southern University at Shreveport's 5.3 percent increase over last fall was the largest locally.

SU-Shreveport added 119 students, pumping its enrollment up to 2,349. SU-S officials are predicting larger increases next year when dormitories are built on campus.

John Alaк, interim director of SUSLA's institutional research and planning department, said unique allied health programs like dental hygienist and radiologist training are top draws.

■ See **ROLLS** 2A

Couple flees Ivan only to lose dog — here

By Alisa Stingley
astingley@gannett.com

Fleeing Hurricane Ivan 10 days ago, Justine Everett and her husband arrived in Shreveport fearful they might lose everything.

When they returned to their Mobile, Ala. area home a few days later, it had only minor damage. But they had lost something.

Allie.

The couple's 3-year-old Australian shepherd escaped out of a fenced back yard in Shreveport sometime the night of Sept. 15.

That was only hours after the couple arrived to stay with friend Meredith King and her son, the Rev. Todd Hanks, who live on Timberlane in North Highlands neighborhood.

"(Allie's) an escape artist. She managed to somehow open the gate. ... The friends we were staying with continue to search."
Justine Everett, Alabama resident who lost her pet here

Finding Allie

She is a black, long-haired Australian shepherd with a natural bobtail and brown eyes. She weighs 50 pounds and was wearing a crimson-colored collar with a rabies tag. Call collect at (251) 649-3510 if you find the dog.

■ See **DOG** 2A

Child seat training course helps officers save lives

By Keri Kirby
kerikirby@gannett.com

When Bossier City police officer Lindsey Kutz first heard about the child safety seat certification course she took this week, she couldn't imagine why it would take five days to complete.

She changed her mind around day three.

"There's been a lot to it. It's definitely worth five days and I can see how it could take longer," she said as she took a break from installing an infant seat inside a truck. "There's a lot to know."

Kutz is one of 33 officers from area law enforcement

More information

If all child passengers less than 15 years old were restrained properly, it is estimated that more than 600 U.S. lives could be saved and 182,000 injuries could be prevented annually
Source: Louisiana SAFE Kids

agencies who will complete the 32-hour course today with a public child safety checkup from 1 p.m. until 4 p.m. at Kroger's, 1867 Nelson St.

Trooper Kevin Allen, state police Troop L spokesman and a lead instructor for the course, said the goal of the training is

in the United States. Correctly installed and used child safety seats reduce the risk of death by 71 percent for infants, 54 percent for toddlers, and reduce the need for hospitalization by 69 percent for children under 5.

for the officers to go home and pass their knowledge on to parents in their communities.

"This is such a big issue because nine out of 10 child seats are installed incorrectly in Louisiana," he said.

Shane Bevel/The Times
Bossier police officer Amanda Faith practices securing a child seat in the back of a car at Caddo Correctional Facility.

■ See **SEAT** 2A

Weather

High: 83 Low: 65
Details: 2A

Index

Advice	4D	Lottery	2A
Classified	1E	Money	6B
Comics	3D	Movie Ads	2D
Crossword	4D	Scoreboard	7C
Deaths	5B	Sports	1C
Editorials	11A	Stocks	6B
Living	1D	T. Greening	1B
Local/State	1B	Television	5D

Figure 8.10.
Copyright 2004, *The Shreveport* (La.) *Times*. Used with permission.

D-300 bus drivers plan to file grievance

Union upset by district's decision to hire company for deLacey routes

Board weighs in

On Monday, the District 300 school board is likely to decide whether to approve the contract with Jones Transportation. The meeting starts at 7:30 p.m. at the administration center, 300 Cleveland Ave., Carpentersville.

By DERRICK GINGERY
dgingery@nwherald.com

CARPENTERSVILLE – District 300's bus drivers union will file a grievance related to the hiring of Jones Transportation Services to handle routes for the deLacey Family Education Center.

Susan Brancamp, president of the Dundee Association of Transportation Employees, the drivers union, said the union wants the district to let its members handle the deLacey routes.

Brancamp said Friday that the union asked the district last week to end its contract with Jones Transportation, then decided a grievance would be necessary.

The grievance will go to the supervisors in the transportation department first but could reach the school board.

"We filed a cease and desist [order], and when they chose not to do that, we asked for a grievance to be filed at the board level," Brancamp said. "[Superintendent Kenneth] Arndt said he didn't think that was appropriate, so we filed at Level 1, which is [Transportation Director] Woody Fitzmaurice."

Brancamp would not say when the grievance would be filed. Arndt said a meeting will be scheduled with union officials to talk about the grievance.

School board members this month agreed to hire Jones Transportation to take bus routes for the deLacey center, used for preschool and early-childhood services.

See D-300, page 2A

Gilberts land faces cleanup

Lead contamination spread to property owned by village

By MEGAN EDWARDS
medwards@nwherald.com

GILBERTS – The village owns about 10,000 square feet of lead-contaminated land surrounding public works buildings on Railroad Street, U.S. Environmental Protection Agency officials said Friday.

The buildings are a few feet from the eastern edge of 5 acres owned by Next Media Inc. that was found to be contaminated in July. The contamination is the result of a lead-salvaging business that operated on the property in the 1960s and 1970s, officials said. Auto batteries were broken open, and the lead inside was removed.

Gilberts owns about 20,000 square feet of land adjacent to Next Media's property between Tower Hill Road and Railroad Street, near the Chicago & North Western Railroad, EPA federal on-site coordinator Mike Ribordy said.

"About half of that is contaminated," he said.

Lead can be harmful if swallowed or inhaled. It can lead to brain and kidney failure or cause learning disabilities in children. But if the contamination remains underground and out of the groundwater, it poses little threat to the public, officials said.

Who pays?

EPA officials said they will determine whether the village will have to pay for the cleanup after determining how the property was obtained and used.

See LEAD, page 2A

DEVICES HELP TREAT CARDIAC ARREST

Gene Niemann of Woodstock works out at Health Bridge Fitness Center in Crystal Lake. Health Bridge complies with a new state law requiring automatic external defibrillators in places where people exercise.

Ryan Rayburn / Northwest Herald

Taken to heart

Clubs, schools quick to adhere to defibrillator law

By JESSICA PERSONETTE
jpersonette@nwherald.com

They've never used them, but they are glad they have them.

Several area health clubs, schools and park districts already are in compliance with a recent state law requiring automatic external defibrillators in places where people exercise or play sports.

The device delivers an electric shock to a person suffering from cardiac arrest.

Cary fire Lt. Andy Veath said the most common heart rhythm during a heart attack is called ventricular fibrillation, in which there is no discernible beat or pulse and the heart "quivers." Defibrillators send a shock to help the heart beat normally again.

"What's really helpful about this in the field is, the longer the heart is in fibrillation, the more resistant it becomes to shock and medications we use to stimulate it," Veath said. "So if someone can have [a defibrillator] and provide that shock early on, the chances of turning that into a heart rate is very good."

See HEART, page 6A

Personal trainer Dome Paroongsup displays an external defibrillator that Health Bridge Fitness Center keeps on hand. The center has had a device for three years.

Ryan Rayburn / Northwest Herald

Trouble mounts in Iraq

Violence belies happy message of Allawi's visit

By JIM KRANE
The Associated Press

BAGHDAD, Iraq – Prime Minister Ayad Allawi and President Bush have declared that Iraq is on the road to stability, with the Iraqi leader saying elections will be possible in all but three or four of Iraq's 18 provinces.

But the map of Iraq is scarred with violence every day. The capital is wracked by kidnappings and bombings. And September is shaping up as one of the deadliest months for American soldiers.

Westerners are fleeing Iraq with reconstruction projects half-finished. Town markets sell grisly videos of beheadings. And U.S. troops grapple with an increasingly potent insurgency that appears to easily recruit fighters.

Allawi's assessment accurately describes conditions in parts of northern Iraq under Kurdish control and some Shiite towns of the south.

But his upbeat message masks the violence in the major cities of Baghdad and Mosul, and in the Sunni towns north and west of the capital.

Problems persist

▪ U.S. officials debate key details of the planned Iraqi election in January.

▪ Six Egyptians and four Iraqis have been kidnapped, police say.

Page 13A

See IRAQ, page 2A

Illinois Secretary of State Police secure the rotunda of the State Capitol in Springfield on Monday after a co-worker was shot and killed. Secretary of State Jesse White stands by his office's policy of not requiring guards to wear bulletproof vests.

AP photo

White backs bulletproof-vest policy

Guards not required to wear protective shields despite availability

By RYAN KEITH
The Associated Press

SPRINGFIELD – As hundreds mourned a slain security guard at the state Capitol, Secretary of State Jesse White on Friday defended his office's decision not to require guards to wear bulletproof vests.

The office has 18 bulletproof vests available, and White said wearing one could have saved the unarmed guard's life. But he said no reason existed before the shooting to make guards wear them.

"The vests have to be fitted for them to be worn, and whenever there was a spirit of unrest, when they felt that their life was in danger, they could use them," White said in an interview after a service for William Wozniak, 51.

Wozniak, one of about 80 Capitol guards, had little if any warning Monday when a gunman walked through the main entrance and fired a shotgun blast into his chest, killing him.

See VESTS, page 2A

Jesse White

Figure 8.11.
Copyright 2004, the *Northwest Herald*, Crystal Lake, Ill. Used with permission.

signment editors and their reporters negotiate lengths for their stories, and the assignment editor must tell the designer if a story is running longer than anticipated. This information enables editors to begin designing their pages, making minor, and sometimes major, adjustments as news develops.

When editors want a story cut to a certain length, they put the desired figure at the top of the story. The copy editor calls the story onto the screen, noting the headline orders and the story length. The copy editor then trims a few phrases or sentences to shave the story by an inch or so. If that isn't enough, a paragraph or two, sometimes more, may be deleted. The computer tells the copy editor when the correct length is reached.

Avoiding pitfalls

Anyone designing newspaper pages should keep in mind the knowledge of typography accumulated by researchers. (Typography was introduced in Chapter 7.) For a newspaper to gain maximum impact with the reader, experts in typography advise certain design guidelines. Here is a list of things to avoid:

1. **Don't "tombstone."** Heads of similar size and weight side by side resemble grave markers in old cemeteries.
2. **Avoid "squint-size" headlines.** The reader should never have to squint to read headlines. Twelve-point heads are all right on one- and two-paragraph stories, but a longer story ought to have a bigger head. Multicolumn heads should be at least 30-point, unless there is a corner above an ad to fill on an inside page.
3. **Never crowd the page.** Headlines should not take up every millimeter of space, and captions should not be jammed against their pictures. On the other hand, too much air gives readers the feeling that they bought a lot of blank paper.
4. **Avoid letting headlines "bump."** Heads should be separated vertically by body type, rules or art so that each one stands clearly by itself. This sometimes is impossible at the top of a page, but even there the heads can show contrast.
5. **Stop body type from forming ponderous blocks.** Break up lengths of type with subheads. Use multiple columns. This gives the impression that reading the story will not be arduous. Even an editor, upon seeing a long, ponderous story in print, tends to say, "That looks interesting. I'll have to read it when I have more time." They never do.
6. **No headline should "cry wolf."** If a story is of little consequence, let the headline admit it. A reader justly feels cheated if the head grossly exaggerates the story's value.
7. **Don't let a story escape its headline.** Tucking the last few lines of a story someplace in an adjoining column is sloppy design. It confuses

the reader and makes the type look sidetracked. Keep the story under the shelter of the head.

Taking positive steps

Other rules accentuate the positive:

1. **Try to put associated stories together.** Otherwise insert a refer somewhere near the beginning of the major story.
2. **Enliven the corners of the pages.** They can look like dead space unless strong typography is planned to give them life.
3. **Choose headline typefaces that contrast but don't conflict.** Perhaps this harmony of type can be explained by comparing it to harmony of dress. A man who wears a plaid jacket with a vertically striped shirt and a diagonally striped tie may find the combination overwhelms the eye.
4. **Use few typefaces.** Most publications specify what typefaces are appropriate—generally only from a family or two. Use of too many different faces results in a gaudy look that editors should avoid.

Pictures in design

Editors designing pages on a big newspaper usually have a large selection of photos from wire services and staff photographers. Even if there are only a few really good pictures on a given day, the editor tries to avoid printing any poor art and aims for a large proportion of excellent photographs. The average quality is kept high this way, even though the number of pictures may have to be reduced some days.

Some papers have a rigid policy on art: There must be a picture on every news page. This restriction frequently forces the editor to use poor pictures. A better policy would be to have a picture on every page if a good photograph is available. Well-designed papers that try to mix art and news are not bothered if several pages lack art. Their editors believe that a solid page of type is better than one diluted with a photographic cliché, such as city officials sitting around a table or a governor signing a bill.

Increasingly, editors print a few pictures of beauty or to illustrate some offbeat scene, such as railroad freight yards or water gushing through a hydroelectric plant. The beautiful and the odd may not offer much information, but they can provide a change from the conventional news photo. Picture editing is discussed in more detail in Chapter 9.

Newspapers have staffs of artists who produce informational graphics, or infographics for short, to help illustrate complicated stories. These, too, are "art" and often provide information that a picture cannot. A well-designed diagram can help readers understand how events unfolded, or how a new gizmo works, or simply show where a news event occurred.

Internet News Site Design

Editors for news Web sites (sometimes called producers) generally have much less flexibility when it comes to design. The sites they work for are, for the most part, rigorously formatted; instead, Web site editors are working continually on updating and rearranging content within their sites' structural confines. Still, it's important for Web editors to understand the functions of design and to have more than just a passing knowledge of HTML and digital photo preparation.

The Web site structure

Most news sites have a framework that does not change from day to day. Editors at these sites use computer programs known as content managers to update the information on these sites. These content management programs have taken the necessity out of hard coding stories, photos, audio and video content for the Web; the coding is done in the background by the computer. For example, all the Web sites operated by the Knight Ridder news media chain use a common content management program developed for that company. Off-the-shelf Web site authoring programs include Adobe's GoLive and Macromedia's Dreamweaver.

The transfer of text content from print to online is for the most part automated. For example, at the *Contra Costa Times* in Northern California, a copy editor each night goes through a category checklist for each story appearing in the next morning's editions. On these checklists, the editor designates what regions from the newspaper's coverage area the stories come from, what topics they discuss (for example, crime news), and other identifiers unique to that market. After the newspaper goes to press, the online computer system queries the news production system and routes copies of those stories to the appropriate Web pages on the publication's Web site. The next morning, the online editors check for transfer glitches, process and add photographs and then build the *Times'* home page. At the *San Jose Mercury News*, a reporter or editor includes tags on stories that designate Web site categories at the top of each story, and the stories are then automatically routed by computer to the appropriate areas on MercuryNews.com.

Some examples of news site design appear as Figures 8.12–8.17.

Visitors to news Web sites will find that, although content is changed frequently, the layout remains constant. Atop the home page, visitors find the name of the publication and, typically, an advertisement. Across the screen and beneath the flag are navigation buttons that users can click to move about the site. The main section of the page is usually di-

vided into three or four columns, often called rails. The left of these almost always is a more detailed navigation bar that helps visitors get to where they want to go. The second rail typically contains the top stories, photographs and editorial content. The third and fourth rails provide more advertising and links through the site.

Home pages rarely contain full stories. Rather, the news is presented as headlines and short paragraphs that describe the stories, called blurbs or touts. Site visitors interested in reading the full story click on a hyper-

Figure 8.13.
From the *Dothan* (Ala.) *Eagle*. Copyright 2004 Media General. Used with permission.

link to view it. If the story was written for print, the blurb may be the same as the lead, but often the print lead does not lend itself to online publication, so the online editor needs to recast it for the Internet audience. Sometimes this involves finding the nut paragraph, two or three paragraphs down into the story. Sometimes it involves rewriting the lead for immediacy, such as by using present tense.

The Internet provides space that print publications simply cannot provide. Online editors create packages with their stories that the newspaper does not have room for. Photographers can provide extra pictures. Hyperlinks to full-text documents cited in stories can be created. Audio and video can be added to enhance the story online. Editors can create online polls. They can host online chats with people in the news, or re-

Figure 8.14.
Copyright 2004, the *Green Bay Press-Gazette*. Used with permission.

porters and columnists in the newsroom. They can host forums to which readers can respond to events in the news. Online editors need to constantly think about the various alternative ways that stories can be told and create ways for readers to interact.

HTML

Documents on the World Wide Web are coded in HTML, XHTML and XML, languages that Web browsers read and then convert into images

Figure 8.15.
Copyright 2004, the
Joplin (Mo.) *Globe.* Used
with permission.

on individuals' computer screens. Because of the use of content management programs, it's no longer necessary for online editors to be experts in these computer languages. Those tasks can be relegated to the webmasters. It is important, however, for online editors to have a rudimentary understanding of HTML so that they can fix errors when they crop on their sites. This book does not attempt to be a comprehensive guide to HTML; many good books as well as online guides are available, including the introduction to HTML that is available from the National Center for Supercomputing Applications, at http://archive.ncsa.uiuc.edu/General/Internet/WWW/HTMLPrimer.html.

Commonly Used HTML tags

HTML coding comes in the form of tags, which are instructions inserted between brackets. For example, the start of an HTML document carries the tag <HTML> and closes with </HTML>. Some other basic tags (opening and closing tags):

<title> The document name that appears atop the browser window
     </title>
<H1> For the largest headline. </H1>
<H2> For a smaller headline. </H2>
<H3> For the next smallest headline (and so forth). </H3>
<body> For body text. </body>
<P> Each paragraph needs opening and closing paragraph tags. </P>
<P ALIGN=CENTER> Creates a centered paragraph. </P>
<P ALIGN=RIGHT> Creates a flush right paragraph. </P>
<UL> Starts a bulleted list. Each item in the list then begins with <LI>.
     </UL>

 Forces a line break without creating a new paragraph.
<A HREF="http://www.whitehouse.gov"> Creates a hyperlink to the
     URL within the quotation marks. </a>
<IMG SRC=imagename> Inserts an image.
<A HREF="mailto:user@internet.com"> Creates an e-mail link to the
     address listed. </A>

Figure 8.16.
Copyright 2004, *Los Angeles Times*. Used with permission.

Many manuals that explain HTML in more detail are available, as are online tutorials. One is "A Beginner's Guide to HTML" from the National

Figure 8.17.
Copyright 2004. *The Nashua* (N.H.) *Telegraph*. Used with permission.

Center for Supercomputing Applications at the University of Illinois, which developed HTML. Go to http://archive.ncsa.uiuc.edu/General/Internet/WWW/HTMLPrimerAll.html.

Typography online

The World Wide Web was originally conceived as a way for scientists to swap information. Typography and design were not on their minds. Typeface use was set by the browser user, out of the control of Web site designers. For example, if a user set Times New Roman as his or her default font, all the text in the page appeared in Times New Roman, in the size specified in the HTML tags. Now, through the use of cascading style sheets (CSS), designers can specify the typefaces and styles that will be displayed on users' screens—provided that those typefaces are installed on the users' computers.

As with print typography, it's important for Web sites to strive for a clean look with readable text. Designers should be limited to specified type families to avoid a hodgepodge look. Some typefaces that have been designed for readability on computer monitors include Times New Roman, Georgia, Verdana, Arial and Trebuchet.[7]

More Resources for Designers

Front pages from the around world, updated daily:
http://www.newseum.org/todaysfrontpages

Society for News Design:
www.snd.org

National Center for Supercomputing Applications' Beginner's Guide to HTML:
http://archive.ncsa.uiuc.edu/General/Internet/WWW/HTMLPrimer.html

Eyetrack III: Online News Consumer Behavior in the Age of Multimedia,
http://www.poynterextra.org/eyetrack2004/index.htm

Notes

1. Mario Garcia, *Contemporary Newspaper Design*, 3rd ed. (Englewood Cliffs, N.J.: Prentice Hall, 1993).
2. Mario R. Garcia and Pegie Stark, *Eyes on the News* (St. Petersburg, Fla., Poynter Institute for Media Studies, 1991), 25.
3. Marion Lowenstein, Greg Edwards, Deborah Tatar and Andrew DeVigal, *Stanford-Poynter Project/EyeTracking Online News* (Poynter Institute for Media Studies, 2000), http://www.poynterextra.org/et/i.htm.
4. Steve Outing and Laura Ruel, *The Best of Eyetrack III: What We Saw When We Looked Through Their Eyes* (Poynter Institute for Media Studies, 2004), http://www.poynterextra.org/eyetrack2004/main.htm.
5. Mario Garcia, *Pure Design* (St. Petersburg, Fla.: Miller Media, 2002), 87.
6. Tim Harrower, *The Newspaper Designer's Handbook*, 5th ed. (Boston: McGraw-Hill, 2002), 22.
7. Patrick J. Lynch and Sarah Horton, *Web Style Guide*, 2nd ed. (New Haven: Yale University Press, 2001).

CHAPTER 9

Editing Photos and Graphics

No news presentation is complete without photographs or other art-work. Art enhances even the most deft storyteller's prose. Good reporters know that good photographs help draw readers into their stories. Photographs can instantaneously convey messages of joy, angst, sorrow—the whole range of human emotions. Who can forget the Pulitzer Prize–winning picture of the firefighter holding the bloodied baby after the bombing of the federal building in Oklahoma? Or the pictures of an airplane crashing into the World Trade Center? Or the charred bodies of dead Americans hanging from bridges in Iraq? Or the photo of a South Vietnamese military officer shooting a suspected Viet Cong soldier in the head?

Online news publication has enhanced the still photographer's ability to help bring the news to audiences. Where print publications might only have room for a single picture, the infinite space of the Internet allows the creation of galleries of a dozen or more photos. Some news sites, such as that of the *New York Times*, add reporter narration to these features. At some publications, still photographers have added capturing video to their newsgathering abilities.

The visual companion to photographs is the informational graphic, or infographic. Infographics also enhance storytelling by breaking out key information and presenting information visually through maps, charts, graphs and diagrams. Something as simple as a map can help a reader place a news event in his city, in the country or across the globe. Or it can help him understand how a budget process works, or the life cycle of a 17-year cicada.

Just as editors work with reporters to develop stories, so they work with photographers to find and choose the best pictures, and they work with graphic artists in the conception and design of informational graphics. Later, on the copy desk, copy editors write captions for the pictures

Figure 9.1.
Photographers shooting sporting events should go beyond the usual action shots and capture the emotion of the event. Photo by David Martin Olson/*The State Hornet.* Used with permission.

and check that the photos work together as part of the larger package that also includes the headline and possible sidebars. Copy editors also check informational graphics, reviewing them critically as they would a story, making sure that the story and the graphic match and that the graphic is free of errors.

What Makes for a Good Photo

Good photos do not come easily. They must be taken by skilled individuals, using first-rate equipment. Photographers must have time to explore ways of getting outstanding pictures. Encouragement helps, as it does in any craft.

As part of the writing-editing-design, or WED process (see Chapter 8), editors involve photographers early in the process of a story in order to get the best pictures. Often, a reporter and photographer will go together on the same assignment. A photographer assigned to come up with a picture as an afterthought rarely can produce an image as compelling as she would if she were involved from the beginning.

News photographers are journalists, and as is true of reporters and editors, they must sense what makes news. Someone has said that a good photojournalist is an "informed talent," understanding the fundamentals of politics to photograph political figures, for example, or corporate world intricacies when photographing a tense stockholders' meeting.

The person in charge of photography is, not surprisingly, called the *chief photographer* or the *picture editor*. Larger publications may also have a director of photography. Working together with their photographers, picture editors decide which pictures to use and how they will appear in the paper or online. On smaller publications, an editor who works with reporters may also be responsible for picture choice. These staff limitations too often mean that picture editing is treated carelessly or casually. Pictures are not selected thoughtfully, and photographers receive only sketchy direction about the purpose of the picture and its possible use.

Figure 9.2.
A photographer on an assignment about an orchestra can present the editor with a wide picture of all the musicians and close-ups with more details. With space, designers can create nice packages with more than one offering. Photos by David Martin Olson/ *The State Hornet.* Used with permission.

Pictures at such publications tend to be used as typographical devices to relieve the monotony of a page of print.

Yet, staffers at such smaller publications can still learn to reject ordinary pictures, to crop good ones to make them better and to push photographers to do more than line up a few people and snap the shutter. After some practice and study, almost anyone with a good news sense can sort through a dozen pictures to choose the best two or three, rejecting the routine shots and picking those with originality. The staffer can learn to say, "Not one of these pictures is much good." In such cases photographers must be encouraged to seek different angles, to avoid contrivances such as phony props and to wait until a good picture is possible.

Good photo chiefs and editors try to get each side to understand the other's needs. In the end, of course, the photo editor must decide which pictures get into the paper and in what form. Photo editors may have their decisions overruled by a higher editor from time to time, but in general they have the final say.

At some news operations, picture editors are little more than technicians and liaisons between other editors and photographers. They pass on assignments, decide a certain amount of policy and select, crop and size pictures. This may lead to some organizational efficiency, and it is better than having no photo editor, but such a system usually produces uncreative photographs.

The Art of Quality

Figure 9.3.
For a story on feral chickens on a college campus, a photographer could come back with just a bird in the picture. Better, though, is a picture that sets the bird on campus. Photo by David Martin Olson/*The State Hornet*. Used with permission.

Brian Horton of the Associated Press explains three facets involved in making photographs: composition, style and cropping. Composition refers to what's in the photograph. Each photographer develops his or her own style that's consistent. Cropping refers to deciding what elements are included or excluded from the photograph, either by the way it is framed as the picture is taken or as it is edited on a computer.[1]

Good picture editing starts with high-quality photos, which means technical excellence and superior visualization of the content. Every publication must, from time to time, print some mediocre photographs. A family brings in a tinted photograph on soft mat paper to go with an obituary for a local newspaper, or a reporter persuades the parents of an injured child to lend a badly lighted snapshot of the victim. Such pictures fall short of photographic excellence in several respects, yet they will be published, perhaps even in large sizes, because they help tell the story. Computers can sometimes enhance the original image for improved reproduction or Web publication, but technicians must be careful not to otherwise alter the photograph.

The routine photograph is often shot straight on at eye height. For a fresh approach, the photographer may crouch for a low angle—or go up a ladder for a high one—or walk around somewhere to the side to get an unusual viewpoint. Consider the usual shot of a man giving a plaque to another. Instead of the obvious straight-on shot, the photographer can try taking the picture at a low angle, showing the winner grinning up at his framed certificate, which has been hoisted up to his shoulder.

When a president was on the White House lawn signing a bill for more parks, a photographer climbed a tree and shot the scene through the leaves. Both of these examples involve routine assignments, and the photographers had to figure out ways to escape the monotony of such assignments.

News photographers sometimes strive for artistic patterns in their pictures. These may be rows of bleachers or bottles, lines of fence posts or windows. Highly patterned backgrounds that detract from the focal point should be avoided. Yet the best photo artist, seeking aesthetic results, sometimes violates tradition. Fuzziness, at least of some parts of a photo, may create a mood. Because stopping the action can mean a dull sports picture, there may be more drama in the blur of a moving arm or leg, and racing cars with lines of motion may simultaneously seem to whiz and be beautiful. It is difficult to do these well. If a blurred picture is less than outstanding, using a conventional shot is better.

Besides capturing a strong center of interest and a different camera angle, good photographers try for appropriate special effects. For example, the illusion of depth comes from using an angle that puts a pertinent subject in the foreground—shooting down at a seminar table over the shoulder of a teacher, for example, or including a firefighter with hose at the edge of the picture of a building fire. This effort is similar to *framing*, another useful approach.

Good news pictures should have people in them, tell a story and show action. A mug shot of a senator, for example, shows no action and tells readers only what the senator looks like. Action obviously is limited in most pictures; few news pictures show someone felling a tree or knocking down a circus tent. Most photographed action is more subdued: a secretary of state leaning forward to hear a question; a corporate trader looking warily at two investors. But how dull they would look if they merely sat, smiling at the camera.

A picture of a lake at dawn may show great beauty, but interest soars if it includes a man gliding across the water in a canoe. Even the implication of life helps; a picture of a mountainside cabin with smoke rising

Figure 9.4.
A protest picture can be made more interesting by framing the protesters in front of the state Capitol. Photo by David Martin Olson/*The State Hornet.* Used with permission.

Figure 9.5.

Pictures from a rally can take on life when people are interacting. Notice how the photo of the discussion is more interesting than the cliché photo of a man waving a flag. Photos by David Martin Olson/ *The State Hornet.* Used with permission.

from the chimney gives some human attachment. A few pictures without people will make the grade, however. Who can resist lingering over Ansel Adams' pictures, which rarely include people?

Many news publications illustrate feature stories with portraits of their subjects, sometimes also called environmental portraits because they depict the subject in their environs. Great portrait photographers reveal character in their pictures. Portrait painters encourage us to spend a minute or two over their work, searching for insight into another human face. Meticulous news photographers sometimes can come close to such artistry. But an even better approach is for the photographer to spend some time with the subject and capture a photograph of the subject *doing something.*

As in the theater, props can be valuable to the news photographer. A picture of a woman talking on the telephone is hackneyed but probably better than a fast shot of her looking at the camera. Good photographers often wait until their subjects unconsciously grasp some prop, such as a football, trophy or paperweight, before taking the best shot. Props let the subject relax and appear natural.

Fakery with props must be forbidden. One photographer dropped candy into a sousaphone and got a great shot of a little boy crawling into the horn. It was a fraud, however, for the child never would have crawled there without a rigged inducement. Other contrivances, such as a pointer, a funny hat or the old hula hoop, get labeled fake in most readers' minds.

Items already in use by the photographic subjects, however, can help produce excellent pictures. The feature shot of a little girl trying on hats before a mirror, for example, or the picture of an old man trudging home from the river carrying one fish can have great impact. The devices are not really props, so their use looks natural.

The photographer, to turn out quality work, avoids gimmickry and corn, such as a politician wearing a cowboy outfit or drinking milk from a huge bowl. The routine shot of a routine action, such as the signing of a bill, should be forsaken. So should clichés such as handshaking (sometimes called "grip and grin") award presentations, ribbon cuttings and gavel passings. Worst of all is the lineup, where three or four persons face the camera. The picture editor must take a pledge never to give assignments that result in corn, routine pictures or clichés.

Judging Pictures

A picture editor learns to evaluate photographs as a news editor learns to judge stories, by experience and by observing how other journalists operate. Some pictures are obviously great, others blatantly dull. But the majority of pictures are in between and only a fraction of them can be used. Those chosen will depend on the day's needs and the editor's personal tastes.

Through market research, picture editors can determine what subjects interest readers. However, picture editors should not blindly follow what market research tells them. Ultimately, they have to understand intuitively what will interest readers. What will interest editors probably will interest subscribers. If they exclaim, "Wow!" about a photo, it probably means that readers, too, will feel its impact. So photo editors must learn to understand themselves. Each editor will naturally have some enthusiasms, but they should not become hobby horses. Or an editor may temper dislike of a certain type of picture because experience has shown that readers react favorably to it. Editors give readers "what they want" if in good conscience they can, but they usually select what their judgment says is the best photojournalism.

Ethics of Illustration

The tension between what readers want and what they should have suggests problems in ethics that the picture editor also confronts in making selections. Some readers may want the macabre or near-pornographic

Figure 9.6.
Picture editors must consider technical quality when choosing photographs. In this set, the top photo was taken without a flash; the bottom picture with the flash better exposes the woman's face. Photos by David Martin Olson/ *The State Hornet*. Used with permission.

photo, yet may criticize the paper that uses photographs in bad taste. The picture editor must sometimes walk the hazy, wiggling line between the acceptable and unacceptable.

Until the Vietnam War, pictures of bodies were generally forbidden and grisly shots were used sparingly. During the "first televised war," however, television network news ran color pictures of slaughter and gore nearly every day. Since then news publications, although cautious about bloody scenes, have been more willing to print pictures of brutality.

Some readers were angry when the *New York Post* printed a front-page picture of a young woman leaping to her death from an apartment building. The newspaper came under harsh criticism from the journalism community as well. Geneva Overholser, former editor of the *Des Moines Register*, called the display a "naked grab at emotionalism."[2]

Television and the Internet have, however, made the public more willing to accept other gruesome scenes. Reports of starvation in East Africa in 1985 included pictures of thousands of people, many of them babies, only days from death. These pictures so shocked the world that major relief efforts were started almost overnight by public and private groups. When photographs of men beheaded in Iraq became available on Internet, many users went to have a look.

Although photo manipulation dates back decades, computer technology has made it easy—perhaps too easy—to do. A journalist's primary function is truth-telling, and that applies to photographers as well. Pictures capture a true moment in time. When computers are used to alter the photos, they are no longer true—they are a fabrication. In 2003, a *Los Angeles Times* photographer in Iraq was not satisfied with the pictures he took of an evacuation, so he used a computer to combine elements from two photographs taken moments apart into one. The photo ran in the *Times* the next day. When the fraud was discovered, the photographer was fired and the *Times* apologized.

Digital Photography

Most news photographers now use digital cameras—a big improvement from the days of film. Before, when a photographer was finished shooting pictures, she had to return to the darkroom to develop the film, review the negatives for the best pictures, and then print the pictures. Now, photographs can be sent instantly to the newsroom by telephone or wirelessly, to be published online within minutes or be prepared for the print edition the next day.

Sources of Photos

Newspapers and news Web sites get more of their photos from the wire services than any other source. AP sends streams of pictures, usually of good quality, to its customers, and the supplemental news services make available the work of news organizations around the country.

Local sources

Some small news operations use reporters as photographers, but the idea of the photographer-reporter has never really caught on. A major reason is that many editors contend that a person can't report *and* photograph well. Many reporters and photographers will agree. Yet some picture editors feel that a reporter who is out on a story might as well have a camera along and shoot some pictures. They give their reporters "point-and-shoot cameras"—those with automatic focus—and let them take photographs as they cover their beats. Pictures taken by reporters may be adequate, but they rarely are a substitute for pictures taken by professional photographers using first-rate equipment. News operations seeking quality pictures and reporting will use specialists for each field.

Free-lance photographers place some pictures with news organizations as well, especially their magazine sections. Some of the most famous news photographs have been taken by amateurs who just happened to be on the spot. The Oklahoma City bombing photo of the firefighter with the baby is an example.

Some other local pictures are provided by news sources. Families may supply photographs for obituaries. Brides bring in their pictures for wedding announcements. Sometimes a reporter wangles a portrait from the family of a victim or a suspect. Some news subjects come into the newsroom's studio for a picture. Although there is the ever-present danger of stilted photography, this plan works well for such things as awards and some feature pictures.

Public relations sources provide many more newspaper pictures than readers realize or most editors admit. Most of those glamour pictures come from press agents of screen and television celebrities. Photographs in the family section that feature new fashions, modern interiors and luscious foods are often from publicity sources. Local companies provide varied pictures for the business pages. And, as publicity workshops never tire of pointing out, the good photograph from the publicity chairman of even the PTA or hobby groups may see publication. Editors should accept such pictures, however, only if they show quality and genuine news value. Most public relations pictures are distributed for one purpose: advertising. Journalists should be wary of being used for such purposes.

Newsrooms have one other important source of pictures—their own libraries and databases. Older pictures are filed in folders established by subject; newer ones are kept electronically in searchable databases for easy retrieval. From such files, news publications can rush into publication photographs of newsworthy people when they speak, win, lose, get into trouble or die. (Only careless editors use pictures that are obviously 10 or 20 years old; however, there are stories—such as the death of a once-prominent tycoon—for which an old picture is better than none, but in those cases the date of the photo should be indicated.)

Picture editors for print publication usually have many times more photographs than they can use. The task is to pick the best without making some staffers feel unneeded. If the newspaper has an online operation, additional photographs can be placed on the Internet, with a reference in the newspaper indicating that.

Cropping and Sizing

Picture editors are involved in both the cropping and sizing of photographs. Cropping refers to eliminating unwanted or unnecessary content from a photo by trimming it from the edges. Sizing refers to adjusting the dimensions of a photograph to fit the needs of the newspaper or Web site. These steps are sometimes, but not always, done in tandem.

Cropping

The first crop occurs when the photographer makes the picture, by virtue of the way she frames the shot. In the newsroom, the photographer and picture editor together look at what she has and decide whether further cropping is necessary. Many pictures require little or no cropping, because the photographer focused on the essentials. The experienced editor, however, may wish to crop severely, cutting out anything that seems to detract from the point of the picture, but should only do so with the photographer's consent—in much the same way that an assignment editor works with the reporter when a story needs to be revised.

Editors sometimes crop and size in relation to page design, which may require a long one-column orientation or a more horizontal picture three columns wide. Usually, however, the picture is cropped to attain the best photographic result and the page design is adjusted accordingly. So editors cut out busy backgrounds, superfluous people and objects and other distractions to bring the picture out of the photograph. Cropping should accentuate the focus of interest—the part of the picture that catches the eye.

Advice on cropping may sometimes seem inconsistent, but the wise editor follows the rules that will make the picture most effective. They should try to retain the essential composition of a good picture. They should not crop ruthlessly, cutting off the tops of heads or bodies from the waist down. They should crop only when it is necessary to improve the picture and to emphasize dominant points of interest.

Figure 9.7.
At full frame, this picture is of a student looking at vandalized campaign signs. Cropped, it becomes a less interesting view of just the signs. Photo by David Martin Olson/*The State Hornet.* Used with permission.

As they crop, editors and photographers should keep these other pointers in mind.

1. Look for other than the "obvious" crop, to get unusual results.
2. In head and shoulder shots, leave a bit of space on the side toward which a person faces.
3. Emphasize the action by leaving space before the thrust of an action, whether a racing car or jumping basketball player.
4. Avoid spoiling a hairstyle or cutting off legs at the ankle.
5. Keep vertical lines vertical.
6. Retain horizons for perspective, but be sure they are horizontal.
7. Avoid fancy and irregular shapes, unless there's a strong reason for them.
8. Experiment. Keep asking, "How can this be improved? Can I honestly dramatize the picture some way? Am I cropping out something essential?"

To visualize the picture when cropped, picture editors can make the trims on a computer and decide whether they like the look. If they don't, they can revert to the original image.

There is no problem of sizing or scaling if the editor simply crops out of the picture an area exactly the size that the picture needs to be. For example, it is no problem to mark an area a column wide and 3 inches deep. But rarely does the picture fit designers' needs so exactly.

Sizing

Computers are used to size photographs. Many news operations use Adobe Photoshop to process pictures, although other programs are available. A page designer will decide what size he would like to use a photograph—let's say three columns—and will either size the photo-

Figure 9.8.
At full frame, this photograph describes a track-and-field event. Cropped, it tells the story of the athlete. Photo by David Martin Olson/*The State Hornet.* Used with permission.

graph himself or send the photo to technicians skilled in preparing digital images for the press. The photograph can then be imported into a page using a page design program such as QuarkXpress. The editor can then adjust the size of the photo to work with his design. It's OK to reduce the photo during page design, but if the designer decides he wants to use it larger, he should send the photo back to be resized by the technicians in order to preserve resolution of the image.

Some page designers still use proportion wheels to calculate the approximate size of a photograph, particularly if they use paper dummies in their initial planning of a page's design. To use a proportion wheel, a designer must first know the original dimensions of the photograph and one dimension of the printed size—usually the width. The designer lines up the original width on the inside of the wheel with the width on the outside and then finds the original depth on the inside of the wheel. It lines up with the new depth on the outside of the wheel.

It is in cropping and sizing that picture editors have the opportunity to employ the real drama of modern news photography. If the conventional method is to reduce everything to two or three columns, they will break away to put the best pictures into sizes five and even six columns wide, where they will leap out at the reader.

Writing Captions

The picture editor must see that every photo has a *caption*, (sometimes called *cutlines* or just *lines)*. Sometimes simply the name suffices for the picture with one person, such as a head shot or a bride's portrait. Necessary explanation for a picture should be in short, clear sentences.

As with headlines, captions are in the present tense: "Crewmen try to check flames. . . " or "Joe Doakes of Middle State hurls a javelin. . . ." Of the five W's usually part of the news lead, the captions should include at least the *who, where* and *when.* Most of the *what* is told by the picture itself.

Writers tend to worry too much about *what.* If the picture is good, an unmodified, simple verb is enough. It is amateurish to write "smilingly accepts" or "express delight about." The expression "is shown" and "is pictured" waste space. However, if the reason for a smile or gesture is not self-evident, the reader deserves an explanation.

Editorializing or ascribing emotions can be dangerous in captions.

"Club-swinging policeman" may cast an onus on the officer, but "eyes blazing defiance, the looter" may shift prejudice in the opposite direction. Let the reader decide from the look of the clubs and eyes. Unless they misrepresent the full story, cutlines should be deadpan.

Here are some other tips for caption writers:

1. Identify people, places and things correctly. Identify people "from left," not "left to right."

2. If a story accompanies the picture, explain the picture, not the story.
3. Tell the reader what to look for in the picture.
4. Don't leave the reader baffled. Clear up any ambiguities.
5. Don't libel anyone.

Typographical devices are sometimes used to lure the roving eye to the picture. Often this is two or three words of boldface caps that kick off the cutlines:

CANDIDATES GATHER—Democratic leaders. . .

Or there may be a small headline in a larger type than the cutlines:

Candidates gather

Democratic leaders from upstate counties barbecue. . .

Other Artwork

Very few news publications gave much thought to graphic illustration of news stories until the debut of *USA Today* in 1982. (See Figure 9.9.) That newspaper's approach to color and visual illustration of the news started a revolution in the newspaper industry. Now, readers would be hard-pressed to find a news publication that does not use informational graphics of some kind to enhance its storytelling.

In his book on news page design, Tim Harrower talks about the various types of graphics in use today: fever, bar and pie charts; fact and bio boxes; lists and checklists; glossaries and quizzes; tables; ratings; diagrams; and maps.[3]

At most publications, an art director or graphics editor works with artists in the conception and production of infographics. This editor also works with assignment editors, designers and copy editors to make sure the infographic fits as part of a larger news package presentation. The editing of infographics goes through several layers, including the graphics editor, the assignment editor and a copy editor. The approach to editing infographics is the same as the approach to stories: Do they make sense? Are they grammatically correct? Do the numbers add up? Also important is that the information in the graphic must be consistent with the information in the story. If a graphic reports a proposed tax increase of 3.3 percent and the story talks about a 3.4 percent figure, an editor needs to reconcile the figures.

Notes

1. Brian Horton, *The Associated Press Guide to Photojournalism*, 2nd ed. (New York: McGraw-Hill, 2001).

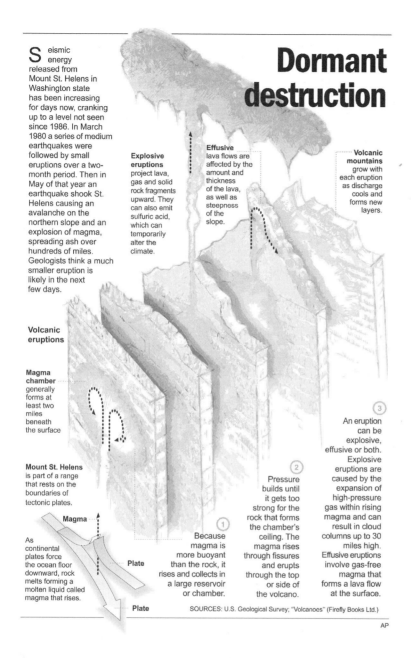

Seismic energy released from Mount St. Helens in Washington state has been increasing for days now, cranking up to a level not seen since 1986. In March 1980 a series of medium earthquakes were followed by small eruptions over a two-month period. Then in May of that year an earthquake shook St. Helens causing an avalanche on the northern slope and an explosion of magma, spreading ash over hundreds of miles. Geologists think a much smaller eruption is likely in the next few days.

Dormant destruction

Explosive eruptions project lava, gas and solid rock fragments upward. They can also emit sulfuric acid, which can temporarily alter the climate.

Effusive lava flows are affected by the amount and thickness of the lava, as well as steepness of the slope.

Volcanic mountains grow with each eruption as discharge cools and forms new layers.

Volcanic eruptions

Magma chamber generally forms at least two miles beneath the surface

Mount St. Helens is part of a range that rests on the boundaries of tectonic plates.

Magma

As continental plates force the ocean floor downward, rock melts forming a molten liquid called magma that rises.

Plate

Plate

(1) Because magma is more buoyant than the rock, it rises and collects in a large reservoir or chamber.

(2) Pressure builds until it gets too strong for the rock that forms the chamber's ceiling. The magma rises through fissures and erupts through the top or side of the volcano.

(3) An eruption can be explosive, effusive or both. Explosive eruptions are caused by the expansion of high-pressure gas within rising magma and can result in cloud columns up to 30 miles high. Effusive eruptions involve gas-free magma that forms a lava flow at the surface.

SOURCES: U.S. Geological Survey; "Volcanoes" (Firefly Books Ltd.)

AP

Figure 9.9.
Informational graphics of varying kinds are now a staple of news publications. Editors must give them as much attention as they do stories and photographs. Copyright 2004, the Associated Press. Used with permission.

2. Geneva Overholser, "N.Y. Post Readers Upset Over Suicide Photo," *Poynter Online* (March 11, 2004), http://www.poynteronline.org/column.asp$id=54&aid=62282.

3. Tim Harrower, *The Newspaper Designer's Handbook*, 5th ed. (Boston: McGraw-Hill, 2002), 153.

CHAPTER 10

Editing News Services

Ever since the invention of the telegraph, news from afar has been sent by wire. Civil War reporters used telegrams to get stories to their newspapers. Later some papers had stenographers listen to stories coming by Morse code and typed the stories. Late in the 19th century, the Teletype was invented, bringing stories on paper to newsrooms. Now teletypes are museum pieces.

They were swept aside by computers and satellites. Once, copy was received at 66 words a minute; now it arrives nearly instantaneously, flooding newsrooms with stories and pictures from the Associated Press, the *New York Times*, the *Washington Post*, the *Los Angeles Times* and other publications.

Wire editors decide what state, national and world news is used in the newspaper or online. They select and edit perhaps 25 to 30 stories each day so that those stories will give readers at least an adequate report of what is happening in their world. To accomplish this goal, a good wire editor must have wide knowledge, careful news judgment, an eye for typographical display and a skeptical attitude.

Knowledge lets the editor understand what is going on in the audience's state as well as the nation and world. Knowledge of history, politics and social change helps put the news in perspective. Skepticism helps keep the editor from being misled or even fooled by inaccurate or false information. Judgment lets the editor apply the knowledge to the stories at hand so that the information is clear, fair and reasonably complete. The typographical eye helps the editor envision how certain stories will look in print and online.

People who like to deal with national and international news often seek the wire editor's job. They relish the task of reading hundreds of stories each day, selecting the ones they consider most significant and trimming them to fit the available space. At small publications, wire editors may edit the news, write headlines for the stories and even report some local news or edit city copy. On midsize publications, they probably concentrate on the wire editing and headline writing. On somewhat bigger papers they only skim most of the wire stories and select the ones they want. Copy editors then edit the stories and write the heads.

On the largest metropolitan papers, the wire news may be divided, with the city editor or state editor getting the stories that originate close to home, and other copy going to foreign, business and national desks. Sports wires feed directly into the sports department. Copy streams into the newsrooms of the biggest papers from a half-dozen wire services.

The Associated Press

The Associated Press is the dominant wire service in the United States. Other services lack the breadth of coverage that AP provides. Technically a news cooperative, the AP covers events in the smallest towns and the biggest cities. It has full-time correspondents in most major cities, and in lesser places, at home and abroad, it has part-timers, called stringers, to file stories whenever events warrant. Additionally, as part of membership in the AP, its subscribers agree to provide content for use on the service. One of the tasks of editors in newsrooms is to send copies of stories that they think may interest the AP.

Supplemental Services

In addition to the Associated Press, many publications also subscribe to what are known as supplemental wire services. These services provide a depth of coverage that the AP's breadth typically cannot provide. The *New York Times* sells its own service to more than 600 American and Canadian papers. In addition to stories from the *Times*, its service also provides subscribers with reports from the *Arizona Republic*, the *San Francisco Chronicle*, *Los Angeles Daily News*, the *Boston Globe* and other news publications. It also provides photographs and informational graphics. The service provides editors around the country an early peek at what *Times* editors are putting on the front page—which influences story nationally.

Another service, the Washington Post-Los Angeles Times, provides articles from those publications as well as other partners. Knight Ridder/ Tribune provides the coverage of newspapers owned by Knight Ridder and Tribune Publishing, including the *Chicago Tribune*, the *San Jose Mercury News*, the *Philadelphia Inquirer* and the *Miami Herald*. Still other supplemental services offer publications the news reports of Newhouse newspapers, Scripps-Howard newspapers and McClatchy newspapers.

Feature Content

The wire services provide far more than straight news reports. They have feature staffs, picture services and a special wire for radio and television stations. The radio wire provides national and state news, and every hour a number of news items, taking about four minutes to read, are pieced together. With one minute of commercials, they make the five-minute newscast.

Editing the Wire at a Newspaper

Wire editors at daily newspapers arrive at work about eight hours before the first edition's deadline. They tap a few keys and up pops the news digest, which once was called the budget (and many editors still often call the digest the budget). The digest summarizes the major stories planned for that day. Editors skim these summaries to get a feel for the day's activities. Their thought processes go something like, "Hmmm, the hurricane story certainly is the hard news of the day. I'll keep an eye on the damage reports and see how bad it gets. That story about the Sept. 11 anniversary is certainly important—many people around here knew people who died. That could be the centerpiece. The story about bin Laden seems a little vague; I'll need to see what their sourcing is."

AP News Digest

Here is the top of the Associated Press news digest for newspapers publishing editions on Sept. 12, 2004. Note how each item contains a dateline, a short description of the story, the story's slug and the availability of art with the story.

AP News Digest

Sunday AMs

BULL BAY, Jamaica—Hurricane Ivan's monstrous waves and torrential rains smash homes, uproot trees, topple utility poles and kill at least two people in Jamaica, but a last-minute "wobble" spares the island the full force of the storm's 155-mph fury. The course change could be good news for hurricane-fatigued Floridians. Next in Ivan's path: the Cayman Islands and Cuba. BC-Hurricane Ivan. AP Photos HAV102, 109, XWA106, AP Graphics HURRICANE IVAN, IVAN PROJECTED PATH.

NEW YORK—Their voices breaking, parents and grandparents stand in pairs at ground zero and recite the names of the 2,749 people killed exactly three years ago at the World Trade Center, among them their own sons and daughters. "We'll never forget you because you're in our hearts forever," one father says, looking skyward. Others commemorate their loss at the Pentagon and in a field in Pennsylvania. BC-Sept 11 Anniversary. AP Photos.

BAGRAM, Afghanistan—A top American commander says al-Qaida chief Osama bin Laden and his No. 2 Ayman al-Zawahri are still pulling the strings in an increasingly violent Afghanistan three years after the Sept. 11 attacks. The general says the bin Laden trail is cold but insists that attacks like the recent suicide car bombing of a U.S. security firm in Kabul bear the al-Qaida hallmark. BC-Afghan-Al-Qaida. AP Photo KAB105.

CHICAGO—When Louis Zapata returned from Iraq, the toddler he had left 15 months earlier had matured into a talkative "little lady." His wife had learned to handle the bills and child-rearing on her own. His former co-workers had been promoted, while the license Zapata needed to return to his job in security had expired. For Zapata and other National Guardsmen activated since the Sept. 11 attacks, the return to civilian life has been much harder than they expected. BC-Soldiers-Coming Home. AP Photos CX301-CX303.

The digest may include a dozen items, and many editors will use nearly all the listed stories. In addition, the wire service will provide advisories every few hours, notifying editors about other stories that are in the works. With these digests and advisories, editors can get a quick summation of the day's news and plan which stories will get good display. They can get more specific details about the day's events by hitting a few more keys to glance at the first paragraph of all stories filed to date. The computer will sort the stories by categories—national, state, political— and can even be programmed to flag editors to stories that mention their communities. Printouts of these summaries can be made for easy reference or to show to other editors.

Next, wire editors choose lesser stories and send them to the news desk for design and headline assignment. Someone on the rim will edit the story and write the head. The slot editor will check the story and head and alert the page designer that the story is ready to go.

The most important stories are discussed in a late-afternoon news meeting, also attended by the news editor, picture editor, city editor, state editor and managing editor. The best stories in each department and the best pictures are described briefly. After some debate, the managing editor might say, "Do we agree that we should lead with the proposal for a new city tax? And put on Page 1 the Park Service story, the fire at the tire factory and the governor's plan to increase the state budget only 2 percent? Two pictures on the fire. If the hurricane story amounts to much, we will bump the Park Service piece."

The wire editor then works on the top 10 or 12 stories, cutting them a little if necessary and putting them into the news editor's queue. Those stories, with headlines assigned, go to the copy desk and then on to the press.

Smaller papers may have no news editor, and the editorial conference may consist of little more than a conversation among editors at their desks.

At the largest publications, the wire-editing duties may be split among a number of editors. For example, one might be responsible for editing the national news, another the foreign news and a third the state and regional news. Editors at news organizations that subscribe to a number of supplemental services need to be highly organized to deal with the sheer volume of copy that they must sort through while deciding what to use and how to use it.

Online Wire Editing

Immediacy is the power of online news publications. Editors working for news Web sites receive wires in the same way: The stories come by satellite and are sorted by categories; digests and advisories let them know what's coming. But after a story moves, an online wire editor can post it immediately; he doesn't have to wait until the presses roll again, five or six hours later. This immediacy requires that online wire editors stay constantly tuned in to what's going on by frequent scanning of the wires for updates, listening to the radio and monitoring television reports.

Because such stories are coming in constantly, the online wire editor needs to be organized and keep ahead of the pace. He also needs to understand his Web site's audience. What stories from the wires will interest readers? What stories should be discarded? Web sites keep statistics of what content is driving the most traffic, and editors can use that information in deciding the best material for online distribution. At the *San Jose Mercury News*, for example, the online editor particularly checks for wire reports from California and the Bay Area as he updates MercuryNews.com throughout the day.

How Services Operate

The AP divides its material into various categories. The A wire carries national stories other than those out of Washington. Stories out of Washington move on the W wire. The I category is for foreign stories. Regional wires have different labels, and they provide news of a state or region. One regional wire covers all of New England. Pennsylvania and Delaware make up another region. The F wire contains financial news and the S wire, sports.

The AP sends out significant breaking news under three priority categories: urgents, bulletins and flashes. Newsroom computers are programmed to alert editors to when stories under such categories arise. Urgent is the lowest of the categories and is used almost every day. Bulletins are reserved for larger news events, whereas flashes are reserved for stories that represent "a transcendent development," such as presidential assassination attempts. Years may go by without the use of a flash.

Some Wire Service Terminology

When a story moves on the Associated Press wire, it will be topped with a slugline that looks like this:

AM-Congress, Bjt, 350

The AM refers to the news cycle; in this example, it would be for morning publication. PM would be for afternoon newspapers, and BC for both cycles. Congress is the slug of the story, and should be the same as the slug used on the news digest. Bjt indicates to the editor that the story is one of those listed on the digest (or budget). The number refers to the length of the story in words.

If the AP needs to update the story during the day, it may move just a new beginning known as a top, telling editors to pick up the rest from the story that previously moved on the wire. It might look like this:

AM-Congress, Bjt, 1st Ld., a0325

This indicates that the story has a new lead; it also provides the number of the previous story that moved. Continued updates would be marked 2nd Ld, 3rd Ld and so forth. The service may move additional pieces of the story and designate them as 1st Add, 2nd Add and so forth.

Because transmission times are now instantaneous, new leads that pick up text from previous stories are rare. Instead, the AP moves complete new stories so that editors don't have to cut and paste. The service designates those stories this way:

AM-Congress, Bjt, 1st Ld-Writethru

The "writethru" indicates that the service has written through the previous story and this one is complete. Except on deadline, editors should wait for writethrus rather than piece together separate takes of stories.

A Busy Day at the Associated Press

Early in the morning of Sept. 25, 2004, Hurricane Jeanne was bearing down on the Atlantic Coast of Florida. It was the fourth hurricane to hit the Sunshine State in six weeks, keeping reporters and editors at the Associated Press busy keeping its clients updated.

The first story of the news cycle moved at about 2:50 a.m., with the following lead:

BC-Hurricane Jeanne-Florida,Bjt,0924

Hurricane Jeanne forces more than 800,000 in Florida to evacuate

Eds: At 2 a.m. EDT, Jeanne was near latitude 26.5 north, longitude 75.6 west. Next advisory at 5 a.m.

With BC-Hurricane Rumors

AP Photos NYET250, FLROC105, FLPE103-104

By Jill Barton

ASSOCIATED PRESS

FORT PIERCE, Fla. — Hurricane Jeanne forced the evacuations of more than 800,000 residents Saturday as it bore down on Florida with winds near 105 mph and threatened to strengthen into a major storm.

As the storm moved closer to shore, the AP continued to file updates about the evacuations and preparations for the storm's onslaught. It went through more than 20 writethrus through the course of the night, until the hurricane finally made landfall just after midnight on Sept. 26. At that point, the AP moved the following news alert:

BC-APNewsAlert,0031

STUART, Fla. — Forecasters at the National Hurricane Center in Miami say Jeanne has officially made landfall near Stuart with 120-mph winds.

The wire service continued to update its main story as more information became available. The last story of the cycle was the 25th Lead-Writethru, which looked like this:

BC-Hurricane Jeanne-Florida, 25th Ld-Writethru,1277

Jeanne hits Florida with 120 mph winds; up to 2 million urged to get out
Eds: UPDATES throughout with latest position, wind speed, detail; should stand for AMs. At 1 a.m. EDT Sunday, Jeanne was centered near latitude 27.2 north, longtitude 80.4 west.

AP Photos FLDA105, FLPAP111, NY113

AP Graphic HURRICANE JEANNE

By Deborah Hastings

ASSOCIATED PRESS

STUART, Fla. — Hurricane Jeanne sent wind and huge waves crashing ashore as it slammed into storm-weary Florida late Saturday, forcing thousands into shelters and tearing part of the roof from a hospital. The storm made landfall three weeks after Frances ravaged the same stretch of the state's central Atlantic coast, and hurled debris only recently cleared from earlier hurricanes.

Special services

In addition to news stories, the wire services offer a variety of material. They provide columnists who deal in humor, foreign affairs, business, Hollywood, TV, finance, agriculture and religion. The services also have departments that provide detailed timely and timeless features. Both services file advance stories, many for use in Sunday publications. These often are filed several weeks in advance of the publication date. Sunday feature stories are in particular demand because most Sunday newspapers are bulky, yet little news is made on weekends. By getting such stories early, editors can prepare during slack periods and "close" some pages a few days early.

Combining Stories

The AP gathers news at its domestic bureaus, and AP stories with national interest are sent to New York headquarters for further editing. Regional stories are handled within their areas; New York doesn't see them. Stories from abroad come directly to New York and then are sent to subscribers across the country.

Sometimes editors combine reports from different wire services. They might lead with the first two paragraphs from the *New York Times*, for example, and then insert a couple from AP and close with a half-dozen from the *Washington Post*. The job requires a little transitional writing to make sure that the language moves smoothly and essential information has not been left out. When compiling or interweaving wire stories, the editor should be sure to give proper credit to the various services used.

Some editing systems allow editors to work on two stories on the same screen, making it easier for editors to blend a few paragraphs from each to make a thorough story. In some instances the editor can insert parenthetically a fact gleaned from another service. If the main story is from AP, it may be strengthened with a paragraph from another source: "(The *Boston Globe* reported, meanwhile, that the president had decided to stay two more days in Hawaii.)"

Occasionally, the dateline of a story will change. If a major unexpected event occurs in Lynn, Mass., the first news may be filed from Boston. An hour or so later reporters may have firsthand reports in Lynn and can dateline stories from there.

Sometimes a wire service discovers that it has made a serious error, one that would cause embarrassment or possibly produce a libel suit against the service and all papers using the offending story. In that case a bulletin kill is sent to its members, advising editors to kill a story or part of one. If the errant story should have happened to get into a few papers, the fact that the service filed a bulletin kill might reduce damages in any libel suit. Introduction of the bulletin kill as evidence in court would indicate that the service made a serious and speedy effort to correct the error.

As mentioned in an earlier chapter, all editors want to watch for ways to localize stories. The wire editor, in particular, should remain alert for ways that the reader can say unconsciously, "Ah, here's a story close to home." Such stories get read much better than ones that seem to have no direct interest to readers. In January 2004, the Associated Press moved a story that started as follows:

After years of marketing itself as "America's No. 1 Wired City," Tacoma has earned itself a new, more dubious distinction: "America's Most Stressed-Out City."

In a survey based on divorces, suicides and other factors, the industrialized port city of 195,000 people topped the list, followed by Miami, then New Orleans, Las Vegas, New York City and Portland.

The *San Jose Mercury News* recast the story to emphasize the California angles:

Tacoma is the nation's most stressed-out big city, says the BestPlaces Web site, based on divorces, suicide rates and other factors. It was followed by Miami, New Orleans, Las Vegas, New York City and Portland, Ore. Stockton-Lodi ranked eighth, the only California metropolitan area among the Top 10. San Jose was No. 56.

Tying for least stressful were Albany-Schenectady-Troy in New York and Harrisburg-Lebanon-Carlisle in Pennsylvania. Orange County, Calif., was the third least-stressful region.

Criticism of Wire Services

The flaws of the wire services might well be the flaws of journalism generally. Editors often cling to stereotypes, demanding a stream of stories that report conflict, oddities and speculation. Many of these stories are read today and forgotten tonight. Nationalism has been reduced, but once AP's general manager had to warn the staff to report international conflict fairly, without cheering for one side or the other. Still, nationalism does creep in.

Similar reflex reporting can creep into copy when handling stories about countries with different forms of government. Ideologies are rarely simple, and reporters should avoid giving them simple labels, such as pro-American or pro-Chinese. It probably is fair, however, to describe a country's position *on a certain issue* as pro-American. Perhaps it would be more helpful for the reader if reporters abroad did not scurry about with some kind of invisible measuring device to see whether another country's policies are favorable to the United States. A report on *what* happened and *why* it happened would be better. Wire editors would be advised to sniff copy carefully for nationalistic bias and eliminate it.

The wire services, in common with the better newspapers, also have moved to eliminate any hint of payoffs to reporters. Free lunches, a packet of free football tickets and free trips once were common. Now the wire services accept free entry to a game or a theater to cover a legitimate event, but all other "freebies" are banned.

The wire services are not totally to blame when significant information does not reach readers. Wire service writers and editors know that sometimes their best stories remain in the computer, never seeing publication. One enterprising AP bureau did a thorough job of finding that almost a quarter of the property in the state was not assessed or was grossly underassessed for tax purposes. Many papers in that state ran the stories but several others did not. And few followed the state information with careful evaluation of tax assessments in their own communities. Fortunately, wire service staffers contend that an increasing number of papers print the best wire service copy. This stimulates the staffers, for they know that millions of people have access to their stories.

Guidelines for Wire Editors

Individual wire editors must struggle to give readers full, accurate and important news within space limitations. They may accomplish this by careful use of wire stories. They may persuade the publisher to buy a supplemental service. They should broaden their own knowledge by spending an hour a day reading other news publications. This reading will help them test their own news judgment. Editors in the East should read the *New York Times*, the *Wall Street Journal*, *Washington Post* and the *Christian Science Monitor*. In the Midwest they should read at least a couple of Eastern papers, plus Chicago publications and the *St. Louis Post-Dispatch*. In the South they should check the *St. Petersburg Times*, the *Miami Herald*, and the *Atlanta Journal-Constitution*. In the West they should examine the *Los Angeles Times*, the *Denver Post* and the *Dallas Morning News*.

In addition, good wire editors need to cultivate these qualities:

1. **Knowledge.** They keep up in the social sciences, particularly the history of the world during the last 50 years.
2. **Wariness.** They are cautious in handling fad stories, such as child abuse, juvenile crime or high school dropouts. They remain skeptical of unsubstantiated reports, stories based on unnamed sources and tales of medical "cures." Planted stories, trial balloons, "media events" and calculated leaks should trigger sham-detectors.
3. **Awareness of goals.** Their picture of needed coverage should encompass tomorrow's world as well as today's.
4. **Alertness.** Wire editors spot the news that will attain maximum readership in their areas.
5. **Organization.** Stories need careful placement in the news pages, rather than being dropped helter-skelter into any hole that fits. Related stories should be kept together.
6. **Balance.** Editors should mix major and minor stories effectively and be able to leaven the basic seriousness of the publication with humorous items.

An editor who successfully does all these things will present the information that the public needs to function as citizens in a democratic society.

CHAPTER 11

Imagination in News Editing

One news publication appears tired, listless, routine; another impresses its readers as being fresh, dynamic and challenging. The difference often is imagination. An editorial team, given the freedom to use its creative powers, can generate new and improved publications in the same way as other professionals discover new methods to save hearts or make homes more livable.

Imagination is needed in many details of headlines, story structures and display. But imagination is involved in three major aspects of a news operation: excellence of product, the progress and reform of the community and the people's right to know.

Imagination and Excellence

Too often, excellence is thought of merely in terms of preserving and imitating what is good. American editors never tire of asserting, somewhat chauvinistically, that they produce the best news publications in the world. It may seem to them logical that all they have to do is keep doing the job they've been doing. The challenge, however, should be to make their news operations each year at least slightly better than they were the year before.

True, if there is a better newspaper in a community down the freeway or in a city a thousand miles away, the editor can copy its superior features and, using imagination, learn and adapt from other editors. But the real challenge of editing is to create and test new journalistic concepts and forms.

Imaginative editing, by definition, can't be frozen into a textbook of rules, for it is impossible to anticipate the freshness and creativity that working editors must discover in themselves. Still, some hints can be given for applying editorial imagination to problems of modern coverage and the use of specialized writers, editors and critics.

Creative thinking

The key to creative journalism is the editor's ability to generate imaginative story assignments. It is easy to assign a reporter to cover a city council meeting, a school bond referendum or an explosion at the grain elevator. Editors can sharpen imagination in assignments by constantly asking as they read, hear and see, "Is there a story in this for our readers?" In most cases there is not. But perhaps once in 20 or 30 times there is. Articles from magazines offer information and insights about problems of general interest, and creative editors always should consider how these articles could apply at home.

The big-circulation magazines such as *Esquire* and the *New Yorker* include solid reporting. The smaller magazines, however, are better sources of insight about trends in social change. Scholarly magazines, too, are filled with articles that may seem dry but sometimes contain fresh and even startling ideas. News assignments on politics, foreign policy, economics, sociology and other topics spring from these articles to an alert editor's mind.

The same potential lies in current books. An editor need not read them completely to get practical ideas. First chapters, for example, often can be skipped or skimmed. Tables of contents usually give clues to important chapters, allowing an editor to pick and choose the material and thereby digest some books in an hour or two. Obviously, some volumes deserve careful attention, and a good editor identifies them quickly and gives them extra time.

Creative assignments

Having found an idea for a story, editors must ask themselves where the staff can obtain necessary information. Will a state official have a few facts? Will someone in city hall be able to add a few details? Is there an expert in the community who could supply more information? Could that expert direct a reporter to other sources? Is there someone who knows the practical difficulties? Do staff reporters have clues about where to find information?

After editors clarify ideas on how to get the facts, they should make assignments to the reporter in detail. A mere "Get a little story on the pollution of Hickory Creek" produces "a little story" with few facts. That article will bounce off the reader, and the next day, concern for Hickory Creek's foul condition will evaporate. Rather, the reporter and editor should discuss the idea in detail so that there is no doubt that a thorough story is desired and that certain sources probably are most promising.

It is important, too, that the editor assign the story to a reporter who is interested in the subject. A writer who is unconcerned about an issue—and unable to get concerned—will do a poor job and may even consciously or unconsciously sabotage the idea. But the editor should not expect a reporter to signal an interest. Sometimes the quiet person sitting in the corner is itching to dig into a serious and important subject.

Creative encouragement

In the best newsrooms, ideas for stories will come from reporters. After all, they're closest to the communities they cover. Some city desks have a suggestion box into which reporters, photographers and copy editors can drop notes proposing stories. This source will dry up in a hurry if the editor ignores the suggestions. When editors use a tip, they should thank the donor; when the tip can't be used, the editor should explain why. Some papers can even give a small bonus for an unusually good idea.

A word of praise for a professional piece of reporting also helps. So does posting a good story on the newsroom bulletin board. Mention of outstanding work in a staff publication stimulates more exceptional reporting, and so does a monetary bonus.

If editors take stories as they come, never suggesting changes or seeking more information, reporters' imaginations wilt. If editors lack enthusiasm, if they are as unconcerned about the discovery of a step toward a cancer cure as about the Cub Scout cookout, they drive away good reporters and encourage the mediocre.

Insightful Coverage

Good news organizations today offer detailed coverage. The superior ones of the future will search for significance with even more imagination and care. They will seek to discover trends, strive for insight into complex issues and explore ways to relate their findings to reader concern and coverage interest. Consequently, leading editors will turn more and more to subjects that have not been covered and are not easily accessible. Recognizing the difference between imagination and imitation, they will resist following fads. Few editors today are so perceptive. They think they are being imaginative when they run stories about a current social problem that has seized the general attention of the moment. Such subjects come and go, like clothing fashions, and then fade into the background. A few years later they may take center stage again. Better editors go after subjects not because everyone else does but because of their own thoughtful judgment.

Television critics some years ago chastised network documentaries for dealing only with obvious issues, such as race relations, troubles with the space program and the size of the federal bureaucracy. The same criticism could have been made against some news publications, for they often worked and reworked popular subjects. It's easy, of course, to think of stories on the national debt, the incidence of cancer and the plight of farmers.

But more recently, journalists have delved into more unexpected issues: nutrition, health care, education and the environment.

Journalists have become more aware that society changes, producing almost imperceptible changes in attitudes and activities. For example, over several years high salaries in business and finance motivated thousands of young people to prepare for business careers. Students often gave salary as their top consideration when choosing an occupation. This development continued for several years before journalists paid attention. Such trends and value changes should be picked up earlier and their effects evaluated.

Journalists are not the only ones to neglect changes and trends until they explode into spot news. Academic specialists as well sometimes fail to grasp what is happening under their noses, and often political leaders badly misread public moods and attitudes. Because of humankind's insensitivity to change, many problems are full-blown before they are recognized. To some extent this is inevitable. People seem almost incapable of paying attention to minor problems. Only when they become gigantic—and almost impossible to solve—are they tackled. Even then, it is tempting simply to reduce those problems rather than eliminate them.

Examples are everywhere. Air pollution was dismissed as an irritant until it killed many people. Nothing serious was done about water pollution until at least one of the Great Lakes became a cesspool. Mental health is little more than an unmentionable subject in a family until nearly every member realizes that one of them is in torment. Even when the ills of society are obvious, many people ignore them, apparently assuming that they will go away.

Fusing interest and importance

It is difficult under these circumstances for editors to publish the news readers need if they are to act as responsible citizens. Criticize editors for not using much of anything about Central Africa or South America, and they may reply sadly: "We printed stories about Africa, and a readership survey showed that only 6 percent paid any attention. The same thing happened to our South American articles. We can't fill up the paper with stories that only 6 percent will read."

Though the argument sounds irrefutable, there is a flaw in it. The editors are right in implying the news organization must publish what most readers want if it is to survive. But they are wrong in suggesting that everyone has to be interested in everything in the paper. Most items must appeal to large groups of readers, but this principle leaves room for some material that will be read by a minority, even a small one. Of the solid, important story, the editor should say, "The public needs to know this even though many readers will not read it. So I am going to print it. If the majority of readers skip it, they will still find plenty of other items to interest them."

The editor has to keep in mind why people read newspaper stories. Wilbur Schramm, the communications researcher, argues that people read because they expect a reward. They find information satisfying even when it may be "bad news" because it provides a negative reward. College students avidly—and perhaps angrily—read about a tuition increase. Motorists read with satisfaction about the elimination of a dangerous stretch of highway, but they also read with concern about the closing of a shortcut. Young people read about the perils of AIDS. Older people carefully follow the obituaries. Probably none of these readers, however, will pay much attention to an election in Uruguay or a disease in Tanzania. Such subjects are too remote from their own concerns.

The task of the editor is to attempt to link these socially and politically important subjects to the legitimate interests and concerns of readers so that they anticipate and find some reward. This is not easy. The editor, working with the reporter, photographer, designer and artist, must plan with care and imagination, striving for a compelling blend of text and art. In some ways, the task is easier today than several decades ago. More readers have attended college; more have traveled, read and broadened their awareness through television news reports and the Internet and documentaries. Also the political and economic involvement of the United States with the world has created a new global awareness.

It is easy, however, to exaggerate the increase of interest in peripheral subjects. College does not always educate. Almost everyone knows college graduates who are narrow, ignorant and scornful of intellect. Many who have traveled extensively are less enlightened about foreign culture than the faithful reader of *National Geographic*. So the alert editor must search for relevance, attempting to make the readers, through their self-interest, aware and concerned.

Presenting news imaginatively

Good reporting must be supported by imaginative presentation. To write a story and slap on a two-column head is not enough. Major pieces deserve major treatment. They require striking art, and they must jolt the reader's interest by presenting the drama of the facts.

Ideas for good visual presentation can be obtained from newspapers that consistently do a good job of combining words and art. Some Sunday magazines published by newspapers manage this effectively. Their small format helps, for if two facing pages offer type and artwork, the reader's eyes will have no distractions from the spread. Editors who actively examine their designs will discover ideas for exceptional visual presentations that can be adapted to the needs and character of their own paper.

Interpretative pieces need not be lengthy. It has become fashionable to run "The Depth Story," in which a reporter writes at length about every facet of one problem in a single report. By itself, the report may be outstanding. But an editor should worry that well-intentioned readers may become overwhelmed and put it aside, saying, "I'll have to read that when I get time." Others may go through the whole thing but forget the single impact after a few days. Because memory must be refreshed, continuing problems need big, medium and small stories every week or so.

This kind of presentation is not cheap. It may take capable, well-paid reporters, photographers and artists weeks or even months to do a short series. This sometimes means spending thousands of dollars, which only the wealthiest news organizations can afford. But smaller publications can do excellent work a little less elaborately. The pictures can be good, if not superb. The writing can be colorful and thorough. The material can be put together in an attractive way.

All this takes additional time and money, but it is worth it if the reader lingers with the paper or on the Web site. It may even be financially profitable in the long run. Advertisers should prefer a publication on which people spend an extended time to one that is skimmed and tossed aside.

Trends to Specialization

The specialized editor has come into prominence since World War II. Specialization probably will continue and spread beyond reporting. Some newsrooms, such as the *Oregonian* in Portland, are organized into topical teams. Such teams can include not only specialized reporters and assignment editors but also copy editors and photographers.

The generalist

Though specialization is the trend, the generalist remains immensely valuable. Copy editors who can do a good job of editing copy about an uprising in Bucharest because they are fairly well-informed about Eastern Europe and who also can handle a story about heartburn because of considerable knowledge about medicine are good to have around. Besides, some specialists get into the bad habit of writing only for other specialists. They gradually take on the jargon of the specialty and sometimes become part of the specialty's establishment. Well-informed generalists can help the newsroom minimize such dangers of overspecialization.

A generalist, even a new reporter, may be able to spot a story that the expert overlooked because the expert was too close to the scene.

A cityside reporter, for example, may examine with fresh eyes what many see as excesses in college football and basketball programs. Someone who normally does not write about education may look into teacher training or whether university administrations keep growing while faculty and the student body do not. The specialists may not only be too close to the subject but also depend too much on the opinions of their regular sources.

Imaginative coverage of trends, however, usually requires specialists. Expert coverage has been long established in three journalistic fields: politics, sports and business. For decades no editor would have dreamed of sending a football writer to cover the stock market or a police reporter to cover the World Series. It is perhaps some kind of wry commentary on American culture that experts were ordinarily demanded only in these three areas. More and more, however, the educational level of our culture demands expertise in science, health, labor, religion, education and the arts.

The Critical Function

To many, critical writing about music, drama and other arts is simply a form of news coverage. Some critics, however, see their work as another art, as comment upon a presentation that will guide ticket-buyers and help shape taste. But whether it is art or news, criticism is something that the imaginative editor has to ponder how to improve—or inaugurate.

Except those in the smaller cities, news publications are doing a reasonably good job of covering the arts. Bigger news organizations have full- or part-time critics for film, music, art, dance and even architecture. Medium-sized papers, in recent years, have used staffers who can judge the arts capably or hired specialists on a free-lance basis.

The culture boom

"Culture" no longer is limited to big cities. Touring theater groups and orchestras come to cities of 150,000 people. Cities smaller than that have their own orchestras. Little theater groups are everywhere. Colleges and even high schools turn out quite good theater. Museums have sprouted in hundreds of cities and many are excellent. In any city of 50,000 or even fewer, one person could be kept busy most of the time covering cultural events, and even if the reviews are only moderately good, the growing number of educated readers will find the local newspaper more vital because of the coverage.

This observation especially pertains to motion pictures. If attendance is a criterion, the movie houses are the local institutions most deserving critical coverage. Traditionally, smaller newspapers have printed puffs about movies in return for ads and perhaps "comp" tickets. The system is unfortunate, for the paper gives away valuable space and the film business encounters a generation of people who don't believe what they read about the pictures. It appears that there is a trend toward better cinema criticism in small and middle-sized as well as large communities. Although honest and objective reviews may cause some turkeys to lose money, they may contribute to the success of good films. Sound criticism in news publications around the country might improve the motion picture industry.

Newspapers and news Web sites hold the same potential for criticizing television, though syndicated criticism makes it more difficult for the local TV critic to contribute properly. Some viewers, however, want to know what others thought, just as they do when they bring the subject up at the coffee break the next morning. Some spot criticism of bigger shows would be appropriate, just as some local editorializing on global issues is. Where local television shows do something out of the ordinary in documentaries or entertainment, the local news publication ought to take critical note, for other media will. Probably the greater opportunity for TV criticism in most cities, however, is to criticize, from a local perspective, what networks, producers or certain shows are attempting to do over time.

Progress and Reform

Imagination should be used both in reforming news organizations and in reforming the community. Traditionally, the good journalist has served as messenger, watchdog and crusader. As editorial emphasis moves from deadpan objectivity to depth reporting, it also advances leadership and guidance. What values are behind interpretative articles? What standards and goals are being suggested by the very fact of their appearance? The imaginative editor goes beyond the search for internal excellence to visualize, plan and help build a better community.

Challenging power

Crusades seem to have gone out of fashion. It is true that many news organizations, fat and complacent, don't make waves. But the fact remains, as the annual Pulitzer Prize and other awards testify, that some newspapers still campaign for progress and reform.

Crusading often means bucking the powerful people in the community. Wealth means power, and more often than not political leadership is tied to that power. The newspaper publisher and the chief managers are probably close to the Establishment of the community—meeting on committees with them, golfing, dining and drinking with them. It is not easy for a paper to break with and confront this aggregation of power, which provides much of the paper's own economic energy. Picking at the petty politicians may not be difficult, and may even be a pleasant sort of sport, but hitting at the real political, social and economic power of the city takes more nerve.

A few observers, however, contend that journalists form a power bloc themselves. Journalists associate with bureaucrats, professors, other professionals and other journalists. They rarely spend much time with high corporate executives, military officers, labor leaders or police officers. The assumption is that journalists deal with people of new power, not the old, monied interests whose power once manipulated city councils, state legislatures, congresses and even presidents.

Surely, some of the old power is gone, but it seems unlikely that much power has been spread to the professional classes. Now power comes from new money—money gained by inheritance, investments and shrewd deals. It is new money that finances lobbying, political fund drives and influence. Reporters, copy editors, editors, librarians, doctors, most lawyers and professors simply are not in the same league. Editors, journalism educators and journalism students should investigate and debate where power lies, watch for its misuse, seek progress and reform and crusade where necessary.

Editors must realize that there are altruistic people who work hard for changes that offer them no financial rewards. They toil only for what they consider will make a better world. Among these people are those who work for preservation of green space, recreation, family planning, safer highways, improved education, political reform and dozens of other worthy goals—and even some goals the editor may consider mistaken. These people also make news—news of progress. One satisfaction of journalism is observing up close a spectrum of the human race, from scoundrel to saint. The editor should not assume, despite confirming evidence on certain days, that everyone is a scoundrel. Imaginative editing includes also the search for good news of change.

Campaigning against prejudice

Impressions, not necessarily accurate ones, are picked up by people from their news reports. These impressions are the result of hasty reading, poor memories and habits of noting only what bolsters their prejudices. A good news publication should challenge such impressions by printing, from time to time, the cold facts of a situation. For example, every year or so it may be necessary to recap the concrete actions concerning school integration in a community or state. Not everyone will read such facts, of course, but some will, and perhaps by steady effort the myths, half-truths and incorrect assumptions can be given a needed burial.

Political figures and others who frequently make public pronouncements often only repeat what is common prejudice. In some instances prejudices are studiously promoted by certain people or groups, and the newspaper must report the correct information. A sizable proportion of the public, for example, has accepted the idea that everyone on welfare is a loafer. It is commonly said that women on welfare have babies so that they can get more money. The editor should check these common impressions. How much more does a woman on welfare get if she has another child? How much does a welfare family get? If a person on welfare got a job for one day, would the income be deducted from the welfare check—and thereby discourage looking for part-time work? The truth would make a story.

Or what about the impression that most college football players major in physical education? Why not a story examining the facts?

Dozens of other illustrations could be cited. Although these are examples of national impressions, in most towns at least a few local misconceptions are bandied about without correction. Good editors will do their best to get at the truth, even though they may suspect that most subscribers would rather read editorials and stories that reinforce their incorrect impressions.

It helps also to consider whether a person making a proposal has a concealed ax to grind. This does not mean that editors must always suspect evil motives. But they should be skeptical. A senator once introduced legislation that would forbid imports of foreign firearms. This sounded like good news to those who supported gun control, but there was a joker in the proposal: The senator came from the state that produced most of the nation's firearms. A ban on foreign weapons presumably would endear him to home industry and the home work force.

Covering varied viewpoints

Complex issues have more than just pro and con sides. There are various angles that a news operation has an obligation to cover in both news and editorial pages. A major criticism of newspapers is that they present a narrow range of opinion. As presidential candidates and voters tend to cluster to the middle of the road on issues, so do newspapers. There have always been a number of right-wing columnists, from William Buckley to George Will, but columnists much to the left of center have been used sparingly. A major challenge to imaginative editors today remains that of finding and developing columnists who can go beyond regurgitating the conventional wisdom and present fresh and stimulating ideas and viewpoints. They may infuriate hidebound readers, but even optimists agree that the country's survival requires creative thought that will jog us out of ruts. Many news organizations have found exceptional columnists of various races and ethnicities who do not limit themselves to comment on difficulties facing those groups.

Imaginative editors also could turn up local writers who would present strong viewpoints. That happens, but, in a quite human way, editors too often print or reprint "a terrific piece" that is terrific only because it endorses their views. Alert editors should also go after articles from the sociologist who wants a much more basic attack on ghetto problems, the minister who opposes (or endorses) a war and the teachers' union president who feels a strike may be necessary next fall.

Some dissenting comments will automatically come in as letters to the editor. Editors should take particular care to print those which intelligently present views different from their own. Some editors try to print at least the nub of argument in every letter received. Others pride themselves—wrongly—in throwing away those from their opponents. Every publication receives a certain percentage of "nut letters" that deserve little space, but nothing angers the readership more than knowing that they have no chance of seeing their arguments published.

The Right to Know

In their running battle with government, journalists for some time have emphasized the people's "right to know." Embedded in constitutional law is the idea that citizens must be fully informed to participate intelligently in government. Publishers and top editors like to boast how carefully they watch government, but the facts don't bear them out. Reporters dutifully show up at press conferences, ask some obvious questions, and run to their computers to report what the official said. Bob Woodward and Carl Bernstein, the chief journalistic probers of Watergate, have called such reporters "sophisticated stenographers." Some editors deserve the title of "sophisticated chief stenographer," for they print only what the powerful utter. Some readers understandably are curious why, for example, reporters hang on every presidential word but can't seem to walk two blocks to cover a hearing on why insurance rates differ so greatly. Instead of nit-picking with critics, good journalists should listen to the criticism and correct their own flaws. Editors even could hope that more readers would demand better journalism. Their demands might make it easier to get a better budget, hire more and better staffers and put out an improved publication.

The reader's needs

In some ways the flaws of news organizations are the flaws of the modern university. Students pick courses in history, political science, economics and literature. Unless they are unusually sharp, they may not see how economics affects politics and how history affects literature. Some educators and some students would like to figure out how to mesh these subjects.

News publications provide a similar smorgasbord. There are stories about politics, economics, social movements, education and the environment, but there is little effort to correlate them. Editors, if they think of it at all, apparently assume that the reader will put all these subjects into some loose order. It is quite an assumption, for most of the nation's editorial pages reveal that editors themselves are not gifted in catching the ties among all the subjects they cover.

Many editors are, of course, concerned about this fragmentation and try to relate one piece of news to another, so perhaps it is a safe prediction that more and more newsrooms will try to help audiences understand the relationships of events that pass before them. Today, we are limited to grouping of associated news events, an occasional news analysis and a boldface insert directing the news reader to check an editorial on the subject. Good as this is, it is not good enough. Part of the solution may be in the blend of the visual and the written word.

How can the editor meet the demands of the better-educated and more skeptical reader? Many press observers think that modern editors should function with these goals in mind:

1. To discover what the readers want to know and to sense what they need to know. The need can be met, in part, by careful reading, listening to intelligent critics and diligently observing the community.
2. To keep alert to developing events, even though those events may not be worth a story for several days or weeks.
3. To report government and education in the community with thoroughness and care.
4. To explain how the reader can make a successful living, which would include money, job satisfaction and the simple pleasures of life.
5. To assist consumers so that they avoid buying, for example, shoddy merchandise and poor quality food.
6. To report the truth on economic conditions.
7. To examine events to see whether the traditions of news reporting should be altered to reflect changes in society and in the reading public's needs.
8. To be alert to assaults on human liberty and to educate the public about democratic principles.
9. To be as fair and honest as possible, for a newspaper's most precious asset is credibility.

The reader's nature

Perhaps the ideal editor would be one who is pushing constantly to get readers to attend to the serious events and trends of their time. Without such an editor, the newspaper is little more than an entertainment sheet. The job of prodding and luring the reader requires subtlety and patience. A reader will not get interested in Africa or even air pollution by reading one story. William Rockhill Nelson, founder of the *Kansas City Star*, talked about the need for patience by citing his paper's campaign for a new bridge across the Missouri River. For years, he said, his paper ran news stories, feature stories, editorials, pictures and cartoons about how the bridge was needed, how it would be needed even more in the future and how commerce would be assisted with a new bridge. The effort paid off. The bridge was built, but only after an editorial campaign that lasted 10 years.

Such hammering at the public consciousness must be done if citizens are to grasp the significance of what is all around them. To accomplish this hammering, without boring or irritating the reader, requires imagination. The editor must be able to present this information in dozens of different ways and, in most instances, ways in which the reader thinks offer a reward.

Stories that result from investigation should not be pelted at the reader. A story today may be followed up in a couple of weeks. An editorial or a cartoon could be run from time to time. More ideas might be produced. Is there a conservation group? What does it propose? What is being suggested in other areas? Would those suggestions apply here? These local stories can be reinforced with national stories about water pollution. In so selecting and highlighting vital issues, the editor meets the readers' needs.

CHAPTER 12

When News Breaks

To many outsiders, the word "newsroom" evokes an image of excited people bellowing at each other, telephones ringing like fire alarms and newsroom assistants frantically darting from desk to desk. This picture may be great for dramatic presentations, but it would be a horrible way to produce the news. If such turmoil were routine, the news would never get out at all, let alone on time, and the staff would be ready for strait-jackets in less than a month.

Newsrooms may not be as serene as libraries, but the noise level is almost always low and people seldom shout. Most sounds come from the barely audible clicking of computer keys. Staffs go methodically about getting the news ready for publication. It's a task that requires organization and orderliness.

On smaller newspapers the task is simpler because they put out just one edition. Because most papers of less than 30,000 circulation put out only one edition a day, they avoid the emergencies of edition changes. Even so, the staffs of smaller papers are usually kept busy by the problems of a normal news day. In an emergency, they have trouble handling all the extra work. Bigger papers usually can take care of crises more easily because they have a large enough staff to cope with late-breaking stories. Online news operations' ability to adjust to breaking news depends on their size, which can vary from having a single editor to a dozen or more reporters, editors and producers. The key is flexibility: Editors willing and ready to quickly alter course cope better than those who stubbornly want to stay on an earlier agreed-upon path.

Various emergencies can disrupt news production. The press may break down, illness might keep three or four key people home, or heavy storms might knock out telephone and power lines. In such times staffers may work by candlelight and hope that their cell phones still work. The paper may have to be printed somewhere else. A Web server may be unreachable. Such emergencies are highly unusual. The more routine "emergencies" come from unexpected news.

If the news is spectacular, dozens of reporters and editors may drop what they're doing to concentrate on the story. Some reporters handle the main part of the story while others get sidebar material. The editors get stories online as quickly as possible and remake the newspaper's front page, directing reporters and photographers at the same time. If the news breaks shortly before deadline, the reporters and editors will be able to provide only sketchy details no matter how quickly they act.

If the news is catastrophic, such as the events of Sept. 11, 2001, the entire newsroom will drop what it's doing. At the *San Jose Mercury News*, for example, editors who usually work at night reported to work early in the morning to prepare an extra edition and to keep MercuryNews.com updated. Other reporters and editors came in early or on their days off to contribute to the effort. The newspaper increased the news hole both that day and for days later to cover the most important story in decades. The newsroom buzzed all day in a unified effort to give readers a comprehensive package about what had happened and why. (See Figure 12.1.)

Fortunately, there are few such crises. Lesser emergencies, however, are frequent. For example, a major decision by the Supreme Court handed down minutes before deadline suddenly becomes the lead story of the day. Or the governor may take an unexpected step involving the city, and the staff must hustle to report the effects. Editors must adjust quickly. One way they adjust is to expect the unexpected. Each day first-rate editors ask themselves the question that they keep in the back of their heads: "What am I going to do if a big story breaks today?" By knowing the alternatives, they can come up quickly with emergency plans.

Preparation and Routines

The well-ordered newsroom is, of course, prepared for all kinds of unexpected news. It has a good library and online archive, for one thing, where stories and pictures of past events are quickly found. Reference books are readily available. One or two reporters can gather new material while editors juggle the story mix.

Some newsrooms have material prepared in advance for a news break involving prominent persons. Using background supplied by wire services, a staff working in slack periods can prepare obituary material and pictures on famous persons who are ill or aged.

To newcomers, writing an obituary before the death may seem ghoulish. Nevertheless, it enables a newsroom to cover fully and swiftly the death of someone famous without straining the staff. News publications had for years prepared for the death of President Reagan so that when he did die, they were already well ahead of the story. But newsrooms must also be careful not to accidentally release pre-written obituaries. The Associated Press accidentally released an obituary of Bob Hope several years before the actor-comedian died.

Figure 12.1.
The front page of the *San Jose Mercury News* on Sept. 12, 2001, was a culmination of a intensive, unified effort of the entire newsroom. (Figure copyright 2001, *San Jose Mercury News*. Used with permission.)

In a crisis, staffers should not get so excited that they make the news melodramatic. Editors should take pains to double-check their news judgment. The managing editor or news editor might even warn the staff to be certain of the accuracy of information gathered hastily from people whose judgment and powers of observation may be impaired in the excitement.

Editors should consider all the angles that need covering. Should the police be checked? Will comment from the mayor be appropriate or irrelevant? Should the governor be called? Are reporters available to cover not only the main event but also the subsidiary news? While decisions are made on coverage, at least one newspaper editor will have to decide what stories to change on Page 1, and even how to alter inside pages.

A newspaper's front page almost always has something expendable: a routine picture, an entertaining but insignificant feature story, a news story that had barely made the front page in the first place. One or all of these pieces could go, or each story could be cut. Even two or three good but lengthy stories may be reduced to accommodate the late news. The news editor can plot a fresh design as soon as it is clear what stories are being written. A truly big event displaces the lead story, and space may have to be opened for two or three sidebars.

Everyone's productivity picks up astonishingly at these times. The excitement apparently pumps the adrenalin needed for reporters to write more swiftly and editors to handle copy at double speed. Everyone relishes the chance to get at least moderately excited, and the experience undoubtedly is a main attraction of journalism.

Updating the Newspaper on Deadline

In most lesser crises, one reporter quickly writes the story. A single editor edits the story, writes a headline and posts the story online. Another editor will juggle something on Page 1 to quickly get a new front page to the press. The change is almost routine.

Because late press starts cost publishers money, editors rarely hold the press for late news. Instead, an early version of a story will be placed on a page to get the press rolling. Then, as updates are ready, the presses can be stopped and new plates attached. The run can then continue. This process means that some subscribers will not get late developments, but many more thousands will get the complete story.

Readers nurtured on old movies may believe that when a spectacular news event occurs, the paper dashes out an extra. Although such extra editions were common when newspapers faced numerous competitors in town, they are now extremely rare.

One such occasion was the terrorist attacks on the United States in the early hours of Sept. 11, 2001. Many newspapers across the country produced extra editions that morning. The next day, their expanded coverage of the attacks filled page upon page without advertising. They printed and sold thousands more copies than usual. Publishers gave editors carte blanche to cover the news, regardless of the cost. The chief executive of Knight Ridder, one of the nation's largest newspaper chains, told journalists: "Please leave no stone unturned in pursuing this story. Do the right thing by readers."[1]

Newspaper Edition Updates

All news organizations deal with changes, and bigger ones deal with them constantly as every edition rolls on a different deadline. The number of changes, however, has been declining as most newspapers have reduced the number of editions. There is little commercial reason for so many editions, because readers buy fewer papers on newsstands or from racks than they did a generation or more ago, and some newspapers have given up on outlying areas that are expensive to serve. Besides, the solid, detailed stories most papers print today do not need changing every hour or two. Big city papers stand ready, however, to replate if a story of real merit comes along. While the presses spin, they quickly get a story and headline ready, make modest changes in the page, produce a new plate or two, stop the presses briefly, and get the new plate locked onto the press. Today, papers are putting out zoned editions, as noted before, and these usually require altering a couple of inside pages for regional news but not the main news sections.

The *Sacramento Bee*

The *Sacramento Bee* is the only daily newspaper in the most populous state's capital. It reaches from south of Sacramento 300 miles north to the Oregon border, and from west of Sacramento 100 miles east to the Nevada border. Editors at the *Bee* produce two editions each night. Most of the editors' efforts go into the first edition, called the state edition, which is delivered to about 30,000 subscribers in the far northern and eastern outreaches of the circulation area. The state edition closes at 10 p.m., with the presses rolling by 10:15 p.m. The second edition, the final, must be finished by 11:30, with the presses starting at 11:45 p.m. Most of the *Bee*'s subscribers get this edition, with a press run of about 270,000. Changes to the edition typically include story updates and corrections from the first edition. New stories that were unavailable for the state edition are subbed in. After the presses are rolling, *Bee* editors can make changes to the final edition as well, substituting pages with what are called chasers. Pages can be chased as late as 1 a.m.

The *Sacramento Bee* also produces seven zoned regional sections on Thursdays and four zoned sections on Sundays. These zoned sections contain local stories and photos targeted to different parts of the *Bee*'s circulation area. A regional copy desk designs and edits these sections, ahead of the deadline for the daily newspaper. Late-breaking stories are more likely to make the *Bee*'s Metro section than the regional sections because of their early deadlines.

News Updates Online

When news breaks, things get more hectic for online editors. Unlike their counterparts at the newspaper, online news sites operate on a constant news cycle. Online audiences want the news now. This creates pressures similar to those that newspaper editors face on deadline—only they can occur at any time during the day.

This is an easier matter when the news comes from a wire service. The online editor decides whether the news is important enough for her audience, and, if so, prepares it for posting on the site. She may consult with an assignment editor to explore local angles to the story. If it's an unfolding event, she updates the story online as more details become available, and assembles links to related matter elsewhere on the news site or on the Internet. For local stories, the online editor must wait for the reporter to gather the information and must carefully edit the story before posting it—that may be the only edit the story gets. With some breaking news, it's best to get a few paragraphs online right away and then provide a fuller story later as the reporter gathers more information and writes it.

The online editor also works with the picture editor to illustrate the story, perhaps creating a slide show to accompany the reporter's account. A reporter equipped with a recorder can provide streaming audio to accompany the story. Again, time is of the essence to serve readers who want the news right away. (See Figures 12.2A–E.)

Piecing Together Parts of Stories

Some breaking stories can be written in parts—even the last part first. There is a system for handling this kind of story, too. Assume that a gas main explodes at a busy downtown corner. One or two reporters and a photographer would be sent to the scene, another would check library clippings under "Explosions" and others would telephone the gas company, police, fire department headquarters, the county morgue and hospitals. Each reporter might gather bits of news that would be worth a couple of paragraphs. But in the confusion, no one can be sure immediately whether anyone was killed, how many were injured, what caused the blast or how much damage resulted.

Although attempts are made to find out all this information, it occasionally helps to get as much of the story written as possible. So the city editor directs one reporter as the lead writer and tells the other reporters to write what material they have and to send it to the lead reporter.

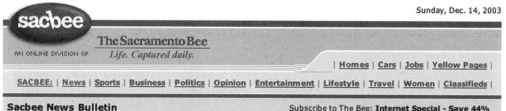

U.S. captures Saddam

American forces captured a bearded Saddam Hussein as he hid in the cellar of a farmhouse near his hometown of Tikrit, ending one of the most intensive manhunts in history. The arrest, eight months after the fall of Baghdad, was carried out without a shot fired and was a huge victory for U.S. forces. "Ladies and gentlemen, we got him," U.S. administrator L. Paul Bremer told a news conference. "The tyrant is a prisoner," Bremer said.

More Coverage

* World leaders thrilled by news of Saddam's capture
* U.S. shows evidence captured man is Saddam
* Iraqi official says Saddam buried himself as U.S. forces closed in
* Profile of Saddam Hussein
* Events in the life of Saddam Hussein
* Blair welcomes capture of Saddam
* Celebratory gunfire greets news of Saddam's capture

Figure 12.2A.
Sacbee.com, the Web site of the *Sacramento Bee*, kept readers updated about the capture of Saddam Hussein on Dec. 14, 2003. Subscribers to Sacbee.com's news alert service received an e-mail bulletin about the capture (Figure Copyright 2003, *The Sacramento Bee.* Used with permission.)

Other reporters at the scene call in the information by telephone. The lead writer pounds out the facts as they dribble in. The top of the story will be written last, giving the fullest account of the who, what, when, where, why and how. When the final information is available, the story can be topped and then is ready for editing.

Some stories can be written in advance and topped later, saving the reporter and desk time on deadline. For example, on election nights, results often come in near a newspaper's deadline. In the afternoon, reporters will write background information about the individual races, known as A-matter, that will serve as the bottom of the story. When results become available late in the evening, the reporter then writes a lead and perhaps two or three additional paragraphs, and then picks up the A-matter. Reporters and editors can use this technique for any news that is expected to come on deadline, such as city council and school board meetings.

The whole newsroom staff, but editors in particular, must keep searching for ways to make big emergencies seems like small ones and to eliminate the small ones. Little things are important, such as having names and telephone numbers of key sources close at hand and main-

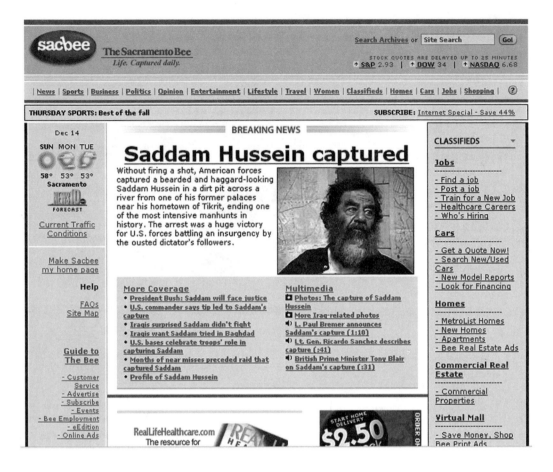

Figure 12.2B.
Early in the afternoon, the Web site had comprehensive coverage of the capture, including slide shows and streaming audio of statements by officials in Iraq and British Prime Minister Tony Blair. (Figure Copyright 2003, *The Sacramento Bee.* Used with permission.)

taining a good library. Planning for emergencies is essential to avoid turmoil and to provide quality coverage.

Above all, journalists should strive to discover how to reduce trivia and how to improve newsroom efficiency. The new technology provides much more efficient news operations. It will pay young journalists to apply their own enterprise to make that technology even better.

Sign up for e-mail alerts for area highways
Including Highway 50 construction info from **CORRIDOR.com**

THE BEE'S IN-DEPTH COVERAGE

Current time in Baghdad
3:45 a.m. Monday

RELATED INFO

Sign up for traffic alerts!

Saddam Hussein captured

By HAMZA HENDAWI, Associated Press
Last Updated 3:34 p.m. PST
Sunday, December 14, 2003

BAGHDAD, Iraq (AP) - Without firing a shot, American forces captured a bearded and haggard-looking Saddam Hussein in a dirt pit across a river from one of his former palaces near his hometown of Tikrit, ending one of the most intensive manhunts in history. The arrest was a huge victory for U.S. forces battling an insurgency by the ousted dictator's followers.

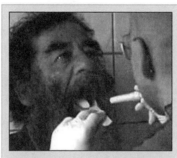

Captured former Iraqi leader Saddam Hussein undergoes medical examinations in Baghdad on Sunday, Dec. 14, 2003, in this image from television.

AP Photo/APTN

In the capital, radio stations played celebratory music, residents fired small arms in the air in celebration and passengers on buses and trucks shouted, "They got Saddam! They got Saddam!" Eager to prove to Iraqis that Saddam was in custody, the U.S. military showed video of the ousted leader, bearded and disheveled, being examined by a military doctor.

"The former dictator of Iraq will face the justice he denied to millions," President Bush said in a midday televised address from the White House, eight months after American troops swept into Baghdad and toppled Saddam's

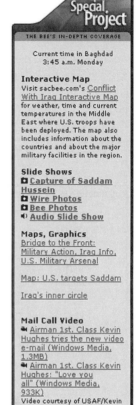

Interactive Map
Visit sacbee.com's Conflict With Iraq Interactive Map for weather, time and current temperatures in the Middle East where U.S. troops have been deployed. The map also includes information about the countries and about the major military facilities in the region.

Slide Shows
▣ Capture of Saddam Hussein
▣ Wire Photos
▣ Bee Photos
◄ Audio Slide Show

Maps, Graphics
Bridge to the Front: Military Action, Iraq Info, U.S. Military Arsenal

Map: U.S. targets Saddam

Iraq's inner circle

Mail Call Video
▬ Airman 1st. Class Kevin Hughes tries the new video e-mail (Windows Media, 1.3MB)
▬ Airman 1st. Class Kevin Hughes: "Love you all" (Windows Media, 933K)
Video courtesy of USAF/Kevin Hughes

Figure 12.2C.
Clicking on the main story link brought readers to the Associated Press' main story about the capture. (Figure Copyright 2003, *The Sacramento Bee.* Used with permission.)

Figure 12.2D.
Sacbee.com had 27 different stories available. Later in the afternoon, when most people were aware of Saddam's capture, editors recast the headline on the home page. (Figure Copyright 2003, *The Sacramento Bee.* Used with permission.)

The Sacramento Bee

MONDAY December 15, 2003 ★★★   www.sacbee.com   ★★★★ Final edition **50 cents**

A FALLEN MAN: Saddam defiant but defeated, Iraq's new leaders say / **page A9**

ANALYSIS: Victory for Bush could benefit his Iraq strategy and re-election prospects / **page A10**

CAR BOMB: Three attacks at police stations leave at least 25 dead / **page A13**

CAPTURED

U.S. forces pull Saddam from his hole

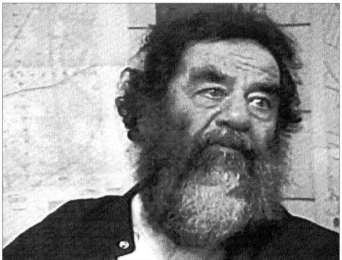

The Saddam Hussein pulled out of a hole outside a farmhouse near Tikrit looked bedraggled, not like the dictator he once was.

Associated Press Television News/U.S. military

A relative gave a vital clue to his location

By Barton Gellman and Dana Priest
WASHINGTON POST

BAGHDAD, Iraq – Thirty-eight weeks after the United States began stalking Saddam Hussein with an arsenal of lethal force, technology and coercion, it fell to a soldier with a spade to flush the fallen leader from a hole.

Perhaps a mile from his nearest palace, Saddam, 66, spent his final minutes of freedom in an underground chamber of hard-packed dirt, just wide enough to permit a man to recline. After decades as self-proclaimed heir to the iconic 12th-century warrior Saladin, Saddam surrendered meekly without a shot from the pistol he clutched in his lap.

The clues that led to Saddam's capture emerged three weeks ago, officials said, when intelligence analysts and Special Operations forces shifted the focus of their hunt from Saddam's innermost circle to the more distant relatives and tribal allies who they suspected had been sheltering the deposed president.

U.S. officials in Baghdad and Washington, speaking on condition of anonymity, said the new strategy led to the capture in Baghdad on Friday of a relative from Saddam's Tikriti clan. Under interrogation, the man contributed a vital, though still undisclosed, clue to Saddam's whereabouts.

► CAPTURE, page A12

Iraqi tribunal likely awaits

By Neil A. Lewis
NEW YORK TIMES

WASHINGTON – After U.S. officials finish interrogating Saddam Hussein, he is expected to become the principal defendant before a special Iraqi-led criminal tribunal that was formally established only last week, Iraqi and American officials said Sunday.

Since the end of major combat in the Iraq war, Bush administration officials have consistently said they want Saddam and his senior aides tried before an Iraqi-led judicial body for war crimes, crimes against humanity and even genocide for his actions against Iraqi Kurds, Shiite Muslims and others.

But as they go down that road, they are certain to draw opposition from critics who urge a judicial proceeding with greater international involvement. The Iraqi Governing Council put forward regulations Wednesday creating a five-member court empowered to try Iraqis on charges stemming from activities from July 17, 1968, the day Saddam's Baath Party came to power, until May 1, 2003, the day President Bush declared major hostilities over.

► TRIAL, page A12

Celebration in Baghdad

Rasul Hamed Khaled, top, celebrates the capture of Saddam Hussein with her family Sunday at the Iraqi Communist Party headquarters in Baghdad. Many, especially Shiites and Kurds treated harshly by Saddam, rejoiced, but others lamented his capture. ► Story, page A11

Los Angeles Times/Carolyn Cole

Bush: Dark era is over for Iraq

By James Rosen
BEE WASHINGTON BUREAU

WASHINGTON – A somber but satisfied President Bush said Sunday that the capture of Saddam Hussein means that "a dark and painful era is over," and he told Iraqis that his goal is to bring them sovereignty, dignity and the chance for a better life.

American soldiers, executing a raid dubbed Operation Red Dawn, pulled the bearded and haggard Saddam from a coffin-sized hole in the ground Saturday evening at an isolated farmhouse outside his hometown of Tikrit.

It was an ignominious end for Saddam, one of history's most brutal dictators, whose image was displayed Sunday on television screens worldwide. He looked like a desperate fugitive, not an all-powerful president who had ordered his army to fight to the death.

Maj. Gen. Ray Odierno, commander of the 4th Infantry Division, whose troops captured the former Iraqi dictator, said Saddam had a pistol but was captured without a shot being fired. He said soldiers found $750,000 in $100 bills

► SADDAM, back page, page A18

Figure 12.2E.
The next morning, Saddam's capture dominated the newspaper's front page. (Figure Copyright 2003, *The Sacramento Bee*. Used with permission.)

State could take lessons from Maryland

By Deb Kollars
BEE STAFF WRITER

The small state of Maryland offers some big lessons for California on what it takes to overhaul a school funding machine:

Take your time. Bring in outside experts and listen intently. Never underestimate the force of a personality. Count on compromising at the very last minute.

"We knew we had to do something different," said Barbara Hoffman of Baltimore, a former Democratic state senator viewed as

PAYING FOR SCHOOLS

Last of two parts

the driving force behind the effort, which was completed last year. "We were spending over $2 billion a year on education and not getting a good product."

Compared with the $41 billion California spends on public education, Maryland's school bill looks tiny. Yet in many ways,

Maryland's reform experience was born of the same problems faced by California.

The state was wrestling with funding inequities among districts. School after school was begging for more money. Cash was going out based on special-interest politics. State leaders felt they were blindly pumping money into schools that were failing to educate children, especially the most disadvantaged.

Maryland had some things going for it that

► SCHOOLS, page A17

Notes

1. Joel Davis, "Publishers and Editors Put Forth 'Extra Effort,'" *Editor & Publisher* (Sept. 24, 2001), 3.

Front pages from around the world reporting the events of Sept. 11, 2001, can be found at: http://www.newseum.org/frontpages/911.htm

CHAPTER 13

Editing and the Law

An editor opens a story about a trial. In the ninth paragraph is this sentence: "When Rogers finished his testimony against the sheriff, Judge Bart Wilson launched into a bitter attack upon the sheriff, calling him a 'scoundrel,' a 'woman-chaser' and a 'lewd, lascivious old man.'" The editor has to consider some important questions: Is it libelous? Will the sheriff sue? If it is libelous and the sheriff sues, how much could the news organization lose?

What if a reviewer says this of a play: "Smith did an adequate job of playing Ophelia, but she might have done better if she had laid off the booze before curtain time." Is this caustic sentence going to get the publication into court?

Suppose a story about the mayor starts, "Mayor Hector Adamson was convicted of stealing a car in 1955, and he served three months in jail for the offense, the *Gazette* discovered today." Is it safe to dredge up a story a half-century old, even if it is true?

These examples are hardly typical of stories that editors deal with, but they show why editors must be constantly alert to the possibility that tucked away in an obscure story is a sentence that will send someone running to a lawyer. That lawyer may decide to call on the publisher to see about a tidy out-of-court settlement. He may even reinforce his efforts by stopping off at the courthouse to file a libel suit.

The lawyer may decide to sue any editors who had their hands in the job. A suit also could be filed against the reporter who wrote the story. The working crew rarely gets sued, however. With only a heavily mortgaged house, a 3-year-old car, two children free and clear, and $3,000 in the credit union, an editor would be too small a target. The news organization is not. Most newspapers or news sites, if they had to, could borrow many thousands. In addition, most news organizations have libel insurance, and lawyers know it.

The Costs of Libel

Libel suits are expensive—even when the news organization wins. And when they lose, the judgments can be enormous. Imagine what the future would be for an editor whose error let his news organization get socked for a million dollars. In 2000 alone, the average libel award was $5.6 million, according to the Libel Defense Resource Center. On the losing ends of these suits have been ABC, *The Wall Street Journal*, Time Warner and the *New York Post*.

The cost of losing a libel suit is not only the judgment handed down by the court. The news organization has to hire trial lawyers, and good ones do not come cheap. Defense attorneys have to be paid even if the news organization wins. The average cost of defending a libel suit has been reported at about $100,000.

One of the early big judgments involved Wally Butts, athletic director at the University of Georgia. The *Saturday Evening Post*, then a weekly, published a statement that a telephone conversation between Butts and Bear Bryant, football coach at the University of Alabama, revealed that Georgia was going to throw the football game with Alabama. The *Post* story quoted only one person, who said he overheard the conversation by accident. Both Butts and Bryant sued. At the trial in the Butts case, no one else could corroborate the statements of the sole witness. The witness also had changed his story somewhat and, besides, his reputation was attacked. Butts was awarded $3 million, although this was cut to $400,000 on appeal. Bryant settled out of court for $300,000. This catastrophe contributed to the death of the weekly *Post*.

Almost 20 years later, entertainer Carol Burnett sued the *National Enquirer* because the paper had reported that she had been rowdy in a Washington restaurant. The original judgment was $1.6 million, later cut to $800,000, and then settled for an undisclosed amount. Burnett gave the sum to the University of Hawaii for the study of journalism ethics.

A former Miss Wyoming won a $26.5 million award from *Penthouse* magazine, but a judge reduced the judgment to $14 million. An appellate court threw out the judgment, ruling that the magazine article would not reasonably be understood as describing the actual facts about her.

Almost all whopping judgments are reduced sharply on appeal or even thrown out. Only about 30 percent of libel cases are ultimately won by the plaintiff. Many suits are filed partly to give the plaintiff a feeling of vengeance, and they are dropped after lingering for a couple of years in the courts. Nevertheless, libel today is serious, and anyone in the newsroom ought to have a good knowledge of libel law. If such knowledge tells an editor that something is libelous, he or she should tell a superior, "This looks dangerous to me." If the superior agrees, he or she can rephrase the offending words, remove the risky part of the story, or ask the news organization's lawyer for advice. In most cases the lawyer is not consulted unless the editors, hoping to run the story pretty much as written, want to be as sure as anyone can be that the story will not cost the paper a libel suit.

Journalists should realize that civility provides one of the best protections against libel. A University of Iowa law school study found that many aggrieved persons call a newspaper to complain that their reputations have been sullied. Instead of getting a polite consideration of the complaint, the study found, a writer responds harshly or the caller is given the runaround. The result is that the complainant, already irritated, becomes angry and hires a lawyer. The study has prompted warnings in many newsrooms to be courteous to such callers and to funnel complaints to one specific person, whose job is to placate the irate.

Online Resources on Media Law

U.S. Copyright Office: www.copyright.gov

Student Press Law Center: www.splc.org

Reporters Committee for Freedom of the Press: www.rcfp.org

California First Amendment Coalition: www.cfac.org

Electronic Frontier Foundation: www.eff.org

University of Iowa Internet Resources on Media Law (including Cyberspace): http://bailiwick.lib.uiowa.edu/journalism/mediaLaw/

Media Law Resource Center: www.ldrc.com

First Amendment Law Review: http://falr.unc.edu/indexmain.html

Copley First Amendment Center: http://www.illinoisfirstamendment-center.org/

1st Amendment Online: http://1stam.umn.edu/

First Amendment Center: http://www.firstamendmentcenter.org/

What Is Libelous?

Libel is usually defined as *written defamation,* and it applies also to most radio and television programs because newscasters and performers are reading from a script. Libel law applies similarly to information disseminated on the Internet, although questions persist about jurisdiction in online defamation cases. For libel to be actionable, four conditions must exist:

1. The information was published.
2. The person bringing the action is identified in the publication.
3. The information is defamatory.
4. The information is false.

Three Defenses

The law offers three main protections for publications that disseminate defamatory information. These legal defenses are the same in each of the 50 states and the District of Columbia. At the heart of the protection is the idea that the public has a right to know many things that are considered defamatory, so papers are given rights, or "defenses," to print such defamation. Theoretically, a person could still sue, but a lawyer would advise against a suit because the news organization stands behind one of these three protections for the public interest:

1. **Truth.** But absolute truth is often hard to prove.
2. **Privilege.** This often is called *qualified* or *statutory* privilege because states let news media print *accurate and fair* stories about the activities of the courts and government agencies. A plaintiff cannot win a libel suit over a fair and accurate report of privileged government proceedings or records, no matter how defamatory—or false.
3. **Fair comment.** A news organization may criticize the activities of public officials and works or performances open to the public and publicly displayed, such as books, art shows, concerts, plays, athletic contests and nightclub acts.

Truth

Truth, under law, is not simply what news editors believe is the truth or what someone told a reporter is true. From a legal standpoint, truth is what can be proved in court to be true. Occasionally, therefore, a journalist will say, "I know the guy is a crook, but I can't prove it." So, a story about him is not published.

Sometimes a news organization running an investigation will obtain someone's promise to testify to the truth of a charge in case the story ever comes to court. But suppose the trial date approaches and Mr. Witness is nowhere to be found? Because the truth cannot now be proved, a plaintiff perhaps collects at least a few thousand dollars and the publication collects experience. Instead of relying on a witness to appear in a case of libel, some news organizations take pains to have their sources give them affidavits to be used in case someone sues. The affidavits are sworn statements by the informants that certain assertions made by the organization are true. Some even try to forestall the threat of suit by telling the readers, in effect, that they have the goods: "At least three police officers operate as bookmakers in their spare time, two former officers *declared in affidavits signed* Friday." Assuming that the three accused officers are named later in the story, they and their lawyers are forewarned that the newspaper has sworn statements for court proof.

Privilege

Because the rights of privilege do not, in all states, apply to *all* courts and *all* deliberations of public bodies and *all* public records, editors should be familiar with the restrictions in their own states. Editors should also be aware that accounts of committees of Congress and state legislatures are covered by privilege. The protection does not apply to closed legislative committee hearings. However, any publications issued by such committees are covered by privilege, even though the publications may be filled with material that would be libelous if printed by anyone else.

It is always advisable to remember that application and interpretation make the law flexible. The courts may rule at one time that such-and-such is the law. Within five or 10 years, with a different political climate and with different evidence, fresh decisions may result in the opposite interpretation. As an illustration, many of the laws made in the 1940s and 1950s to restrict radical political activity were invalidated by the Supreme Court within a decade or two.

Moreover, as is true of the protection of privilege in many states on juvenile court proceedings, other laws are not clear. The police blotter, or record book, is a privileged document in some states, but in others either it is not or the law on the subject is fuzzy. In some places, what a police officer says about a case is also privileged. It is clear, however, that once a lawsuit has been filed—is in the hands of the clerk of the courts—the contents of the file are privileged.

Any part of the trial that is removed from the court record is not privileged. If the judge strikes testimony, the protection is taken away. The same applies when the judge *clears the court*, for reporters either must leave the courtroom at such times or must not print anything that happens in the court after the judge has cleared it.

No story during or preceding a trial should provide any editorial evaluation of the guilt or innocence of the accused. Stories should stick to what has been said for court record. No story should refer to a person as a "killer" or a "burglar" until he has been convicted of such crimes. Obviously, this applies to headlines as well.

Some people have the mistaken idea that if the word *allegedly* is tossed into a story, the news organization will avoid a libel suit. It will not. It's best to avoid the word altogether. What if a reporter wrote, "Johnson allegedly pried a sliding door lock to enter the house"? This says the news organization is making the allegation. It's better to attribute accusations of crimes to official sources: "Johnson pried a sliding door lock to enter the house, police reports said." Reporters and editors should not assume, however, that what a police officer tells them is privileged. They should check the rules in their state.

An arrest, however, is privileged. Nevertheless, it is worth being cautious about. Police may get a little overzealous and arrest people for insufficient cause. So an officer, in the midst of some excitement, may reach out and tell someone he is under arrest. The someone may be the vice president of a university. A Web site might post a story of the arrest, only to find that two hours later, the vice president had been taken to the police station and quickly released, with personal and profuse apologies from the desk sergeant, the chief of police, the mayor and, of course, the arresting officer. The privilege might not hold up now, on the grounds that the vice president was not really considered arrested by the police.

Cautious editors print news of arrests only after an *information*, or preliminary charge, is written out at the police station. This precaution applies especially to mass arrests when police sometimes will shove a hundred people into police vans, tell them they are under arrest, take them to a remote police station and release them. Unless a reporter follows through to see that there is an official record of an arrest, police can deny later, after publication, that anyone had been arrested. A denial without a written *information* could leave the paper in a bad spot.

Fair comment and rhetorical hyperbole

Sarcastic and sardonic play reviews flourished in the 1930s and early 1940s. Reviewers struggled to have something snide or devastating to say about at least one performer, if not the whole cast. That approach to play reviewing spilled over into reviews of books, music and art. The exaggeration and the strained efforts to be cleverly derogatory, fortunately, are less common today, but editors still must know where to draw the line.

It is legal to pan a play or performance in exaggerated language. The law provides that anything written about the performance, including how the person looked while performing, is protected by what is known as *fair comment and criticism*. The only qualification is that the writing not be malicious.

One case that has amused law and journalism students for decades concerned a 1901 newspaper review in Odebolt, Iowa. The reviewer covered the stage performance of a singing trio known as the Cherry Sisters. Because horses were common in 1901, the reviewer chose to use equine terms, knowing his audience would appreciate them:

> Effie is an old jade of 50 summers, Jessie a frisky filly of 40 and Addie, the flower of the family, a capering monstrosity of 35. Their long skinny arms, equipped with talons at the extremities, swung mechanically, and

anon waved frantically at the suffering audience. The mouths of their rancid features opened like caverns and sounds like the wailings of damned souls issued therefrom. They pranced around the stage with a motion that suggested a cross between the danse du ventre and fox trot, strange creatures with painted faces and hideous mien. Effie is spavined, Addie is stringhalt and Jessie, the only one who showed her stockings, has legs with calves as classic in their outlines as the curves of a broom handle.

Effie sued and lost. She appealed, but the appellate court ruled against her: "Viewing the evidence in the light of the rules heretofore announced, and remembering that the trial court had the plaintiff before it and saw her repeat some of the performances given by her on stage, we are of the opinion that there was *no* error in directing a verdict for the defendants."

An editor must make sure, however, that a review does not deal derogatorily with the performer's private life, such as drinking habits, sex life and political views. These are considered by law to be a person's own business, until the performer makes them public business by something such as getting arrested for drunkenness.

It is almost taken for granted that the news media can criticize public officials with impunity. Many public officials, notably presidents, have virtually no private life, so criticism of practically anything they do is allowed by custom, although ethics and taste restrain well-edited publications. Scandal sheets thrive on libel of famous persons and usually get away with it because it is hard for them to prevail in court.

Fair comment is a common-law defense that varies from state to state. A constitutional protection for opinion seems to have replaced the fair comment defense to a large extent. Justice Powell in *Gertz v. Robert Welch, Inc.* wrote, "Under the First Amendment there is no such thing as a false idea. However pernicious an opinion may seem, we depend for its correction not on the conscience of judges or juries but on the competition of other ideas."

Although Powell was only referring to the libertarian roots of freedom of expression, lower courts have seized upon the statement as the genesis of a new defense. The rule that has evolved up to this point is that one potentially can be liable for expression of defamatory facts but not for defamatory statements of opinion. The similarity to the fair comment defense is obvious, and the same problem occurs: What is fact and what is opinion? Is it opinion to call somebody a lousy agent? An incompetent judge? An amateurish performer?

Courts apply a three-pronged test when determining whether a defamation is protected by fair comment:

1. Is the comment an opinion statement? Can it be proved true or false?
2. Does the defamatory comment focus on a subject of legitimate public interest?
3. Is there a factual basis for the comment?[1]

One court said it was opinion to assert that a public official voted to "squander property tax funds for Tahoe airport." Another court ruled that it was not opinion to say a judge was "probably corrupt." Allegations of criminal activity are not considered opinion. Editorials and cartoons may contain more than opinion and thus result in liability. Even if journalists cannot be liable for opinion, they can be liable for facts included with opinion or for undisclosed facts that were implied as the basis for the opinion. So, for practical purposes, the ambiguity of the opinion defense should deter editors from relying on it.

Related to fair comment is rhetorical hyperbole. This happens when somebody makes such an exaggerated, unbelievable statement that readers can only conclude it is an opinion. Some examples of cases involving rhetorical hyperbole included a teacher described as a "babbler" and editorial statements that a mayor's zoning proposal involved "extortion" and "blackmail."[2]

Public Figures and Public Officials

Over the past 40 years, the courts have ruled that certain inaccuracies or falsehoods about *public figures* and *public officials* may be printed safely. The landmark decision on this subject was handed down in 1964 by the U.S. Supreme Court in *New York Times v. Sullivan*. About $3 million in judgments had been assessed against the *Times* in behalf of various Alabama figures, including Gov. John Patterson and four Montgomery city officials. One of the officials was L.B. Sullivan, commissioner of public affairs and head of the police department. A full-page advertisement, placed in the *Times*, said that during a demonstration at Alabama State College police had "ringed" the campus, student leaders had been expelled, the "entire" student body had shown its protest by refusing to register for classes and the campus dining hall had been padlocked.

Several of these statements were not true. For example, nine students were expelled, but for demanding service at a downtown lunch counter. The dining hall never was padlocked, and the police did not "ring" the campus.

The Supreme Court ruled this way in favor of the *Times*:

> The constitutional guarantees require, we think, a federal rule that prohibits a public official from recovering damages for a defamatory falsehood relating to his official conduct unless he proves that the statement was made with "actual malice"—that is, with the knowledge that it was false or with reckless disregard of whether it was false or not.[3]

Knowledge of falsity is straightforward: If the publication knew the defamatory statement was untrue, that's actual malice. "Reckless disregard" of the truth, on the other hand, is a little more difficult to get one's hands on. What's required is that the reporter or editor had serious doubts about whether a story was true but published it anyway. This is a difficult standard for plaintiffs to prove and thus provides some protection to reporters and editors who write stories critical of public officials.[4]

The question that faces editors, then, is what constitutes a public official. Anybody elected to public office certainly is. But what about people who work for the government? When are they public officials and when are they merely public servants? The Supreme Court has said that the "public official" designation applies at the very least to those among the hierarchy of government employees who have or appear to have to the public a substantial responsibility for or control over the conduct of public affairs."[5] This means that school superintendents, county administrators, city managers and public university presidents are public officials, but school secretaries, county social workers, city clerical workers and public university professors are not.

One court granted Sen. Barry Goldwater $75,000 in a libel suit against Ralph Ginzburg and his magazine *Fact.* In 1964, when Goldwater ran for president, Ginzburg published a story based on the opinion of more than a dozen psychiatrists that Goldwater was not mentally stable. None of the psychiatrists had ever seen Goldwater. The senator was a public official, all right, but the court ruled that Ginzburg had recklessly disregarded the facts. So at least in that one case journalists learned the outer limits of the public official doctrine.

In 1974, the Supreme Court extended the actual malice defense to cases involving two types of *public figures*: all-purpose public figures who "occupy positions of such pervasive power and influence that they are deemed public figures for all purposes," and limited-purpose public figures, those who "have thrust themselves to the forefront of particular public controversies in order to influence the resolution of the issues involved."[6] For public figures to prevail in libel suits, they also must prove actual malice—the statements were known to be false or there was reckless disregard for their falsity.

The Supreme Court has given editors a little comfort by ruling that libel suits filed by public figures and public officials must be dismissed before trial unless evidence suggests that they can prove libel with "convincing clarity."

The standard of fault is lower for people who aren't public officials or public figures. They need only show that the news publication did not use "reasonable care" when it defamed the defendant.[7]

Strange Rulings

In *Time v. Firestone,* journalists learned to their surprise that those they might commonly consider public figures were not necessarily so in legal terms. Mary Alice Sullivan Firestone, wife of the tire manufacturing heir, frequently had her name and picture in the society pages. She was extremely prominent in the Palm Beach area, where she lived, and the

Firestone name would bring recognition almost any place in the country. She even held press conferences after she filed a spectacular divorce suit. After the divorce was granted, *Time* magazine reported that the grounds for divorce were adultery, the reason cited when she filed for divorce. In the decree, however, the divorce was granted for "lack of domesticity." She sued *Time*, arguing that it called her an adulteress. *Time* tried to argue that she was a public figure and had to prove actual malice, but the court rejected that notion because she had not "thrust herself into the forefront of any particular controversy."[8]

Among others who have not been considered public figures are a research scientist using a $500,000 government grant, a criminal defense lawyer and a man who pleaded guilty to contempt for not appearing at a grand jury hearing on an espionage case. In this latter case, the Supreme Court rejected the argument "that any person who engages in criminal conduct automatically becomes a public figure. . . . To hold otherwise would create an 'open season' for all who sought to defame persons convicted of crime."

The Supreme Court has expressed concern that the media can create public figures merely by giving them extensive coverage, thus creating a privilege to defame in the context of the defamation. So the Court essentially has said that people who might generally be regarded as public figures are not necessarily public figures in the legal sense. An editor therefore should presume that *the subject of a story is not a public figure.* It always will be unclear whether a court will second-guess an editor's judgment, so it may be best to err on the side of prudence. The limitations on the actual malice privilege mean that it is more important now than it has been to rely on defenses such as accuracy and the use of information from the public record.

If editors set out to find just where the public figure borderline is, they may find their publication in court. Sticking to the provable facts is the best way to stay out of trouble. The fact that something is legal is not cause for being sloppy with facts or careless with reputations. A loose news organization is in no position to recommend virtue to anyone else. If an online site or newspaper sticks to what the editors think is the truth and makes a mistake, it can use the public official or public figure defense with ethical justification.

Classes of Libel

Per se *and* per quod

Libel comes under two main headings: *per se* and *per quod.* Libel *per se* can be translated as "libel on the face of it." To be called a communist when one is not a communist has been considered libel *per se* for some years. The plaintiff would have to bring little into court except the offending newspaper clipping to prove the point. With libel *per quod,* on the other hand, one must know the circumstances to determine whether the statement is defamatory. In other words, the plaintiff has to prove that a reputation was damaged.

In two historic cases, the plaintiffs did not want money. All they sought was a ruling by the court that they had been libeled. Theodore Roosevelt settled for a one-cent judgment. Henry Ford was less restrained. He took six times as much.

Civil and criminal libel

Libel is almost always a civil dispute. That is, it is a wrong being argued by two or more people. (Corporations are treated by law as people.) No jail or prison terms are involved.

Criminal libel does exist, but it is so rare it almost can be ignored. To get a criminal libel verdict, the court would have to rule that a publication has committed a crime *against society*. In such instances, the news story is held to have been so inflammatory that a segment of society riots, storms City Hall or tries to blow up the news organization's facilities itself. In recent decades the idea that a news organization could produce a riot was remote and the threat of this type of libel academic. Every few years some zealous prosecuting attorney files a criminal libel action, but nothing comes of it.

Everything Counts

All journalists should be aware that a news organization is responsible for *everything* it distributes: news stories, headlines, features, comics, advertisements, editorials, letters to the editor and pictures. Aside from the question of malice, quoting someone else on a defamation—such as the superintendent of schools or a policeman—does not enable a news organization to avoid a charge of libel. It does not save the newspaper any responsibility if it is someone's signed letter in the paper that contains the defamation. Neither is there any help if the libel is in a paid advertisement. It is no relief, either, to have some letter writer say, "I will stand behind it." Don't bet on it. The newspaper may be assessed, say, $20,000 damages and run up tens of thousands more in legal bills defending itself, and may lose reader confidence. Is the letter writer, who says he will be responsible, ready to cough up $30,000? Editors might cool off demands from hotheaded readers by saying, only somewhat facetiously, "Would you put up a $50,000 bond just in case we get sued for libel?" At the mere thought of such a sum most letter writers would throw their libelous prose into the wastebasket—or at least cross out the offending phrases.

Editors and reporters are often threatened with libel suits. A news source occasionally will shout, "If you print that, I'll sue you for libel!"

Actually it is clear that the person doesn't have the slightest idea of what constitutes libel. So the journalist either ignores the threat or gives an ironic rejoinder. If the threats are based on ignorance, as most of them are, the journalist can take a few minutes to explain why the story is not actionable. If this isn't satisfactory, the journalist can suggest that the source consult a lawyer. A substantial number of people mistakenly assume that they can tell a news organization what to leave out, or put in, and successfully sue if the paper disregards their orders.

In any case the journalist is smart to keep calm, although it is tempting to utter some scornful phrase. To maintain good public relations for the newspaper, staffers should be gentle in handling the irate people who dread exposure in print or online.

Escape Routes

Although truth, fair comment, privilege and, to some extent, public figure status are defenses against libel, there are other ways to avoid a libel suit:

1. **Statute of limitations.** The suit must be brought within a specified time after the offending material was printed. In most states this is one year. If the plaintiff brings suit 366 days after the story appeared, no case.
2. **Out-of-court settlement.** If a news publication agrees out of court that it libeled someone and pays a certain sum of money, that act wipes out any chance of a suit.
3. **Consent.** This rarely occurs, but if a reporter showed a news source a story or recited the facts or charges that were going to be in the story and the source made no objection, the court assumes that the source "consented" to them.

After a publication gets embroiled in a libel suit, its publisher, editors and lawyers have to figure how to beat it. In many instances there is no real way out. The publication then tries to show that it tried to mitigate the effects of the defamation as soon as it became aware of its error.

The best evidence of mitigation is a *retraction*. The most effective retractions appear in about as prominent a position in the paper as the libel did. If the libel appeared in a banner headline on Page 1, the retraction at least would have to be in a prominent position on the front page. In many states, publication of a retraction will bar any further legal action by the defamed party.

These other proofs of the news organization's good faith may help:

1. The offending story was omitted or "cleaned up" in later editions.
2. An honest effort was made to retrieve the papers that included the libel. For example, if the libel was noticed 10 minutes after the press

run was started, the paper would have tried to call back the delivery trucks.

3. The libelous information had been copied by error.
4. The information came from a normally reliable source, such as a police chief or a judge.
5. The information was *common knowledge*. This claim refers to what "everyone knows." As an illustration, a gangster may never have been convicted of anything, but it is common knowledge that he is a gangster.
6. The newsroom had used normal precautions. This would require evidence that the journalists had double-checked facts before publishing them.
7. There were persistent and public rumors about the case.
8. The plaintiff can be proved to have a bad reputation.

Watchwords

A main cause of libel suits has been careless crime reporting—of names, addresses or size of crime. So the editor must particularly watch stories involving crime and the courts. As noted earlier, it is easy for a reporter to refer to "the killer" instead of "slaying suspect"—he or she is not a killer, legally, until convicted. Sometimes police catch a person red-handed in a criminal act. To be on the safe side the story had better not say, "Joe Johnson was caught breaking into the McTavish warehouse." It would be better to write, "Police arrested Joe Johnson last night, accusing him of breaking into the McTavish warehouse."

Picture cutlines or even placement of pictures can provide grounds for libel. If a sheriff and an alleged criminal are pictured together and the cutlines switch identification, one or both might sue. Also, if a picture runs next to a story so that readers assume they go together, there may be grounds for action.

Implications and insinuations have to be watched with great care. The plaintiff can establish a good case by bringing only two or three people into court to testify that they inferred something defamatory from something the paper printed.

Not naming individuals in stories may be no protection. It is what readers believe is being said that counts. When a column in a college newspaper denounced a football player, but not by name, several readers, at least, thought the column referred to a certain player who had been accused of a serious crime. Actually, the columnist had meant someone else, but the person who some people thought was mentioned might have collected.

As a rule, a group cannot be libeled. It would be hard to convince a jury that something defamatory about a sizable group really applied to every member of the group. A rule of thumb is that the larger the group, the harder to libel. But this depends to some extent on how emotional the public is about the organization. A magazine once implied that University of Oklahoma football players came off the field and squirted dope into their noses. Some of the players sued, claiming that they had shot a peppermint solution into their mouths to relieve dryness. The Oklahoma Supreme Court agreed that the magazine should pay $75,000, which was distributed among some 60 players. The same implications might, perhaps, have been made safely about another large group, say, the Oklahoma marching band. Because band fans are fewer and less excitable than football fans, a court would probably be reluctant to see such an implication as doing an individual harm.

A few other points on libel should be considered. For instance, the dead cannot be libeled, for the simple reason that they can no longer suffer from slights to their reputations. A suit could be filed by the dead person's heirs, but they would have to prove specific injury to themselves, such as loss of income.

The news organization is safe to print charges after they are actually filed at the courthouse, because they have started through the judicial process. But a story had better not report the gist of written charges casually dropped by a lawyer on a desk in the county clerk's office. The lawyer might retrieve them 20 minutes later and throw them away.

A report on what people told a grand jury would not be considered grounds for a libel suit. But because the operations of the grand jury are secret, the presiding judge might decide that the newspaper, or its reporters, are in contempt of court. For that, one can go to jail.

Executive acts are considered privileged, but it is safer to get them in writing than to quote them as given verbally. If the mayor tells a reporter that he fired the police chief "for moral turpitude," it would be helpful if the newspaper could get a copy of the letter dismissing the chief. The copy could be saved in case the chief sues.

Editors should be suspicious of irony. A story that says, "George Zarfoss went to Boston to visit Esmerelda Fisher, a 'friend,'" almost asks for a suit by Zarfoss or Fisher, or both.

Damages

When a plaintiff wins a libel suit, the court may award four kinds of damages:

1. **Presumed.** No proof of injury has to be submitted. These are simply presumed, without evidence, to have resulted from injured feelings or humiliation.
2. **Actual.** These damages are established for injury to reputation and must be proved.
3. **Special.** The plaintiff proves specific financial injury. The actual pecuniary loss is assessed.

4. **Punitive.** The court grants a cash award as punishment. Such damages may be quite high, to discourage the editors from libeling again. (Punitive awards, by the way, are taxable. The others are not.)

Fair Trial

The First Amendment guarantees a free press and the Sixth Amendment guarantees a fair trial. The amendments clash from time to time, for what a newspaper publishes may jeopardize a fair trial, and some people, eager for fairness in court, seek to restrict the press. In a few cases, the courts have ruled that heavy publicity before trials has made it almost impossible for an accused person to receive fair treatment. The publicity may be so widespread in some cases that moving the site of the trial would not help the defendant much. For example, the President's Commission on the Assassination of President John F. Kennedy, chaired by Chief Justice Earl Warren, expressed grave doubts that Lee Harvey Oswald could have received a fair trial, given all the publicity surrounding the assassination. In another case, as hard as it is to believe, a court in Washington, D.C., found 12 jurors who never had heard of the Watergate incident, and the trial of those involved in the cover-up proceeded without incident.

The ethical journalist will want to assure any accused person a fair trial and will try to inform the public about cases before the courts. Careful writing and judicious editing should eliminate nearly all conflicts between those goals. Reporters should be instructed to reject any editorial comment, to avoid inflammatory descriptions of crimes, to underplay grisly details and to concentrate on a story tone that shows respect for the rights of the accused. It is the editor's job, if the reporter fails to follow these guidelines, to edit the copy so that it does.

Privacy

The laws about privacy are fairly new and have not been widely tested in the courts. There has been growing concern, however, about invasions of privacy by the government, particularly with electronic snooping devices. The press has come in for its share of criticism, too, and some of it has been justified. Some reporters and photographers have the idea that anything they want to find or photograph is fair game, never considering whether the picture or story could cause unnecessary anguish.

At one time it would have been enough for an editor to remind reporters and photographers to avoid the keyhole and the transom. But today photographers and their employers may face a lawsuit over what appeared to be a good, newsworthy picture. The charge usually is invasion of privacy, and in a few cases the charges have stuck or have been an annoyance. As a result, many news organizations have photographers get written permission from their subjects whenever a suit seems possible.

When privacy may be involved, the editor is wise to focus on newsworthiness, not sensation. Invading privacy to get an entertaining or titillating story is dangerous as well as unethical. In court, newsworthiness is a defense for invasion of privacy just as truth is for libel. News facts from the public record, for example, would be privileged, as would facts about a public figure. When faced with an allegation of invasion of privacy, courts look at whether the publication of private facts are offensive to a reasonable person and whether the information is of legitimate public concern. If not, the plaintiff will prevail.

Copyright

Copyright is the protection against republication of original work without the consent of the owner. Any work published after January 1, 1978, can be copyrighted for the life of the creator and for 75 years after the creator's death. Material copyrighted before that date can by copyrighted for up to 95 years. Editors should be wary about reprinting such material, to avoid getting the publication into an expensive and lengthy lawsuit.

After a work is created, it is protected by copyright regardless of whether the author or publishers register it with the U.S. Copyright Office. For a copyright owner to sue, however, the copyright must be registered. Still, the Copyright Office recommends that authors and publishers include copyright notices with their works; most newspapers and Web sites now provide a notice copyrighting all their content.

The editor's concern with copyright is to avoid reprinting copyrighted material without permission from the publisher. Some publications, particularly small ones, often do reprint without permission material from copyrighted magazines, books and other news publications. In most cases the owner of the copyrighted material throws up his hands and says, "What can I do? It would cost me a thousand dollars of someone's time to get even an apology from the bum. So I'll let it go." Meanwhile, the unscrupulous editor steals editorials, articles and cartoons without pushing any one source to legal action—and without having the courtesy to tell readers about the stolen goods.

Although copyright law on the Internet is still evolving—particularly regarding what constitutes a copy—copyright owners generally enjoy the same rights online as they do in print.[9] Few publications indulge in this kind of thievery, but copyright violations proliferate on the Internet.

Copyright law does provide some protections for news organizations. For one, facts cannot be copyrighted. A news organization can report the substance of a news event already reported elsewhere without violating copyright laws. What the law does protect is the way the news is presented.[10] Copyright law also provides for the "fair use" of copyrighted material. Among the considerations are the purpose of the use of the copyrighted material and the amount of the material used. For news organizations, material may be used if relevant to a news report or as part of a critique or review of the copyrighted work. Courts will also look at the relative proportion of the copyrighted work used to its entirety when evaluating fair use. The best principle is to quote copyrighted material sparingly. Organizations that republish copyrighted works under the fair use rules should always give the copyright holder credit, as a courtesy.

Notes

1. Don R. Pember and Clay Calvert, *Mass Media Law*, 2005-2006 ed. (Boston: McGraw-Hill, 2005), 230–231.

2. Pember and Calvert, 225–226.

3. *New York Times Co. v. Sullivan*, 376 U.S. 254.

4. Pember and Calvert, 198.

5. *Rosenblatt v. Baer*, 383 U.S. 75 (1996).

6. *Gertz v. Welch*, 418 U.S. 323 (1974).

7. Pember and Calvert, 188.

8. *Time v. Firestone*, 424 U.S. 448 (1976).

9. Pember and Calvert, 504.

10. Pember and Calvert, 513.

CHAPTER 14

Editing and Ethics

Mass media law, the purview of the previous chapter, describes the limits of what journalists *can* do—certainly important for anybody entering a career in communications. But mass media law doesn't prescribe an even more important matter: what journalists *should* do. Many things that journalists can publish legally go beyond the bounds of what most would consider quality journalism. When should the name of a criminal suspect be disclosed and when should it be withheld? When should a rape victim's identity be disclosed, if ever? What community groups can a journalist be active in? When is it acceptable to take gifts from news sources? Is it appropriate to work undercover? How aggressively should certain stories be pursued? Is there a line to be drawn between journalism and patriotism? Between journalism and citizenship? All these questions involve journalism *ethics*, the norms by which journalists conduct themselves and by which editors decide which stories to pursue and which to abandon.

Some recent high-profile ethical breaches have tarnished the reputations of two prominent journalism organizations, the *New York Times* and *USA Today*. At the *Times*, reporter Jayson Blair was found to have plagiarized the work of other publications and to have simply made up some of his reports. At *USA Today*, Jack Kelley resigned after an investigation there found that he had committed the same journalistic sins. At the *Sacramento Bee*, a sports reporter was fired after the newspaper discovered he had reported about games that he had not attended. For online publications, the ability to post news nearly instantaneously has led to the publication of erroneous information that is hard to retract.[1]

A Hypothetical

The sports editor of a university city newspaper talks earnestly with the managing editor. "We have evidence," she tells the ME, "that two former

Figure 14.1.
New attention focused on journalism ethics after *New York Times* reporter Jayson Blair resigned in a plagiarism and fabrication scandal. The executive editor and managing editor also resigned. *New York Times*/Getty Images. Used with permission.

football players at the university received gifts worth several thousand dollars when they were players. If such gifts were given to two it seems possible that others also got some. How do you think we should handle the story?"

The managing editor immediately senses danger. The players may be lying, seeking publicity. If they are truthful, how high does the corruption go? Are coaches and university officials involved? If the story is ignored, what might the reaction be? A full investigation could be conducted and perhaps dozens of hot stories could appear. What would happen then? Zealous fans would scream at the newspaper. Circulation would skid. A new managing editor might be hired.

Top editors must make an ethical decision in this case. The publisher, executive editor, managing editor, city editor, sports editor and perhaps the paper's legal counsel will have to decide how to proceed. They know that they could tell the sports editor to forget any story, but their professionalism tells them that they should print news, not suppress it. They also realize that news of any suppression might leak and the paper would look cowardly.

In this fictional case, fortunately, no deadline faces editors. They have several days to make up their minds. In that time they may reach three alternatives: (1) dig for every possible angle to the story and, if the facts warrant, print the results fairly and calmly under big headlines on Page 1; (2) print the players' claims but nothing more, assuming that readers will discount the story; and (3) drop the whole thing, justifying the inaction by saying that the National Collegiate Athletic Association will discover the problem, if one exists, sooner or later.

Each alternative could exact a cost. If the first choice is followed, the paper probably will lose advertising and subscribers. The whole staff will be subject to scurrilous attacks. The other choices will make staffers feel that they work for a spineless newspaper. Some may look elsewhere for work. If the NCAA cracks down a few months later, thoughtful readers may wonder why the paper had been so short of curiosity.

Ethical Codes

An ethical problem of the magnitude of the one discussed above does not erupt every day, but smaller questions that involve ethics crop up every day. Most news organizations set ethical rules as part of their policy. For example, they may require that a person accused of wrongdoing must have a right to reply. Or they will acknowledge that they have a financial stake in some newsworthy project.

Intelligent editors aim for a consistent policy to guide staffs through ethical thickets. Some may adopt the Code of Ethics of the Society of Professional Journalists (www.spj.org/ethics.asp). Others write their own ethical guidelines. Editors don't want a story today handled differently from how a similar story was handled yesterday. Most editors today try to play the news straight so that readers will find their news organizations fair and credible.

Ethical Principles

Bob Steele, an expert on media ethics at the Poynter Institute for Media Studies, has put together these principles for the ethical behavior of journalists.

1. Seek Truth and Report It as Fully as Possible

- Inform yourself continuously so that you in turn can inform, engage and educate the public in a clear and compelling way on significant issues.
- Be honest, fair and courageous in gathering, reporting and interpreting accurate information.
- Give voice to the voiceless.
- Hold the powerful accountable.

2. Act Independently

- Guard vigorously the essential stewardship role a free press plays in an open society.
- Seek out and disseminate competing perspectives without being unduly influenced by those who would use their power or position counter to the public interest.
- Remain free of associations and activities that may compromise your integrity or damage your credibility.
- Recognize that good ethical decisions require individual responsibility enriched by collaborative efforts.

3. Minimize Harm

- Be compassionate for those affected by your actions.
- Treat sources, subjects, and colleagues as human beings deserving of respect, not merely as means to your journalistic ends.
- Recognize that gathering and reporting information may cause harm or discomfort, but balance those negatives by choosing alternatives that maximize your goal of truthtelling.

Copyright 2004, the Poynter Institute for Media Studies. Used with permission.

One catchphrase of ethical coverage is "All the news that's fit to print." That slogan was introduced at the *New York Times* by Adolph S. Ochs, the publisher who brought the *Times* to greatness. It was 1897, when other New York City newspapers were vying against one another in sensationalism, and Ochs used the phrase to emphasize the thoroughness and sobriety of ethical newspaper publishing.

The cynic may say that the slogan should be "All the news that fits," or that fits the editor's whims. Everyone knows that *all* the news can't be printed. But "all the news" implies a thoroughness that will not omit stories because of laziness or pressure. "Fit" implies that the editors will avoid sensationalism or pandering to low tastes. Yet they should find it fitting for the public to know what happens, however distasteful or terrifying and regardless of pressures to leave out some events.

Freedom and Responsibility

Some editors might say that what they print is their own business and not the province of philosophers. They would be right, in the sense that a free press is guaranteed by the Constitution and that professional customs in the United States have evolved for handling these ethical questions. Custom probably controls more stories than editorial ethics do. Yet there are philosophical bases for the rights of news organizations to operate as they do, and managers ignore these at their peril.

In the medieval days of kings and queens, there would have been no argument about whether it was right or wrong to publish news of a scandal, even if there had been printing presses and editors. The monarch felt he or she had authority from God to make such decisions. A long trail of Star Chambers and jailed editors led from such dictatorship to a modern democratic system in which editors, within the framework of law, can print without license or censorship. People at first argued, as in the Declaration of Independence, that they had such inalienable rights from God. More recently, they are claimed as essential human rights.

John Milton provided the practical argument for press freedom. In the *Areopagitica* (1644) he argued for the "free marketplace of ideas." If all ideas were freely published, he said, the best ones would win out. It followed that people must have the right to know all the facts and arguments. So he rationalized the editor's freedom as one of the prerequisites for a working democracy. Thomas Jefferson argued for the citizen's right to the truth, being optimistic, as was Milton, that a benevolent Providence allowed reasonable and moral people to run their own affairs. His idea of press freedom became one of the guarantees in the Bill of Rights.

Freedom implies responsibility. Those who get liberty must use it responsibly or risk losing it, whether in a developing nation or on a college campus. The grant of freedom to editors to purvey the news necessary to a democratic society carries the implied demand that they will disseminate the news. When the media suppress or distort the news, they jeopardize their claim to freedom. The unwritten expectation of American citizens is that the news organizations will give "all the news that's fit to print" or, by extension, broadcast or Internet publication. This is the ethical imperative under which perhaps most editors work.

Codes of Ethics

Recognizing these obligations, news organizations sometimes proclaim idealistic platforms or policies. The Society of Professional Journalists' Code of Ethics is widely distributed. The American Society of Newspaper Editors adopted its own Canons of Journalism in the 1920s, and those canons have since been revised into a Statement of Principles. The problem with such codes is that there is no real enforcement mechanism, beyond perhaps the threat that journalists who transgress them risk losing their jobs or losing face with their colleagues. Few working journalists could quote much of the SPJ Code of Ethics.

The difficulty is that, as with democracy, freedom and responsibility, principles of journalism must be stated as abstractions. Pessimists can readily dismiss pledges of public interest or high trust as pious hypocrisies. The problem is to relate high-sounding dictums to hard cases. Because no news organization and no person is perfect, there are inevitably some tarnishes at the best organizations, not to mention the corrosions at the worst.

Still, an effort must be made to set standards for ethical journalistic behavior. If such moral principles as love, compassion and kindness are given lip service rather than devotion, they serve still as ideals or goals. Journalists need such abstractions to broaden their vision.

Truth

Truth is the word that summarizes many journalistic ideals. But what, philosophy has always asked, is Truth? Working newsmen and newswomen know well enough what truth means on the job and don't worry too much about Truth. They check the truth of small details but also the truth of the big picture, so far as they can discover and portray it. Former *Washington Post* reporter Carl Bernstein has described this as "the best obtainable version of the truth," an acknowledgement that the full truth is sometimes hard to grab hold of and may shift over time as more facts are revealed.

One important facet of truth is *accuracy.* Newsrooms rightly develop a fixation on accuracy about names and addresses. But reporters must be at least as careful about accurate quotation, or about the accuracy of the impression that results from the way facts are put together.

Close to accuracy is *objectivity.* Reporters should keep themselves out of the story, and editors should see that they do. The profession's conventional wisdom dictates that editorializing will be confined to opinion pieces, yet editorializing barbs in stories are always slipping by editors. Some reporters produce stories that are really editorials, and their editors, with sloppy ethics, byline them and publish them as news, becoming a conduit for an organization's position. The editor's job is to see that copy is accurate and free from editorial bias, whether it comes from a novice reporter or a Washington correspondent.

The popular dichotomy of objectivity versus interpretation represents a misunderstanding of the journalist's problem with truth. The short, deadpan news account, the so-called objective story, the feature story and the interpretative piece are all on the side of objectivity. Opposite them is the subjective story by the reporter who, knowingly or unknowingly, distorts the news, whether of a minor accident or of international conflict. The sound interpretative story introduces the writer's evaluations (and these are admittedly subjective, with personal coloring) but does so as fairly and honestly—as objectively—as possible. The corrupt interpretation, by contrast, does not aim at truth but vents the writer's prejudices. (Editorials and editorial-page interpretations, of course, differ from news stories.)

Intertwined with accuracy and the objective search for it is the concept of *fairness*. Human limitations may prevent an organization's being really accurate and truly objective, but readers know whether the editors try to be fair. They treat everybody alike. Ideally, they are as gentle with the poor unknown as with the big shot, with the hated political party or enemy nation as with their own faction or country. Perceptive critics of the press see that it is the standard of fairness that is violated when papers over the years have blandly printed in their news columns accounts that refer to "welfare queens," "white trash," "bums" and so on; the editor may protest that such highly connotative words describe accurately some social moods—but are they ever fair?

The pragmatic editor

Editors often face pressures that may imperil accuracy and fairness. Pressure from government they understand and usually can combat, if they wish. But pressure from advertisers continues to plague journalists. Most of this pressure is subtle, for rarely does an advertiser roar, "You print that and I will yank all my ads from your paper." Instead, the advertisers may call the editor or publisher and express "concern" or "regret" that certain stories appeared. Business executives may lament the "tone" of a publication's coverage. Because the publisher often associates with business people, it is hard to resist this almost constant pressure to bend to the business point of view. In many ways, this pressure is surprising, for most newspapers, being businesses, take a pro-business attitude that filters often into news, features and pictures, as well as editorials.

The ideals of accuracy, objectivity and fairness are all contained in the larger ideal of truth. But are these really phony ideals, used to delude, as hypocrites use the flag and motherhood? Some hard-bitten cynics among editors would doubtless say "yes," and their shoddy news publications reveal what happens when principle crumbles. Yet even the most ethical editors tend to be pragmatic about high journalistic principle. Pragmatism is an American philosophy that holds that the best way is the way that works best. Americans are idealistic, but they are also practical. Editors do not usually mount white chargers. They conform.

The realistic goal for the ethical journalist is to compromise as little as possible, for being pragmatic is not the same as being venal or cowardly. The best editors aim high and therefore hit higher than those who aim low.

Three Key Areas

Much of the ethical problem for editors is one of balance. They must weigh the importance of pressures to distort or omit the news against the demands of their own conscience to be thorough and fair. At the same time, they must counterbalance the frailty and limitation in their own freedom with the need to be socially responsible. They must put the individual's right of privacy in the balance against the obligation to inform the public; and they must weigh a demand for compassion against the utilitarian requirement to do what is best for the most.

Editors, however, are not systematic philosophers who worry much about complete consistency. Pragmatically, and perhaps too hastily, they make a decision, and then another and another. This is journalistic life, and editors have to live with the results. Day-to-day editorial work focuses on three issues of journalism ethics: respect for individuals, maintaining good taste and weighing the potential effects of news reports. Each of them combines the tensions of different ethical problems, and editors must develop attitudes on each of the three that harmonize satisfactorily with their philosophies of journalism and life.

Respect for the Individual

Bob Steele's ethical principles discussed earlier are broken into three sections: seek truth and report it as fully as possible; act independently; and minimize harm. Two of these duties frequently conflict: reporting the truth and minimizing harm. There's no doubt that journalism has the ability to cause great harm to individuals and organizations, and journalists constantly must be aware of that. The balancing act that editors and reporters have to perform is delicate: Is the public's need to know this information greater than the harm that will come, or will the harm to a person outweigh the good to the public? Steele has developed a list of 10 questions for journalists to consider when facing this type of problem. (See the sidebar "Ten Questions to Ask").

Ten Questions to Ask

Bob Steele, an expert on media ethics at the Poynter Institute for Media Studies, recommends that journalists consider these 10 questions when confronting an ethical problem.

1. What do I know? What do I need to know?
2. What is my journalistic purpose?
3. What are my ethical concerns?
4. What organizational policies and professional guidelines should I consider?
5. How can I include other people, with different perspectives and diverse ideas, in the decision-making process?
6. Who are the stakeholders—those affected by my decision? What are their motivations? Which are legitimate?
7. What if the roles were reversed? How would I feel if I were in the shoes of one of the stakeholders?
8. What are the possible consequences of my actions? Short term? Long term?
9. What are my alternatives to maximize my truthtelling responsibility and minimize harm?
10. Can I clearly and fully justify my thinking and my decision? To my colleagues? To the stakeholders? To the public?

Copyright 2004, Poynter Institute for Media Studies. Used with permission.

The right to privacy

The right of privacy is a delicate thing. From the legal side, a news organization can probably get by if its publication of a personal matter is closely related to news events, but privacy is more than a question of law. Sometimes journalism ethics may halt an invasion of privacy that law would permit.

Because much of their most significant work is always close to invading someone's privacy, journalists may have to remind themselves not to be too hard-boiled on the question. Ordinary people, as distinguished from politicians and celebrities, have great sensitivity about "undue publicity." In one case, a woman was incensed because the news media reported that a teenager had shot her passing car with a BB gun. As a misdemeanor, the shooting became a public record, and an editor could see plenty of reasons for printing the news: The public could judge whether juveniles are delinquent, whether the neighborhood had gangs, whether the police were doing their job and whether guns should be controlled. The woman could appreciate none of these arguments. She saw no reason that her age should be printed, and she feared that the teenager, knowing her name, would take reprisals against her or her children. Silly?

From the editor's point of view, maybe yes. But from the point of view of privacy and her feeling about press invasions, it was her own business whether she was shot at. Some journalists have accepted this criticism and have stopped using names in some crime stories and use general addresses rather than specific ones for crime scenes. For example, a reporter could place a burglary in the 900 block of Fifth Street, rather than say it occurred at 903 Fifth St.

Mass labeling

Another level of respect for individuals is in news about whole masses of people, as in wars and urban violence. Communist newspapers for decades often stereotyped the Western world as "imperialistic warmongers." But the American press easily slips into such dehumanizing labels, too. In World War I, it made the enemy inhuman with the word "Huns." Then, in World War II, it was "Japs." In more recent years those who vigorously disapproved of some United States policies were often labeled "Communist." It is much the same when reporters write loosely of "black rioters," leading white readers to react against a whole black community that may in fact be more than 99 percent peaceful.

By taking care of such issues as privacy and mass labeling, news organizations can be a good influence in maintaining respect for individuals. This is an area of the news media's greatest strength. When focusing on the individual because of honest human interest, journalism can repulse the dehumanizing forces of mass society.

Good taste

Journalists must resist the temptation to conform to a debasing popular culture. From the profane and sexist lyrics of hip-hop and rap music to the increasingly disturbing antics of reality television and shock radio, American culture today is rife with mass media messages that can only be categorized as vulgar. Profane language surrounds us at the shopping mall, in the schoolyard, at the ballpark. Journalists, as civic servants, must remain above this fray and instead contribute to civil discourse in society.

The problem of taste in news organizations is not, as many suppose, wholly one of restraint about vulgarity, profanity and sex. There can be bad taste in political writing. In the partisan-press days of the early United States, editors scurrilously attacked political enemies. During the Depression of the 1930s, newspapers indulged in calumny, and in recent years the issues of government scandal—such as the coverage of the Bill Clinton-Monica Lewinsky scandal—have triggered a barrage of bad taste.

Such issues bring up the difficulty of reporting violence with good taste. Riots and wartime killings must be reported to the public with graphic pictures to tell the whole story. Once, news organizations avoided publishing pictures of dead people. Present-day editors must use these pictures of the dead from riots, wars and terrorist attacks. But must they also use photos of the dead from disasters and accidents? Grisly photographs and lurid paragraphs, in almost all cases, must be scratched.

The problem of taste is particularly acute in artwork. Restraint must be shown with photographs of cheesecake and gore. What television uses cannot be the criterion. The fleeting quality of pictures on the screen may lessen the objection to some material on television, but the permanence of the printed picture can make it more titillating or repelling—and thus in poor taste.

So, editors must strike balances. They must satisfy the public's need for the facts, but they must also recall the high professional obligations of a free press in the area of taste as elsewhere. They will not let fears of the Nice Nellies keep them from portraying realistic aspects of the cruel and vulgar world as they are. But in an era when public taste has been cheapened and hardened, their greater concern will be to view journalism as an instrument to lift up culture and even civilization itself.

The effects of news

Editors who say they publish "without fear or favor" emphasize their objectivity. They override outside pressures on what material to use. They learn to overlook the consequences of their decisions, for editorial action is paralyzed or biased if an editor worries about how an item is going to affect the co-worker, mother or friend of a person in the news.

There is a running debate about whether news publications have much effect. Editorials have been discounted as political factors for decades. Communications researchers have been able to demonstrate few clear effects of simple reports and have drawn back from trying to analyze really complex but important problems such as how news reports influence the vote for president.

If the influence of news organizations cannot be pinpointed, can the effects of home or school or church be proved any more convincingly? Are they any less real even so? Would anyone seriously hypothesize that the media have less effect than parents or teachers? A newsmaker does not doubt that publication has an effect. The college football star knows that sports reporting influences his ability to get dates and a pro contract. The embezzler recognizes that at the very least, news stories about his deeds can wreck his credit rating. The woman selling widgets knows her sales go up after an article about them appears.

Editors also know that their publications have an effect from the actions of publicity seekers asking space and acquaintances phoning to try to suppress news. They hope that the effect is good, and one of the strongest arguments for press freedom is that full reporting benefits the democratic process. They like to point to times when coverage has led to ousters of public cheats and when crusades have brought civic improvements. The development of social responsibility theory urges them to be even more concerned about their paper's effect on society.

Chain reactions

As news of one suicide in a mental hospital gets around, other patients sometimes make suicide attempts. From that observation psychiatrists sometimes also conclude that news accounts of suicides tend to trigger other suicides. Some of them argue that accounts of dramatic, "mad" killings stimulate others to attempt such murders. The argument is plausible, since it is obvious that "good" ideas for communities and business catch on because they get news media notice. But can an editor start holding back "bad" news lest it stimulate readers to try the same misdeed?

Suicide is normally played down in news reports because usually the person who kills himself is not of great news importance. One fairly common guideline is that suicides done in private—such as at home—are passed by, whereas suicides in public are worth reporting, particularly if the act disrupts routine activity. Many news publications have followed the practice of giving few details about the method of suicide. They may omit the name of a poison, for example, on the theory that other depressed people may want to take the same "out."

News publications can contribute to widespread panic. Some stories catch the public's attention and thus get sustained play, even if the threat is not as large as the public imagines. Some recent examples of this include the scare over sudden acute respiratory syndrome and mad cow disease, which because of their unusual nature drew much attention—even though Americans are much more likely to die of heart disease than either of those maladies.

Some Common Problems

Underlying the discussion in this chapter is the assumption that the journalist will live up to the ethical standards of the profession and the community. Just as we assume that most cashiers will not dip into the till and that most government officials will not take bribes, so we assume that editors should be honest. They will not accept gifts that will color their judgment, they will not take money to leave news out and they will not promote a pet cause to win favors or preferment. Such general principles are easy to state but hard to practice.

Gifts

Reporters, in particular, move among sources who may offer gifts. In most cases the gift is merely a token: a necktie or some handkerchiefs at

Christmas, a lunch or a ballpoint pen. Sometimes the gift is not a token but a bribe. For example, reporters covering a professional football team some years ago were each given a quality portable electric typewriter at the end of the season. A reporter who accepts a $300 gift can easily slip into softening or eliminating any critical stories about the football team or its management. Wasn't that the purpose of the gift?

Gratuities to journalists are usually far more subtle. An invitation to a special cocktail party, a fancy dinner or a plush weekend sometimes sways reporters into thinking that the merchant in trouble with the Federal Trade Commission is too charming to expose. The reporter's copy reflects this appraisal. Sometimes reporters have been flattered to the point of being obsequious when a president or a governor asks them for advice. Others can succumb to flattery coming from a much lower source. And can a travel story be trusted if a travel agency paid the writer's way to do research for the piece?

Journalists, like everyone else, want to be liked, and it bothers some to play the role, even occasionally, of the skeptic. Perhaps the best advice is that the journalist should at these times ask, "Am I performing my professional obligations?"

Thoughtful reporters in Washington sometimes admit that an invitation to the home of the secretary of state for a "not for attribution" press conference causes them to crawl at least a little way into the secretary's pocket. After all, only a few reporters are so honored. What reporters would not be a bit dazzled if they lunched at the White House? For weeks afterward the reporters could drop into all conversations, "When I was lunching with the president. . . ."

Public duty

Other governmental pressures have ethical overtones. A reporter or editor who criticizes the military is apt to be considered disloyal or at least "not on the team." A dissenter from American foreign policy may be reminded sternly, "Dissent stops at the water's edge." In one case, a famous columnist critical of an administration was subjected to an organized whispering campaign to discredit him. The critic of hometown business operations may be denounced in public as a "carping critic who is bringing scorn to our fair city." These pressures, often not expressed so bluntly, are hard to combat because they are subtle. In addition, the person who is pressured enjoys being praised by the rich and powerful as a person who "has helped our town a lot." What they probably mean is that the journalist has been a faithful puppet of the elite—a mouthpiece for a few rather than a person speaking for the many.

One of the toughest ethical problems facing journalists is when to be silent. All kinds of responsible people—police, industrialists, city officials—will ask the press to withhold information. The reasons are various, but at the highest levels the customary reason is *the national interest*. The best instance of silence in the national interest was President Kennedy's persuading the *New York Times* to soften a story that the United States was planning to invade Cuba at the Bay of Pigs.

Later, Kennedy said the invasion was a disaster that would have been avoided if the *Times* had printed a story saying that the attack was imminent. He added that such a story would have saved him and the nation much embarrassment.

Several years later, the Nixon administration tried to bar the publication of the Pentagon Papers, which detailed the history of U.S. involvement in Vietnam. The *New York Times* first began publishing the story, and when a court blocked further publication, the *Washington Post* began publishing them a few days later. The issue went to the U.S. Supreme Court, which ruled that the government could not bar publication of matter absent a clear and present danger to national security.

All presidential administrations do their best to keep some information from journalists. Staffers are skilled in stalling, diverting attention and keeping secrets. Reporters should be skeptical of information provided by presidents and other high officials.

There are times, of course, when the press is quick to withhold information in the public interest. If the police are about to raid an unlicensed bar or are ready to make an unexpected arrest, the facts are withheld until after the police do their work. But the interest had better be clear; otherwise the press will not be serving the public but rather those who wish to operate in secrecy. Nothing so damages a news publication's reputation and encourages rumor more than the public's realization that it omits news or favors the police, the mayor or the manager of the town's biggest industry.

Political involvement

Another practical ethical consideration for an editor is whether to run for public office or to head a special committee. It inflates anyone's ego, of course, to be asked to run, but as a candidate or an elected official, the journalist puts the news organization in a position to be either partisan or accused of partisanship. How can a news publication maintain a semblance of journalistic detachment in education coverage if one of its reporters or editors is a member of the school board?

One newspaper editor became chairman of a civic committee to investigate new water sources for the city. It was an important job and a position he could fill capably. But the findings of his committee became controversial and the key issue in a mayoral campaign. Much of the public thought that the newspaper was acting as a mouthpiece for the editor's own views on water sources. The newspaper's standing in the community declined even though no bias was ever proved.

The Ethics of Online Journalism

Journalists who work for Internet news publications, who must observe the ethical responsibilities of other journalists, face additional problems unique to that medium. Among these problems are speed versus accuracy, the use of the Internet as a reporting tool and the blurring line between editorial and advertising content.[2]

A reporter working for an online publication faces a pressure that her counterpart in the print newsroom does not: The editor wants the story now, for immediate dissemination. This rush to publish means that the reporter does not have as much time to check her facts nor the time to make an additional call. An ethical question, such as the naming of a criminal suspect, that might prompt a lengthy discussion at a daily newspaper might get short consideration in the rush to post a breaking story. And many online publications have no copy desks, thus leaving them without the essential quality control that copy editors provide at print publications. These factors make mistakes online almost certain. The one upside is that editors can quickly fix mistakes when they are found; the downside is that the error may have been seen by thousands—or more—before being corrected. An editor working in the online medium, therefore, needs to take particular care with sensitive stories before they are posted online.

The Internet has become an invaluable tool for reporters conducting research and for editors checking facts. But it also presents potential problems. For one thing, it could lead to reporters rehashing the same story ideas rather than coming up with fresh angles. For another, the Internet has made it easy for unscrupulous reporters to plagiarize the work of others. Editors need to be on guard against these possible practices.

Advertising that attempts to masquerade as stories generated by the newsroom are nothing new. Journalists have for decades fought to keep such pieces—sometimes called advertorials—from the news pages without being clearly marked as advertising. This problem has now spilled over onto Internet news sites. On some home pages, a user cannot tell whether some links will lead to journalistic work vetted in the newsroom or puff pieces generated by the Web site's advertising department. Online journalists should resist this intrusion and insist that advertising be labeled as such.

Accountability

The Society of Professional Journalists adds a fourth ethical duty that Bob Steele does not include on his list. It requires journalists, and the organizations they work for, to be accountable. Among other things, this means they need to be transparent in how they go about their work, and that they admit it publicly when they make mistakes. Most news publications now regularly run corrections, typically appearing in the same place each time so that readers know where to find them. Many print publications run them on the second page of the front section. The *Washington Post*'s Web site has a link in its navigation bar to a page of corrections.

Sometimes this ethical duty requires news organizations to go further. In the run-up to the U.S. invasion of Iraq in 2003, news organizations were for the most part in step with the Bush administration's claims that Saddam Hussein was harboring chemical and biological weapons and trying to build an atomic bomb. After the invasion, scant evidence of such weapons or attempts to develop such weapons was found. The *New York Times* and the *Washington Post* both admitted in their news and editorial page columns that they had not done enough to challenge the president's justifications for the invasion.[3]

Using Freedom Responsibly

Ethical journalists, of course, work hard to be responsible. They do their best to set aside their prejudices and concern for professional acclaim. They strive to give readers and listeners the truth. Experienced journalists know how difficult it is to get the truth. They interview widely, check their sources' claims with care and examine records. They are wary of being used by others trying to promote their agendas. They write and edit to produce stories that provide solid, pertinent information. Despite their care, they often discover that some important fact or set of facts has been overlooked. A source may have misled them; a record may be inaccurate; the evaluation of some fact could be invalid.

The journalist working on a tight deadline or trying to rush a story online has special problems. It is tempting not to make one more telephone call, check another record or reflect on the accuracy and completeness of the story at hand. The result occasionally is a story without specific error but one that has neglected certain facts or a breadth of opinion.

Too many journalists, who consider themselves ethical, unconsciously gravitate to mainstream reporting. They interview officials and private citizens with conventional views. They even have a list of such sources. Their basic sources may be a press secretary, a few in government, a think-tank expert and a certain professor. Almost all these people come close to sharing the same point of view. Sharply differing opinions or analyses are cited rarely.

Ethical journalists should not flatter themselves by reciting: "I'm careful. I'm fair. I'm accurate. I'm as objective and ethical as I can be." Instead, they might ask themselves, "Am I missing anything? Am I getting tricked anywhere? Am I getting a wide range of viewpoints on crucial issues? Am I simply following the pack, writing stories that reflect the value judgments of my peers? Have I been charmed by a source?"

Such journalists, if they answer honestly, are more likely to produce fair, evocative, factual and valuable information. They also will come closer to printing the whole truth.

Notes

1. Robert I. Berkman and Christopher A. Shumway, *Digital Dilemmas: Ethical Issues for Online Media Professionals*. (Ames, Iowa: Iowa State Press, 2003).

2. For a more detailed discussion of these issues, see Berkman and Shumway.

3. See Howard Kurtz, "The Post on WMDs: An Inside Story," *Washington Post* (Aug. 12, 2004), A1, and "The Times and Iraq," *New York Times* (May 26, 2004, www.nytimes.com/critique).

CHAPTER 15

Policy and Responsibility

Our liberty depends on freedom of the press, and that cannot be limited with-out being lost.
—Thomas Jefferson

In the run-up to the 2004 presidential election, CBS News anchor Dan Rather appeared to have something that no other journalism organization had: documents that reflected poorly on President George W. Bush's record in the National Guard during the Vietnam War. The president had always maintained he had fulfilled his duty during his guard years, but there were persistent questions about gaps in the records document-ing his service. Rather, on the "CBS Evening News" and the news-magazine show "60 Minutes," reported on Sept. 8, 2004, that CBS News had obtained documents from one of Bush's commanders in which he expressed concern that he had been pressured to go easy on Bush. (At the time, Bush's father was ambassador to the United Nations.) This was big news, a big scoop for CBS and potentially a big headache for the president's re-election campaign.

But almost immediately, concerns popped up about the report and the documents. The documents came under intense scrutiny in particu-lar in Web logs, or blogs—Internet diaries that can be created and main-tained by anyone with an Internet account and space on a World Wide Web server. Experts in document authentication questioned whether the documents were real. Even some of the experts that CBS consulted said they had concerns.

About two weeks later, the story unraveled. Rather apologized on the air and said that the authenticity of the documents could not be verified and that the source who had supplied the documents had proved to be unreliable. In essence, CBS had ignored its own journalistic standards in a rush to get a big exclusive on the air—and it admitted as much, launch-ing an internal investigation into what had happened.

Three years earlier, after the burst of the dot-com bubble and a steep decline in the technology business, advertising at daily newspapers was down sharply—particularly at the *San Jose Mercury News*, in the heart of the Silicon Valley. Corporate owner Knight Ridder, worried about a decline in profit margins that would harm its reputation on Wall Street, ordered its newspapers, including the *Mercury News*, to find ways to cut costs. In the newspaper business, that means cutting the size of the paper (to reduce printing costs) and firing employees (to reduce payroll costs). The publisher of the *Mercury News*, Jay Harris, who before moving to the business side had a distinguished career as a journalist, balked. He felt that the level of cuts that Knight Ridder wanted the newspaper to endure would make the *Mercury News* unable to continue with the quality journalism for which it had earned a high reputation. Rather than submit to the cuts, Harris resigned.

"There was virtually no discussion of the damage that would be done to the quality and aspirations of the *Mercury News* as a journalistic endeavor or to its ability to fulfill its responsibilities to the community," Harris later told the American Society of Newspaper Editors. "As importantly, scant attention was paid to the damage that would be done to our ability to compete and grow the business." (For the full text of Harris' speech, go to http://www.asne.org/2001reporter/friday/harristranscript6.html.)

In 2003, the *New York Times* fired a reporter for copying the work of others and for making up information outright. That same year the *Sacramento Bee* fired a sportswriter who wrote an account about a baseball game that he had not attended. The next year, *USA Today* fired a reporter for plagiarism and fabrication. At the *Los Angeles Times*, editors fired a photographer who manipulated a photograph from the Middle East. In Missouri, a sportswriter and movie reviewer was fired for plagiarism. The list goes on.

The problem with plagiarism and fabrication and a rush to publish without sufficient checking: credibility. A news organization's responsibility is to truthful reporting, and at the heart of truthful reporting is accuracy. Without that, a news organization loses its credibility. Without credibility, it loses its audience and cannot survive. A Gallup Poll conducted as the CBS News-Bush documents debacle was unfolding found that only "44 percent of Americans expressed confidence in the media's ability to report news stories accurately and fairly." This reflected a 10 percentage point drop from the previous year and a serious problem for those whose livelihood depends on their believability.

Given current media credibility problems and the increasing-in-frequency black eyes inflicted on the profession, why would anyone want to be a journalist? Why is journalism so important?

To answer that, it's important to understand what the role of journalism is in American society. Here's what Bill Kovach and Tom Rosenstiel have to say about that in their important book, *The Elements of Journalism*:

"The primary purpose of journalism is to provide citizens with the information they need to be free and self-governing."[1]

A Public Trust

Kovach and Rosenstiel's description of journalism's primary purpose may sound idealistic, but it dates to the founding of the nation and the embodiment of freedom of expression in the First Amendment. The Founding Fathers believed in the role of the press—at that time, a highly partisan one—to help hold government power in check and to promote ideas worth considering in the governance of the young nation. As the only enterprise to be protected by the Constitution, the press is in essence a public trust—a profitable one, no doubt, but still a public trust.

One of the traditional roles of the news media in the United States has been as a watchdog over those in power—be that power official or unofficial. Leonard Downie Jr. and Robert Kaiser rank high the responsibility of monitoring of power in their book *The News About the News: American Journalism in Peril.* They describe how American governance is based on accountability, and journalists play a vital role in assuring that accountability. "Anyone tempted to abuse power looks over his or her shoulder to see if someone else is watching," they write. "Ideally, there should be a reporter in the rearview mirror."[2] But, Downie and Kaiser argue, the focus of journalism organizations on profit rather than public service is making this essential role harder for journalists to conduct.

Jay Harris, in his ASNE speech, addressed balancing the needs of profit versus public service:

> "In managing a newspaper or a newspaper company in the public interest, you are faced with these questions: When the interests of readers and shareholders are at odds, which takes priority? When the interests of a community and shareholders are at odds, which takes priority? When the interests of the nation in an informed citizenry and the demands of shareholders for ever-increasing profits are at odds, which takes priority?"

The answer, say Kovach and Rosenstiel, must be the public interest. That notion is among their Elements of Journalism: Journalism's "first loyalty is to citizens." The authors are not alone in their argument that it is quality journalism, not a short-sighted focus on the bottom line and stock prices, that will help journalism businesses grow in the long run.

Kovach and Rosenstiel describe a triangular relationship between newsrooms, the public and advertisers. In a journalistic endeavor, the customer is not the public; the customer is the advertiser. It is advertising that produces the most revenue for the business. What newsrooms, be they a print publication, an Internet news site or a broadcast outlet, do is create a relationship with the public through their journalism. This relationship is then rented to advertisers. In this view, journalistic endeavors must focus on serving the public above all else. The profits will follow.[3]

Harris' speech was seen by many in the journalism community as a call to arms in journalism, to fight against the corporate diminution of journalism by calling public attention to it. For a while, it worked. After Harris' resignation, Knight Ridder reduced its demands for cuts at the *Mercury News*—but only temporarily. A few years later, the *Mercury News* was forced to cut news staff and eliminate an edition.

Those planning careers as reporters and editors should take notice of these trends, but they should not be discouraged. They are the ones on the front lines as journalists; it is here where the battle can best be fought, in an ongoing effort to expose the ills of society. It is on the front lines of journalism where reporters and editors conduct work that has real effects on people's lives. It is on the front lines of journalism where, despite the pressures of corporate cost cutting, reporters and editors do their best work to bring information to the community so that its members can make informed decisions about their lives. This is a battle that cannot and should not be given up. Ever.

Why journalism?

The American Society of Newspaper Editors asked reporters and editors to talk about why they became journalists and why they continue as journalists despite some of the setbacks the industry has suffered. Their motivations and experiences differ, but it was summed up by Jennie Buckner, the editor of the *Charlotte Observer*: "It's true that newspaper work can be hard, sometimes tedious. But there's this payoff: It's work that matters. Newspapers make a difference." The ASNE's report is at http://www.asne.org/index.cfm?ID=4847.

Responsibility and Policy

Every news organization should work out a clear and consistent concept of its aims and operations. The set of principles or guidelines for its procedures—the chart that sets its course—is called its policy. Much of policy is unwritten, carried in the heads of editors. Some points may be vague, some may be inconsistent. But it does offer a kind of "common law" that governs the way decisions will be made.

In the American economy, the publisher's power over policy rests on ownership. Our system does not give control of the press to the state or cooperatives, much less to any interest group. Because the person paying the piper calls the tune, the company that puts up the capital for a news medium decides what it will say and what it will not say.

One indication of confusion on this point is the perennial tendency of some college editors to claim greater power of policy than the colleges are willing to give them. In a private college, individuals put up the capital on which the student paper ultimately rests, and in a state institution, the taxpayers provided most of the original funds. The locus of real power is obscured by talk of campus democracy, by the fact that students may subsidize the paper and by the efforts of wise administrators to give editors maximum freedom. But if there is a libel suit, the institution, not the editor, pays. When student journalists don't like it that way, they quit, perhaps to start their own off-campus publication. Then they meet the bills and pay for any libel suits, and they have a publisher's freedom to publish and not to publish, within the bounds of law and ethics. (Nor would they then, having put energy and money into their paper, probably be inclined to hand it over to others to run as they pleased, without strings! It's not the nature of publishing or ownership.) Though it would be nice to get something for nothing, there is no way to get the freedom to publish as one pleases without paying in energy, money and risk.

Lest the publisher's power appear overwhelming, it should be noted that most publishers are more interested in checking balance sheets than in advancing policies. They infrequently hand down word on policy. More often, they turn day-to-day policy over to those who will formulate policies they approve. When Col. Robert McCormick was running the *Chicago Tribune*, a Northwestern University professor often asked *Tribune* editors whether memos instructed them to be anti-British or anti-labor. The teacher never found that McCormick gave such orders; the staff simply edited the paper on those lines because they thought he wanted it that way. Sometimes, indeed, the true policymaker of a paper is not so much the real-life chief executive as a kind of newsroom phantom the editors see representing the executive's wishes.

Though the publisher or CEO ultimately is responsible for policy and can change it, the top editors may have considerable influence in shaping it. Their first duty is to examine the phantoms for realities. They may find that the staff still worships sacred cows that were slaughtered long ago. Changing conditions naturally demand new policies, which editors can either make or suggest in hope of approval from the top. At minimum, they can try to influence the publisher to adopt the best policy. As policies prove unworkable or unwise, editors also can encourage the publisher to change them. The editor has special professional competence, after all, and a smart publisher will consider any reasoned arguments.

It is possible that a strong and somewhat brash assignment editor will, in effect, change policy by switching content. The publishers or CEOs may not notice it, or they may even approve the change. They could grumble a little but not make the effort to order a reversal. They might be annoyed, of course, to the point of shifting the editor to a different job.

One troubling complication in this owner-policy situation is the ambiguity of absentee ownership, which today is widespread with so many news organizations owned by chains. At its worst, the absentee system means that the owners are interested only in the money the publication makes. Management pinches pennies, lets journalism quality deteriorate and adopts policies designed to save dollars rather than to better a community. At its best, however, absentee ownership may give dedicated professionals the authority to run a good publication.

In looking at the publisher's role, it is also wise not to get too exalted a concept of what policy formation is. The publisher does not send down a code to some Moses. Such a code could no more cover all cases than could the Ten Commandments, and, in any event, it would have to be interpreted by busy copy editors. The news business is practical. Let's say that the publisher decrees the paper should be fair. Fine, but is it fairer to put in this news fact or leave it out? By repeatedly answering this question, writers and editors form policy.

Or suppose a publisher orders that his organization support candidate A. Professionalism decides how far the editors can go with such a policy, and if it is pushed too crassly, the paper—and the publisher's bank account—will suffer. In short, policy is not like a statue, which is formed once and for all. It is more like a hedge, which editors can prune and nurture.

Policies stem from a news organization's objectives. When the goal is full and fair coverage, editors can develop specific policies to reach it. But if the aim is simply to make as much money as possible, other policies are required.

The Editorial Mix

Magazines operate with what editors, borrowing from chemistry, call a formula. The term refers to the combination of ingredients—articles, photos, stories, cartoons and so on—that regularly go into the publication. The shifting nature of the news makes it more difficult to stabilize a news organization's formula or recipe. A heavy mix of foreign news may be best on one day; several local stories may demand treatment on the next. Nevertheless, the concept of a formula helps show how editors develop practices that reach policy goals. The serious publication has one editorial mix, the frivolous another. Descending from the heights of press ideals, practicalities of policy are studied by considering three major ingredients: opinion, news and entertainment.

Opinion

American news organizations, for the most part, separate news and opinion, with the editors' views confined to the opinion pages. Though the ideal may be violated, the policy remains sound. If editorial writers stay within the bounds of law and good taste, few questions are raised about their right to support or oppose candidates or programs. Whether the CEO or publisher sets editorial policy or hands the task to the editors, decisions about the stands to be taken in these opinion columns are a keystone of a news organization's overall policy.

Policy also has to be made for use of columnists. Some news media carry only columns that support their own positions. A more common policy is to select columns that give "both sides." A vigorous, aggressive paper might, however, adopt a policy of selecting—even of finding and cultivating—columnists who will argue a wide variety of stimulating and nonconformist opinions.

Guidelines also must be established for letters to the editor. A sensible and common policy is to publish as many letters as possible and to encourage contributions. If at least a little of every literate contribution is used, the policy wins wide reader support. Online news sites that allow reader feedback must have policies about whether people must identify themselves when posting opinions, and whether to moderate the posts.

News

If accuracy and fairness are desirable goals, independence is a leading virtue in news policy. Selection of the news, as indicated already in discussions of news evaluation and journalism ethics, must be free from influence by editorial page policy, advertising pressures or the biases of the owners or staffers.

Completeness and breadth of coverage are also important in news policy. Editors and publishers of papers outside the largest metropolitan centers sometimes complain when press critics hold up the thoroughness of the *New York Times* as an example. Though news organizations with smaller resources cannot offer such a wealth of news, the goal for even a newspaper of 50,000 should be coverage in breadth and depth of "all the news that's fit to print." By carefully selecting and editing news from local staffers and from the wires, editors can cover world news with at least moderate thoroughness and local news with completeness and enterprise.

News media, of course, publish a great deal of good news. Stories on medical advances, tax cuts or the arrest of a dangerous criminal are all examples of good news. But what is good news to one person may be bad news to another. Democrats rejoice when papers print the good news of their party's victory. To Republicans the news is bad. A boost in the price of XYZ stock is good news to the stockholder but bad news to the person who sold the same stock yesterday.

A sizable number of people wish the news media would play down the bad news. Business executives often want journalists to keep pretending that the economic picture blooms with roses when in fact business is down 8 percent over the previous year. Some sports fans go into rages if their heroes are described as anything less than magnificent. But faking, slanting or distorting the news can be dangerous. People can be badly misled and take steps that cause considerable anguish. As an example, if a local news Web site kept trumpeting how a city was growing, some builders might construct shopping centers or apartment houses that could not be rented, hurting the builders and the city.

A few newspapers for a time tried to promote the positive side of the community by printing lots of stories about civic accomplishments and saying little about crime, accidents and job layoffs. Most of them gave it up after a few months. The efforts usually were strained. Editors were forsaking normal news judgment and the whole attempt smelled of "boosterism," not journalism.

Editors should deal almost daily with some specific policy as a guide. As an example, how should editors handle the story of a crime committed by the 32-year-old son of a United States senator? Should a big story be published? Should the news organization assume that the son has not been under the guidance of the senator for a dozen years and give the story little play or none at all? What about memoirs contending that 30 years ago the author and a famous person had a torrid romance? Is this item fact or fantasy? Even if it is fact, what play should the story receive? What is the policy on stories that sound as though the reporter was overzealous, reaching for a conclusion that was not buttressed by fact? How will editors handle in-house conflicts of interest, such as allowing a business writer to become a bank director? Too many newsrooms let these policy questions go unanswered, and the staff stumbles along until the organization unnecessarily hurts feelings and reputations or embarrasses itself.

Entertainment

It would be foolish for a news publication to have a policy of no entertainment, though some observers apparently feel that should be the goal. It is true that certain publications strive for almost nothing else. On the other hand, in response to the disillusioning development of television largely as entertainment, some editors feel that seriousness is the best competing policy. The policy of a news publication on this score, of course, must be tailored to its public. But, along with opinion and news, entertainment has a legitimate place. It has been a part of newspapers almost since they emerged from flysheets, and it should continue in any editorial formula. The question is, how much of this leavening ingredient should be included?

Sometimes editors beg the question by contending that everything they publish should be interesting and therefore entertaining. That is neither possible nor desirable. Some important developments, such as crises in the oil market, are by their nature dull to ordinary readers. They can be explained clearly and even interestingly, but it would be fatuous to twist these stories into entertainment.

Some people dismiss as entertainment only that which does not fit their own tastes. Some editors will rail against fluffy features, routine pictures and advice columns as a waste of space. They will fight to keep the crossword puzzle, however, because they try to solve it every day.

An honest, objective look at newsroom policy would include an analysis of what is proper to the editorial page, what is real news, and all the rest—comics, advice columns, sports, feature photographs and lifestyle sections. (Editors might differ as to whether cultural coverage or sports is entertainment or a part of the news/opinion spectrum, but such features are part of a good mix.)

Social Responsibility

In the somewhat mixed economy of the United States, journalism today fits somewhere between the old libertarian theory of maximum editorial freedom and the theory of social responsibility. And no matter how ardently Jeffersonians might wish it, news organizations do not today have the freedom to be irascible and irresponsible, as did the editors when Jefferson was president. The role of the news organization in the 21st century must be thought out in new terms—that of a public trust.

The idea of journalism as a public trust dates at least to the deliberations of the Hutchins Commission in the 1940s. The commission investigated problems with a news media seemingly out of control in its coverage. The commission's work resulted in what has become known as social responsibility theory. The main tenets of this theory, as described by Denis McQuail:

- The media have obligations to society, and media ownership is a public trust.
- News media should be truthful, accurate, fair, objective and relevant.
- The media should be free, but self-regulated.
- Media should follow agreed codes of ethics and professional conduct.[4]

The theory also suggests that government should intervene in the news media when necessary, but given the strictures of the First Amendment, it's doubtful that could actually happen.

The image most appropriate for the modern American news media is probably that of public utility. The metaphor is imperfect but instructive. A telephone company or an electric corporation enjoys a monopoly that even free-enterprise enthusiasts rarely question. Though public commissions may control any aspects of the business, such as determining whether its rates are fair, the utility is relatively free to plan, purchase and expand. Yet utility executives recognize that they must serve the whole community and cannot arbitrarily ignore any citizen, provided that bills are paid.

Similarly, a news organization enjoys many protections under the Constitution and by informal tradition. It holds responsibilities both to the community and to individuals, no matter how odd their ideas may appear.

The public-utility concept may help corporate owners and editors form realistic policies for the times. The news organization, as public utility, is a business, but not just any business. It has a responsibility to convey essential information to a democratic society. Citizens have as much right to criticize how well it does this job as they have to criticize telephone service.

News media are also humanitarian enterprises, but not like the Red Cross. Rather, they are businesses like the gas company, which serves people as it earns. Lumber companies may indicate in advertising that their sole interest is in planting trees, but ultimately they exist to produce profits for stockholders. The legitimate money needs of a news medium should not be forgotten in fogs of humanistic discourse.

News media companies often sound hardheaded when they speak of their properties and profit and insincere when they carry on about their ideals. For their part, intellectual critics are inclined to be cynical about the business aspects of publishing and naive about the humanistic potential of our present news media system. Business people and intellectuals might find a common realistic ground if they recognize modern news organizations as public utilities, requiring policies that produce profits and at the same time serve society well.

The public, too, should examine their views with more care. Often critics of the press demand fuller coverage, more courageous reporting and less advertising, yet they might be the first to complain if their demands were met. They most likely would not read the wider coverage and would howl if a courageous reporter raked a little muck in their own back yard.

Any editor, then, should not rush to accept the standards offered by critics. Human beings like to make lofty statements, but they often fail to match those statements with performance.

How does the concept of the public utility relate to policy aims? Such goals as accuracy and fairness, as noted, define the news organization's stance toward information. But related aims emerge from its public utility role: improving the community by reducing racial and sex stereotypes, trying to be sensitive to the feelings of all people and campaigning to eliminate corrupt and tawdry conditions.

Community Betterment

It would be difficult to find a publisher or Web site CEO who would not say that his policy is to improve the community. That goal is minimal, but it is also a major challenge.

Journalists have made great strides in reducing stereotypes. It is somewhat rare to see racial references that have no bearing on the story. Sexist tones still creep into copy, of course, but the instances seem to get sparser every year. Journalists still tend to lump the young and the old as homogenous groups, as though all young and all old are almost exactly alike. Editors need to guard against these flaws. One way to do this is to work toward diverse newsrooms that reflect the community's racial and ethnic makeup. Although newsrooms have made progress here, more needs to be done.

Some journalists have trouble grasping what is outside their experience. They may understand the major religious denominations, for example, but they get muddled on differences, say, between fundamentalists and evangelicals. Too often they don't take time to seek clarification. Sportswriters couldn't believe how a major basketball player, a vegetarian, could perform unless he ate meat. They apparently had never met a vegetarian.

Idealists puzzle some journalists, too, who find it difficult to believe that anyone would put ethics first, ahead of money and prestige. The idealist often is treated as a dreamer or a phony. At the same time, some saintly persons are lionized as flawless.

In the 1960s and 1970s, many reporters and editors were chastised for concentrating on the spectacles in protests. Journalists were accused, often justly, of reporting the statements and actions of only the most militant groups and ignoring the grievances that underlay the protests. The lesson has not always been heeded. Journalists too often still respond hastily to the scathing statement, the exaggerated claim or the rigged event without bothering to seek reasoned and restrained comments. Many politicians have complained bitterly that their meticulous, cautious and studious proposals get ignored by the news media while a dramatic but shallow plan by someone else gets prominent play.

Crusades

It may be the policy of the publisher and editor to pick evils to fight and to conduct what has long been called a "crusade." In news stories, pictures, cartoons and editorials they hammer away to clean out gamblers, build a civic center, get a city development plan adopted or "run the crooks out of city hall."

Crusading easily slips into imbalance and unfairness, but it is exciting journalism. If crusading seems not so general or potent as it was a generation or two ago, the annual recognitions in the Pulitzer Prizes and the Polk and Sigma Delta Chi awards suggest that many newsrooms still have crusading policies. To the crusader, merely giving the news is too slow a road to community betterment. Even when a paper is not seeking a crusade, important events are thrust upon it in such ways that honest journalists are forced to look for the hidden facts if the paper is to meet its responsibilities. Recent Pulitzer Prizes indicate that several papers have plunged into what often would be unpopular frays to correct abuses that involve people's lives or fortunes.

Some of the Pulitzer Prizes have been given in recent years to these papers or reporters:

- Alan Miller and Kevin Sack of the *Los Angeles Times* for their examination of a military aircraft nicknamed "the Widow Maker" that was linked to the deaths of 45 pilots.

- Staff of the *Eagle-Tribune* of Lawrence, Mass., for stories on the accidental drownings of four boys.
- Staff of the *Wall Street Journal* for stories on corporate scandals.
- Clifford J. Levy of the *New York Times* for a series on "Broken Homes" that exposed the abuse of mentally ill adults in state-regulated homes.
- Sonia Nazario of the *Los Angeles Times* for "Enrique's Journey," which told of a Honduran boy's search for his mother, who had migrated to the United States.
- Kevin Sullivan and Mary Jordan of the *Washington Post* for exposing the horrific conditions of the Mexican criminal justice system.

These stories probably did not make news organizations an extra nickel from circulation or advertising. It is also probable that they spent thousands of dollars to get the stories.

Community leadership

Policy also may concern the news organization's role in community leadership. This leadership is continuing, perhaps less intensely than the crusading burst, but in a more vigorous and directed fashion than that necessary for general community betterment. For example, take the perennial issue of schools. A newsroom may work for community betterment simply by giving thorough coverage of what is happening in local education. A crusading news organization may go after the hide of the superintendent or try to get its candidates elected to the school board. But a newsroom oriented toward leadership might search out the opinions of teachers and parents, discuss alternate possibilities on its editorial page and develop interpretative stories showing how similar communities have tackled similar problems.

A news organization may operate on all three levels at different times, or even at the same time. Most of its effort may go to straight coverage and editorials that help the citizens themselves better their community. The publication may crusade on the school drug problem, while, simultaneously, its editors may move in and out of leadership efforts on pollution, street violence or international combats. A news publication will be most effective, however, if the publisher and editors plan a coordinated policy small enough for the staff to handle yet big enough to make an impact. Too often the crusade starts out dramatically and then, like so many heralded grand jury or congressional investigations, it fizzles because of inadequate planning.

In one vital aspect of policy, a news publication cannot avoid contributing to the community's betterment or, perhaps, to its decline. The organization's policies influence what the citizens think about. Television and radio, ministers, professors and clubs all have some part in picking out the big issues for local discussion, but the influence of the newspaper or local news Web site probably outweighs all of them. Television has great influence on the perception of national issues and personalities but little on state and local affairs. Newspapers establish the agenda of concerns as if they were chairing giant town meetings. If the paper prints a lot about muggings, the people worry about muggings. If it gives complete coverage to meetings that deal with school closings, the readers will be talking about the shrinking school system. Riots, pornography, peace activities or drugs become public concerns, or not, depending on whether the local news media cover or ignore them.

Especially through interpretative stories, the news publication sets the agenda of public discussion and action. If it does not cover, say, the desires or demands of the black community, it is difficult for community leaders to generate public concern. If it does publish such material, the public becomes at least slightly aware. Sometimes unobtrusively, sometimes forcefully, the news medium's policies change the community for better or worse. The changes come because readers get facts and analyses of those facts. With that information, the public can decide whether to act.

Journalism versus "Journalism" Online

Press critic A.J. Liebling wrote decades ago that freedom of the press belongs to those who actually own one. What he meant was that only those who can *afford* a press can enjoy the fruits of the First Amendment's free press clause. Printing presses do not come cheap.

The Internet has changed all that. Now, anybody with an Internet account and access to a Web server owns a "press" and can wield the freedom of that "press." Liebling's world of press ownership has grown a millionfold. In the Miltonian sense of a marketplace of ideas, this is a good thing. For busy people in American society trying to make sense of their world, however, it only adds to the confusion.

Does ownership of a Web site that provides information make somebody a journalist? Is someone who publishes rumors and innuendo on his Web site a reporter? Is someone who maintains a Web log, sharing her opinions about any matter under the sun every day, a columnist in the journalistic sense?

The answer: It depends. A blogger who spouts off her opinions without any research or basis in facts can hardly be considered a journalist in the terms that Americans have come to define it. But bloggers whose primary obligation is to the truth, whose reporting is thorough, whose work is vetted by others, fit more into the view of who journalists are.

With the cacophony of information available at the fingertips of Internet users, it's the duty of news organizations to bring some sense to the world. Jack Fuller, president of Tribune Publishing, discusses this in his book *News Values: Ideas for an Information Age*. "Part of the challenge of those who pioneer the new medium will be to devise ways in which it can meet the audience's yearning for a sense of meaning," he writes.[5]

The Elements of Journalism

Bill Kovach and Tom Rosenstiel describe the main tenets of American journalism in their book *The Elements of Journalism*. They are:

- Journalism's first obligation is to the truth.
- Its first loyalty is to citizens.
- Its essence is a discipline of verification.
- Its practitioners must maintain an independence from those they cover.
- It must serve as an independent monitor of power.
- It must provide a forum for public criticism and compromise.
- It must strive to make the significant interesting and relevant.
- It must keep the news comprehensive and proportional.
- Its practitioners must be allowed to exercise their personal conscience.

From The Elements of Journalism *by Bill Kovach and Tom Rosenstiel. Copyright 2001 by Bill Kovach and Tom Rosenstiel. Used with permission of Crown Publishers, a division of Random House, Inc.*

A good place for reporters and editors to start to think about what they do and why they do it, and apply that to whatever medium they are working in, be it print, online or broadcast, is Kovach and Rosenstiel's excellent book *The Elements of Journalism*. This book is important reading for current journalists and those thinking about careers in journalism.

Notes

1. Bill Kovach and Tom Rosenstiel, *The Elements of Journalism: What Newspeople Should Know and the Public Should Expect.* (New York: Crown Publishers, 2001), 17.

2. Leonard Downie Jr. and Robert G. Kaiser, 2002. *The News About the News: American Journalism in Peril.* (New York: Vintage Books.)

3. Kovach and Rosenstiel, p 61.

4. Denis McQuail, *McQuail's Mass Communication Theory*, 4th ed. (London: Sage, 2000), 150.

5. Jack Fuller, *News Values: Ideas for an Information Age* (Chicago: University of Chicago, 1996), 221.

Glossary

ABC. Audit Bureau of Circulations, which compiles statistics on *circulation.*

Add. The copy added to a story, particularly a wire story; also, one *take* or page of a story, such as "Add 1."

Ad impression. A measurement of the frequency with which advertisements are seen online.

Ad side. The section of the business office where advertising is prepared.

Advance. A story written in advance of an event and held for *release;* also, a story written about a forthcoming event.

Advertorial. Copy made to look as though it was produced by the newsroom but is actually advertising.

Agate. Five-and-a-half-point type, usually found only in classified advertising or lists.

Agate line. A measurement of advertising depth. Fourteen make one inch.

Air. See *white space.*

AM. A morning newspaper. The cycle sent by a wire service to morning newspapers.

A-matter. Copy prepared in advance of the *top* of a story so that the story may be quickly completed on deadline.

Angle. The emphasis of a story.

Animation. Web content that moves on the screen.

AP. Associated Press, a cooperative newsgathering organization.

APME. Associated Press Managing Editors association. The editors represent AP member newspapers.

Archives. A computer database that stores all the publication's past stories, photographs and informational graphics for easy retrieval. Also called a *database.* See also *clips.*

Art. Any illustrative material, such as pictures, graphics and sketches.

Art head. A headline given special typographic treatment beyond a publication's regular style.

Ascender. The portion of a *lowercase* letter rising above average letter height; contrast to *descender.*

ASNE. American Society of Newspaper Editors.

Bad break. An unattractive or confusing division of type in a story of more than one column. A column may end with a period, giving the impression that the story has ended, or there may be a prominent *widow.* Also used to describe when associated words are split between lines of a headline.

Balloon. A device used in comic strips to make words appear to come from a character.

Bandwidth. How much data an Internet connection can handle.

Banner. A headline running across the top of a page; also called *streamer*, *line*, *ribbon*.

Banner ad. An advertisement that appears on the top of a Web page.

Bastard width. Type that differs from the standard column width of a print publication.

Beat. The area assigned to a reporter for regular coverage; also, an exclusive story, or *scoop*.

BF. The abbreviation for *boldface*.

Bite. To cut a story so that it fits the space allotted to it.

Blanket. See *offset*.

Blanket head. A headline covering several stories, each with secondary headlines.

Bleed. To run an image right off the edge of a page.

Blind ad. A classified ad that gives a box number instead of the advertiser's name.

Blind interview. An interview story that does not reveal the name of the source, referring to him as "a high-ranking government official," and so on.

Blog. See *Web log*.

Blow up. To enlarge printed or pictorial matter; the enlargement so made.

Blurb. See *tout*.

Body. The story itself, as distinguished from the headline and the illustration.

Body type. The type normally used for news stories. The size is usually 8-, 9-, or 10-point in print.

Boil or **boil down.** To reduce a story substantially.

Boiler plate. A derisive term for poor, inconsequential stories.

Boldface. Dark or heavy type, as distinguished from *lightface*. **This is boldface.**

Book. A group of several stories on the same general subject, usually from a wire service. Also, a newspaper section.

Border. Column rules surrounding an ad, story or headline.

Box. To enclose a story or headline with four *rules* to give it more prominence; also, such an enclosure.

Break. The division of a story continued from one page to another or from one column to another. Compare *jump*, *bad break*, *break-over*, *wrap*, *carryover*. Also, a story breaks when an event occurs or when the news becomes available to reporters.

Break-over. The part of a story continued to another page; also called a *jump* or *runover*. The page on which break-overs are placed is called the break-over page, *carryover*, or *jump page*.

Briefs. Short stories.

Brite. A short, amusing story.

Broadband. A high-speed Internet connection.

Browser. A computer program that reads HTML coding and renders Web pages on a user's screen.

Budget. A listing of stories being prepared for publication; also, the listing of stories expected by a wire service, also called a *news digest*.

Bug. Any fancy typographic device used to break up areas of type, especially in headlines. Compare *dingbat*. Bugs are used with restraint by today's editors. The word also refers to the label of the International Typographical Union.

Bulldog. Once, the newspaper's first *edition* of the day. Now, refers to an early edition of a Sunday newspaper.

Bullet. A large black dot used for decoration, to separate sections of a story, or, at the left edge of a column, to mark each item in a series.

Bulletin. Important and often unexpected news. In wire service parlance only a *flash* is more important.

Bureau. A subsidiary newsgathering force placed in a smaller community, a state capital or the national capital by a news organization or wire service.

Button. A Web graphic that readers click on to be taken to another part of the Web site.

Byline. The reporter's name atop the story.

C and lc. The abbreviation for "caps and lowercase," used to specify the conventional capitalizing used in ordinary writing; contrast to material marked "caps," which means every letter should be a capital.

C and sc. The abbreviation for "caps and small caps," used to set material all in capitals but with most letters smaller than those "capped."

Canned copy. Prepared news or editorials sent by a *syndicate* or publicity organization.

Caps. The abbreviation for "capitals"; also, *uppercase.* Every letter or a word so marked is capitalized. Compare *C and lc* and *C and sc.*

Caption. The words under a picture; a synonym for *cutline.*

Carryover. See *break-over.*

Cascading style sheets, or **CSS.** Coding on Web pages that sets forth that Web site's typographical and design styles; used by browsers when rendering pages on users' screens.

Centerpiece. A prominent display, usually with *art,* on a section front or home page; often accompanied by an *art head.*

Chapel. A union local for printers or press operators.

Chat. Online conversation among Internet users. Some news publications host online chats with newsmakers.

Circulation. The number of copies a newspaper sells in a particular *edition;* the department in charge of distributing the paper.

City desk. The place where the *city editor* and assistants, if any, work.

City editor. The editor in charge of the reporters covering news within a city and its environs.

City room. The newsroom in which reporters and editors work.

Classified advertising. Advertising that runs in categories, or classes, such as the help wanted ads, usually without any graphic enhancement.

Click-through. The rate at which Web users click on links to other parts of the site or to an advertiser's site.

Clips. Previous stories run by a publication, kept in an easily accessed database; for older material, clips are kept in paper envelopes in the library. Online, clips are audio or video content.

Col. The abbreviation for "column."

Color. A story with human interest, often describing places and people in detail. But a "colored" story is a biased, or slanted, report.

Column inch. One inch of type one column wide; a standard measure for newspaper design.

Column rule. A thin line separating columns.

Column sig. Short for column signature. The typographical device that contains a columnist's name and photograph. Compare to *logo.*

Condensed type. Type narrower than the standard width of a particular type *face*, giving a squeezed appearance; contrast *extended type*.

Content analysis. A research method to analyze published material.

Content manager. A computer program that online editors use to process copy for Web publication.

Convergence. The sharing of newsroom resources across platforms: print, online and broadcast.

Copy aide. An errand runner in the newsroom; also called a *newsroom assistant*.

Copy chief. An editor who supervises and checks the work of *copy editors*.

Copy desk. The department for which copy editors work.

Copy editor. A person who edits copy. A copy editor may have other duties depending on the needs of the publication.

Copy writer. A person who writes advertising copy.

Correspondent. A reporter who files stories from places outside the news publication's core area. The person may be on salary or may receive a flat fee or a per-inch rate. See also *stringer*.

CQ. An abbreviation for "it is correct" in copy.

Credit line. A line acknowledging the source for a story or picture.

Crop. To cut away parts of a picture to eliminate unwanted material or to make it a particular size.

Curtain raiser. A story that looks at an event or issue in advance.

Cut. To reduce a story's length; compare *bite*.

Cutline. Any explanatory material under a piece of art; also called a *caption*.

Cutoff rule. A horizontal line used to separate material.

Dateline. The words that give the story's origin and, sometimes, the date on which the story was written.

Dayside. The shift of day workers in the newsroom.

Deck. A secondary, smaller headline on a story that amplifies the main headline. Sometimes called a *drop head* or a *readout*.

Descender. The portion of a *lowercase* letter going below the baseline; contrast *ascender*.

Desk chief. The head of a particular desk.

Dingbat. Any typographical device used for decoration. Compare *bug*.

Directory. A listing of stories available in the computer. Sometimes called a *menu*.

Display ad. All advertising except classified and legal.

Double-truck. A two-page layout, either news or advertising, that eliminates the margin, or *gutter*, between the pages.

Downstyle. A headline style with a minimum of capitalization. Contrast *upstyle*.

Drop cap. See *initial*.

Dropdown. A menu online that displays clickable options.

Drop head. See *deck*.

Dummy. A diagram of a newspaper page used to show where stories, pictures and ads are to be placed.

Dupe. A story that appears twice in the same *edition*.

Ear. Upper corners of a newspaper section front, often containing a slogan, weather information or *refers* to stories inside the section.

Early run. Sections of a newspaper printed in advance of the main press run. Also called a *pre-run*.

Edition. Each *run* of a newspaper *issue*. There may be marked editions, early editions, final editions, and so on.

Editorial. Generally all the nonadvertising and nonbusiness material or operations of a news publication; also, one of the opinion essays of the editorial page.

Editorialize. Putting opinion in a story or headline.

Em. The square of the type size. An em in *12-point* type is 12 points high and 12 points wide.

En. Half an *em*.

Environmental portrait. A photograph in which the subject is photographed in his or her environs.

Evergreen. A timeless story that can be kept ready to go until needed to fill space.

Execution at dawn. A picture of people standing in a line and looking at a camera, as if the photographer placed them there and shot them.

Extended type. Type wider than the standard for a particular *face*; contrast *condensed type*.

Extra. A special, or extra, *edition* published because of spectacular news; now rare.

Face. A particular design of type.

Feature. A story emphasizing the human interest or entertainment aspects of a situation; usually in narrative form. Also, material such as columns and comics bought from a *syndicate*. As a verb, it means to give prominence to a story; to emphasize a part of a story.

Feedback. Online interactive feature that allows Web users to comment on a Web site's content or issues in the news.

File. To transmit a story to the newsroom. As a noun, it refers collectively to the back *issues* of a paper; also, one day's production by a wire service. As a computer term, a single document.

Filler. Short stories, used to fill small spaces in a newspaper.

First-day story. The first published account of an event.

Flag. A newspaper's *nameplate*, often erroneously called the *masthead*.

Flash. The highest priority of news sent by a wire service; used rarely; also, a computer application from Macromedia used to create animation.

Fluff. Inconsequential material.

Flush. Setting type even, or flush, with a margin; *flush left* means flush with the left margin, *flush right* with the right margin.

Fold. The area where a full-sized newspaper is folded. Above the fold is prime real estate.

Folio. The line at the top of the page giving the page number, the name of the newspaper, the city of publication and the date; also, a measure for legal advertising.

Follow (or folo). A story that follows up a *first-day story*; also a *second-day story*.

Follow-up. A story that gives the latest news of an event reported earlier.

Font. A set of particular size and style of type.

Format. The physical appearance of a page, section or book.

Four-color process. A printing process using four different *plates*, each printing one color—black, magenta, cyan and yellow—to create color images.

Fourth estate. The public press.

Front office. The business office.

FTP. File transfer protocol. A process used to upload material to Web sites.

General assignment. A reporter without a beat; available for widely varied stories.

GIF. Graphics Interchange Format. A digital format for images.

Graf. Short for "paragraph."

Graveyard shift. The work period that covers the early morning hours; also called *lobster trick* or *dog watch*. Staffers on this shift may write and edit, but they are there primarily to cover emergencies.

Gray space. A section of a page that has no typographical contrast, giving a gray appearance.

Grip and grin. A picture of people shaking hands or exchanging a certificate or other item and smiling for the camera. Best avoided.

Gutter. The space between columns.

Hairline. An extra-thin *rule*.

Handout. A press release or publicity photo.

Hard news. Stories based on specific, recent, important events.

Head or hed. Short for headline.

Head to come. The notice to the copy desk that the headline will be sent after the story; abbreviated *HTK* or *HTC*.

Head shot. See *mug shot*.

Hits. Measurement of *traffic* on a *Web site*.

Hole. See *news hole*.

Home page. The entry Web page to an online publication's *Web site*. For news organizations, this page usually contains the top stories and pictures.

House organ. A publication issued by a company primarily for its employees.

HTC or HTK. Abbreviations for *head to come*.

HTML. Hypertext markup language, the coding used to build Web pages.

Human interest. The quality giving a story wide appeal. It often contains information on human foibles or oddities or heartwarming and sentimental matter.

Hyperlink. Clickable text on a Web page that takes users to other Web pages, also called a link.

Hyphenation and justification. The function of a computer that hyphenates words properly and provides space between words so that each line is justified. Usually called simply H and J.

Indent. To leave extra space on either side of a column.

Index. The summary of the contents or highlights of a publication.

Initial. A large capital letter at the beginning of an article or paragraph, common in magazines but sometimes used for magazine-style matter in newspapers. Also called a *drop cap*.

Insert. Copy or type to be inserted into a story.

Interface. An electronic connection.

Issue. One day's newspaper, which may have several *editions*.

Ital. or itals. Abbreviations for "italic."

Italic. Type with letters slanted to the right; used for cross references in this glossary. Contrast *roman*.

JPEG. Joint Photographic Expert Group. A format for image files.

Jump. See *break-over*; also, to continue a story. Compare *break*.

Jump head. The headline over the part of the story that was continued, or *jumped*, to another page.

Jump line. A line noting a story is continued (for example, "Continued on Page 6").

Jump page. See *break-over*.

Justify. To use white space between paragraphs to fill out a column; to space out a line of type so that it is *flush* left and right.

Kicker. A few words, usually to the left and above a headline, to give it emphasis; sometimes it serves the same purpose as a *deck*; also, the end of a story.

Label head. A headline, usually without a verb, that only labels the news (for example, "List of Graduates").

Layout. A planned arrangement of stories and pictures on one subject; also, the whole typographical arrangement of a newspaper.

LC or **lc.** Abbreviations for "lowercase."

Lead (pronounced "led"). The addition of white space to fill a column is called *leading*.

Lead (pronounced "leed") **editorial.** The first, and most important, *editorial*.

Leaders (pronounced "leeders"). Dots or dashes to take the eye across a column; often used in tables.

Legibility. The quality of a type style that makes it easily and quickly comprehended or perceived; contrast *readability*.

Library. A collection of clippings, newspaper *files*, and reference books; formerly called the *morgue*; in pagination applications, a file in which frequently used page elements are kept.

Linage. A measure of printed material based on the number of lines; also, the total amount of advertising over a given period of time.

Line. See *banner*; also, *agate line*.

Line gauge. A printer's ruler; also called a *pica pole*.

Link. See *hyperlink*.

Listserv. A list established to send group e-mail. News publications may set up such lists to send news alerts to subscribers. Also called *mailing lists*.

Local. A local news item; usually a *personal*.

Localize. To emphasize a local angle in a story.

Logo. Typographical devices used to draw reader attention to standing features, such as "Campaign 2004."

Lowercase. The small letters of type.

Magazine style. See *upstyle*; also see *initial*.

Mailing list. See *listserv*.

Makeover. To make a new page *plate* to correct an error or to include late news; also called *replate*. May also refer to an edition of a newspaper that includes all replates.

Mandatory kill. An order from a wire service to eliminate a story, probably because it has a serious error or is libelous.

Marginalia. Material placed on the margins of Web pages.

Markets. A section of the news publication that includes news of livestock, commodity and stock markets.

Masthead. A statement of the paper's name, ownership, subscription rate, and so on, which usually appears on the editorial page; often confused with *nameplate* or *flag*.

Measure. The length of a line of type or the width of a column.

Media player. A computer program that allows Internet users to hear and view *streaming audio and video*.

Menu. A computer listing of available stories; also, see *dropdown*.

Modem. Hardware that connects computers to other computers or the Internet.

Module. In newspapers, all the elements of a single story's presentation; online, a container for a story and its associated elements.

Morgue. See *library*.

Mortice. An opening, usually rectangular, in a picture for the insertion of material, often another picture.

MPEG. Moving Pictures Expert Group. A digital format for video.

Mug shot. A picture of somebody's face, usually a half-column wide; also called a *head shot* or *thumbnail.*

Multimedia. Web page content that contains sound, video, animation or interactivity.

Must. An order from a superior that a certain story must publish that day. See also *business-office must.*

NAA. Newspaper Association of America.

Nameplate. The publication's name at the top of the front page or home page; also called *flag* and, wrongly, *masthead.*

Navigation bar, or nav bar. A vertical or horizontal bar on a Web page that contains links to different pages on the site.

New lead (pronounced "leed"). Also called *new top.* A fresh opening paragraph or two for a story.

New top. See *new lead.*

News digest. See *budget.*

News hole. The space in a newspaper allotted to news reports and illustration, the rest being given to advertisements, comic strips and so on.

Newsroom assistant. See *copy aide.*

Nightside. The night shift of a newspaper.

Obit. Short for *obituary.*

Obituary. A story reporting a person's death.

Offset. A photographic method of printing. Copy is photographed and a *plate* made by "burning" light through the negative onto a sensitized sheet of thin metal. The part exposed to light, or "burned," absorbs ink while the rest of the plate rejects it. The plate, wrapped around a roller, transfers, or offsets, the ink to a rubber roller called a blanket, which actually imprints the paper.

ONA. Online News Association.

Op-ed or **opp page.** Abbreviations for "the page opposite"; usually the page devoted to columns and *features* and placed opposite the editorial page; any material that appears on such a page.

Pad. To add useless words to stories or headlines.

Page impressions. A measurement of *traffic* on a *Web site.*

Page proof. A *proof* of a full page. At some publications, editors read proofs before or between editions for final corrections.

Pagination. The process of building pages on a computer.

Personal. A one-paragraph item about minor family news; a kind of *local.*

Pica. A printing measure equivalent to one-sixth of an inch.

Pica pole. See *line gauge.*

Pick up. The instruction at the bottom of copy to tell the printer to pick up other type and add it to the story. In wire copy, it tells the editor where *adds, inserts,* and so on "pick up" into the story.

Pix. Short for "pictures."

Pixel. A digital measurement for pictures and graphics equivalent to a small dot on a computer screen.

Plate. A metal or plastic-coated sheet from which newspapers are printed.

Play. The emphasis given a story, or the emphasis on a certain fact in a story. Facts or stories can be "played up" or "played down."

PM. An afternoon newspaper.

Point. A type measurement equivalent to 1/72nd of an inch. Hence, 72-point type is 1 inch high, 36-point a half-inch, and so on.

Policy. The newspaper's position on how it handles news.

PR. *Public relations.*

Preferred position. An advertising term that refers to an advertiser's receiving a special place for its ads, such as on Page 3 of a newspaper or a banner on a home page. Usually, the advertiser pays extra for this preference.

Prepress. A newspaper department that handles final production tasks, such as color correction of photographs, before *plates* are made.

Pre-run. See *early run.*

Press agent. A person hired to get favorable publicity for an individual or organization.

Process color. See *four-color process.*

Producer. A newsroom worker who prepares content for Web publication. Sometimes, but not always, an editor.

Proof. See *page proof.*

Public relations. The craft of issuing news of and creating a good image for an individual, agency or firm; more professional and comprehensive than work of a press agent. Often shortened to PR.

Puff, puffery. A publicity story or a story that contains unwarranted superlatives.

Pullout. A newspaper section, often a *tabloid*, easily pulled from the rest of the paper; also, material taken from a story and highlighted in a separate design treatment, such as a highlights box.

Pull quote. A quotation taken from a story and given special typographical treatment as a design element.

Put to bed. When all work on a day's issue is complete.

Q. and A. Copy including "question-and-answer" material, as in court testimony or a long interview.

Query. A question raised in a message to a wire service; also, a request by a freelance writer to see whether a news publication is interested in a particular article.

Rail. A vertical section on a news Web page. Most news sites have three to four rails.

Railroad. To publish a story with little or no editing.

Readability. The quality of copy that makes it easy to grasp; contrast *legibility.*

Readership. Research on habits of readers.

Readout. A subsidiary headline that "reads out" (explains in more detail) from a main head; also called a *deck.*

Refer. A typographical insert to a story that refers to related material elsewhere in the publication.

Register. The correct placement or matching of *plates* in color printing so that colors are exactly where they should be for clear reproduction.

Release. The date and time that a news source says information may be released to the public; also, a publicity handout; also, authorization for the use of a photograph.

Reprint. Published material that came from a previous issue or from some other source, such as a magazine.

Revamp. To alter a story by shifting some of the paragraphs but not by rewriting it. See also *rewrite.*

Reverse. Letters printed the opposite of normal, as white letters on a black background.

Rewrite. To write a story again, or to *revamp* a story from a wire service or from another newspaper; also, to write a story telephoned to the newsroom by another reporter.

Ribbon. See *banner*.

Rim. Refers to a group of copy editors. Term comes from when copy editors sat on the outside of a horseshoe-shaped desk.

Rim person. A *copy editor* who sits on the *rim*.

Roman type. The common vertical type that is popularly contrasted to *italic*.

ROP. Short for *run of paper*.

Rule. A line that divides columns, stories or sections; usually one *point* thick, but see also *hairline*.

Run. An *edition*, in the sense that the edition is "run"; also, a *beat*.

Running story. A story—actually many stories—continued for several days or more.

Run of paper. An order meaning that an ad, picture or story could go almost anyplace in the paper.

Runover. The *jump* of a story that continues from another page.

Sacred cow. A person or institution unethically deferred to by being given special news treatment.

Sans serif. See *serif*.

SAU. Standard Advertising Unit, a measure for advertising space accepted uniformly across the industry.

Search box. Web site feature that allows visitors to search for specific terms.

Schedule. A record of stories assigned or already processed.

Scoop. See *beat*.

Second-day story. A story previously published but carrying a *new lead* or some other revision to make it news. Also see *follow*.

Second front page. Usually the front page of a second section; also called *split page*. Sometimes Page 2 or Page 3 gets the name because it carries important news with little or no advertising.

Separate. A story related to another and displayed separately but usually nearby.

Series. Related stories, usually run on consecutive days.

Serif. A tiny finishing stroke or squiggle at the ends of letters in many type faces. A face with simple, square corners is called *sans serif*.

Server. A computer that contains all the files used in a publication's production, or all the files of Web site. The server is accessed from individual computers on the network.

Sidebar. A story that emphasizes one part of a main story and appears alongside it on the page.

Sizing. Determining the size of a picture.

Skyboxes. *Teasers* that run atop the front page, referring to features inside.

Skyline. A line running above the *nameplate*, at the top of the page.

Skyscraper. A vertical ad on a Web page.

Slant. To emphasize a certain part of angle of a story; also, to distort the news.

Slide show. A multimedia presentation online that contains a series of photographs, sometimes accompanied by audio narration.

Slot editor. The editor who directs the *copy editors* sitting around the *rim*; also called a *copy chief*; see *rim*.

Slug or **slugline.** A name for a story or photo, usually one word, for identification as it moves through the editing process.

Small caps. Capital letters smaller than the regular capitals of a particular typeface; see also *C and sc.*

Solid. Lines of type set without space, or *lead*, between them.

Space grabber. A publicity seeker.

Spike. To eliminate, or *kill*, a story.

Split page. See *second front page.*

Split run. The dividing of a publication *run* into two or more slightly different versions, sometimes for research. For example, to check the effectiveness of a new ad, one version would have the new ad and one would have the old.

Spot news. Information about a specific, recent occurrence as contrasted to a story about a trend or continually developing situation.

Spread. See *centerpiece.*

State editor. The person who edits the news from the news publication's area outside the metropolitan region.

Stet. The abbreviation for "let it stand," written above crossed-out words to indicate that they should be kept after all.

Straight news. A story with only the bare facts, without *color* or interpretation.

Streamer. See *banner.*

Streaming audio and video. Sound and video that Internet users can view using a media player.

Stringer. A part-time or free-lance reporter; see also *correspondent.*

Style book or **style sheet.** A specific list of the conventions of spelling, abbreviation, punctuation, capitalization, and so on used by a particular news organization.

Sub. A piece of copy that substitutes for something in a previous story, or a story the substitutes for a previous one.

Subhead. A small headline that appears every few paragraphs to break up *gray space.*

Symmetry. Page design that balances elements on the page so that neither the top nor the bottom, the left nor the right, dominates.

Syndicates. Firms that sell and distribute columns, comics, *features*, and pictures. A wire service technically is a syndicate but is rarely called that.

Tabloid. A newspaper half the size of a regular six-column, 21-inch newspaper. Though some "tabs" are sensational, the term is not a synonym for *yellow journalism.*

Tag. A piece of HTML code.

Tear sheet. A newspaper page sent to an advertiser as evidence that the ad was printed.

Teasers. Elements on a section front or home page that try to get readers to turn to or click on material inside the newspaper or Web site.

Template. A computer document containing the basic formatting for a print or Web page. Editors make a copy from a template to build new pages.

Think piece. An interpretative article.

Thumbnail. Small sketches of how pages might look; also a *mug shot.*

Thumbsucker. A story meant to give readers pause.

Tie-back. A reference in a story to some previous event to help the reader's memory; also a *kicker* that refers back to the lead of a story.

Tie-in. A story or part of a story linked to some other event.

Tight. A situation of little or no room in the whole newspaper, in a particular story or in a line.

Time copy. Material current for days or weeks and therefore timeless; can be run whenever convenient; also called an *evergreen*.

TK. Journalistic shorthand for "to come."

Tombstone. To place similar headlines side by side so that the reader tends to read from head to head rather than from head to story.

Top. The first few paragraphs of a story.

Tout. The text on a home page that summarizes a story and tries to entice the reader to click through; also called a *blurb*.

Traffic. The measurement of visitors to a Web site.

Turn line. See *jump line*.

Typo. Short for "typographical error."

Undated story. A story with no specific geographical focus, such as a war in the Near East, and therefore with no specific dateline. The source of the story is printed at the top, such as "Associated Press."

Unique users. A measurement of visitors to a Web site, determined by computer IP addresses.

Universal desk. A desk that handles copy from several or all departments.

UPI. United Press International, a commercial newsgathering organization. Once a competitor to the AP, it now provides specialized services, such as news photographs from around the world.

Uppercase. See *caps*.

Upstyle. A style that capitalizes more words than most papers do; also called *magazine style*. Contrast *downstyle*.

Urgent. A wire service designation for an important story, but less important than a *bulletin*.

URL. Uniform Resource Locator, a Web site's address.

Web log. An online journal kept by anybody with a Web account. Those who keep Web logs, also called *blogs*, are called bloggers. Not all bloggers are journalists.

Web site. All of an online publication's pages.

Webcast. An event made available live online through *streaming audio* and *video*.

Webmaster. Personal responsible for technical maintenance of a news publication's Web site.

White space. The blank space, also called *air*, around heads, ad copy, and stories; left blank to make the printed material stand out.

Widow. A one- or two-word line at the end of a paragraph; usually unsightly if the last line of *captions* or the first line in a column. See also *bad break*.

Wire editor. The person who supervises the editing of news from wire service.

World Wide Web. The part of the Internet accessible through the use of computer programs called *browsers*.

Wrap. To place type in two or more columns under a multicolumn headline, or beneath a photograph. See also *break*.

Wrapped up. See *put to bed*.

Wrong font. The designation for a letter of type different from the appropriate style.

XHTML. HTML that uses extensible markup language; allows for more programming flexibility.

Yellow journalism. Sensational and often deliberately inaccurate reporting.

Bibliography

Books of Interest to Editors

Agnes, Michael E., ed. *Webster's New World College Dictionary*, 4th ed. (Cleveland: Wiley, 2002).

Arnold, George T. *Media Writer's Handbook: A Guide to Common Writing and Editing Problems*, 3rd ed. (Boston: McGraw-Hill, 2003).

Bagdikian, Ben H. *The New Media Monopoly* (Boston: Beacon Press, 2004).

Baker, Bob. *Newsthinking: The Secret of Making Your Facts Fall Into Place* (Boston: Allyn and Bacon, 2002).

Berkman, Robert I. and Christopher A. Shumway. *Digital Dilemmas: Ethical Issues for Online Media Professionals* (Ames, Iowa: Iowa State Press, 2003).

Boczkowski, Pablo J. *Digitizing the News: Innovation in Online Newspapers* (Cambridge, Mass.: MIT Press, 2004).

Boyd, Andrew. *Broadcast Journalism: Techniques of Radio and Television News*, 5th ed. (Oxford: Focal Press, 2001).

Brians, Paul. *Common Errors in English Usage* (Wilsonville, Ore: William, James, 2003).

Brooks, Brian S., James L. Pinson, and Jean Gaddy Wilson. *Working With Words: A Handbook for Media Writers and Editors*, 5th ed. (Boston: Bedford/St. Martin's, 2003).

Cappon, Rene J. *The Associated Press Guide to News Writing*. (Lawrenceville, N.J.: Thomson/Arco, 2000).

Cappon, Rene J. *The Associated Press Guide to Punctuation* (New York: Basic Books, 2003).

Clark, Roy Peter and Don Fry. *Coaching Writers: Editors and Reporters Working Together Across Platforms* (Boston, MA: Bedford/St. Martin's, 2003).

Craig, Richard. *Online Journalism: Reporting, Writing and Editing for New Media* (Belmont, CA: Wadsworth, 2005).

Downie Jr., Leonard and Robert G. Kaiser. *The News About the News: American Journalism in Peril* (New York: Vintage Books, 2002).

Fuller, Jack. *News Values: Ideas for an Information Age* (Chicago: University of Chicago Press, 1996).

Garcia, Mario. *Contemporary Newspaper Design*, 3rd ed. (Englewood Cliffs, NJ: Prentice-Hall, 1993).

Garcia, Mario R. and Pegie Stark. *Eyes on the News* (St. Petersburg, Fla.: Poynter Institute for Media Studies, 1991).

Garner, Bryan. *Garner's Modern American Usage* (Oxford: Oxford University Press, 2003).

Goldstein, Norman, ed. *The Associated Press Stylebook and Briefing on Media Law* (New York: Associated Press, 2004).

Gove, Philip Babcock, ed. *Webster's Third New International Dictionary, Unabridged*, 3rd ed. (Sprngfield, MA: Merriam-Webster, 2002).

Hale, Constance, ed. *Wired Style: Principles of English Usage in the Digital Age* (San Francisco: HardWired, 1996).

Hale, Constance. *Sin and Syntax* (New York: Broadway Books, 1999).

Harrower, Tim. *The Newspaper Designer's Handbook*, 5th ed. (Boston: McGraw-Hill, 2002).

Kessler, Lauren and Duncan McDonald. *When Words Collide: A Media Writer's Guide to Grammar and Style*, 6th ed. (Belmont, CA: Thomson/Wadsworth, 2004).

Kobre, Ken. *Photojournalism: The Professionals' Approach*, 4th ed. (Boston: Focal Press, 2000).

Kovach, Bill and Tom Rosenstiel. *The Elements of Journalism: What Newspeople Should Know and the Public Should Expect* (New York: Three Rivers Press, 2001).

LaRocque, Paul. *Heads You Win: An Easy Guide to Better Headline and Caption Writing* (Oak Park, IL: Marion Street Press, 2003).

McChesney, Robert W. *The Problem of the Media: U.S. Communication Politics in the 21st Century* (New York: Monthly Review Press, 2004).

McChesney, Robert W. *Rich Media, Poor Democracy: Communication Politics in Dubious Times* (Urbana: University of Illinois Press, 1999).

Merrill, John. *Journalism Ethics: Philosophical Foundations for News Media* (Boston: Bedford/St. Martin's, 1996).

Pember, Don R. and Clay Calvert. *Mass Media Law*, 2005-2006 ed. (Boston: McGraw-Hill, 2005).

Smith, Ron F. *Groping for Ethics in Journalism*, 5th ed. (Ames: Iowa State Press, 2003).

Stovall, James Glen. *Web Journalism: Practice and Promise of a New Medium* (Boston, MA: Allyn & Bacon, 2004).

Strunk, William, Jr., and E.B. White. *The Elements of Style*, 4th ed. (Boston: Allyn & Bacon, 2000).

Walsh, Bill. *Lapsing Into a Comma: A Curmudgeon's Guide to the Many Things That Can Go Wrong in Print—and How to Avoid Them* (Chicago: Contemporary Books, 2000).

Walsh, Bill. *The Elephants of Style*. (New York: McGraw-Hill, 2004).

Wickham, Kathleen Woodruff. *Math Tools for Journalists* (Oak Park, IL: Marion Street Press, 2002).

Williams, Robin. *The Non-Designers Design Book*, 2nd ed. (Berkeley, CA: Peachpit Press, 2004).

Magazines and Journals of Interest to Editors

The American Editor
American Journalism Review
Columbia Journalism Review
Editor & Publisher
Journalism and Mass Communication Quarterly
Nieman Reports
Newspaper Research Journal
Online Journalism Review
Quill

Index